VOICES
ON THE THRESHOLD
OF TOMORROW

145 VIEWS OF THE NEW MILLENNIUM

VOICES
ON THE THRESHOLD
OF TOMORROW

145 VIEWS OF THE NEW MILLENNIUM

Edited by GEORG FEUERSTEIN
and TRISHA LAMB FEUERSTEIN

QUEST BOOKS
The Theosophical Publishing House
Wheaton, IL U.S.A./Madras, India/London, England

The Theosophical Publishing House
P.O. Box 270
Wheaton, IL 60189-0270

A publication of the Theosophical Publishing House,
a department of the Theosophical Society in America.

*This publication made possible with
the assistance of the Kern Foundation*

Library of Congress Cataloging-in-Publication Data

Voices on the threshold of tomorrow : 145 views of the new millennium /
edited by Georg Feuerstein and Tricia Lamb Feuerstein

         p. cm.
Includes index.
ISBN 0–8356–0692–9 : $14.00
     1. Twenty–first century—Forecasts. . I. Feuerstein, Georg.
II. Feuerstein, Tricia Lamb.
CB161.V64 1993
303 . 49 ' 09 ' 05—dc20   93—22751
                                             CIP

9 8 7 6 5 4 3 2 1 * 93 94 95 96 97 98 99

This edition is printed on acid-free paper that meets the
American National Standards Institute Z39.48 Standard

Printed in the United States of America by Versa Press

CONTENTS

VISIONARY PHILOSOPHY, EVOLUTIONARY VISION

THE SOCIAL DIMENSION

SCIENCE, ECONOMICS, AND NATURE

MINDING THE BODY, EMBODYING THE MIND

THE NEW MORALITY

LIVING IN PEACE AND HARMONY

SPIRITUALITY

RECOVERING SPIRITUAL PRACTICE

INDEX   429

Preface

Few books could be more fascinating to create than this anthology. Although it was slow to emerge—requiring more than two years for its birthing—every time we received another essay we felt a growing sense of excitement about the project. Each essay connected us to another voice "out there," another individual struggling with the same issues as ourselves in trying to understand our turbulent times.

Whenever a new contribution arrived on our doorstep, we immediately felt a reassuring sense of kinship with an ever-expanding circle of friends around the globe. We learned that our personal hopes and fears were shared by many others, and that we were by no means alone in our commitment to a more benign future for our children and future generations. We also learned to appreciate that some who are strongly committed to self-transformation and social betterment for all beings do not necessarily share our interpretation of the present historical moment. However, while we may disagree on the conceptual level, we see eye to eye on the moral level, which is the more important, since actions always speak louder than words.

In any case, it was reassuring to find a broad consensus about the present-day crisis and the moral growth demanded of our species to ensure its and other species' survival. We hope that this anthology will be found as enriching by our readers as we have found it, in its process of emergence over the past two years.

We are grateful to all of the contributors for carving out the time from their busy schedules to write their essays and, in many cases, respond to our subsequent queries. We are also very grateful to Brenda Rosen and the Editorial Board of Quest Books for adopting this work.

And finally, we would like to thank Laurance S. Rockefeller for his generous support of this project and for seeing so clearly its possibilities.

Georg Feuerstein and Trisha Lamb Feuerstein
Middletown, Northern California
January, 1993

Introduction

Astronomers recently announced that on August 14, 2126, a giant comet named Swift-Tuttle might crash into the Earth. The impact would cause widespread devastation and possibly even dramatically alter the political balance, whatever it may be at that time. More than that, the impact might have far more serious consequences for life on our planet.

Nature is full of catastrophes, whether caused by cosmic visitors like the Swift-Tuttle comet, or springing from planet-bound forces. Catastrophes represent large-scale changes demanding a high measure of adaptation. But change does not come only in the form of such massive onslaughts. As Heraclitus noted long ago, change is a universal phenomenon.

From our human perspective, we give meaning to change by calling it "evolution" or "history" or "personal biography." Historically speaking, there appear to be times when change is accelerated. This is the case in our own era. Most of the voices included in this anthology echo this belief or would not wish to contest it.

The fact is, a growing number of people think we are living in crucial times of change. This presumption alone can act as a significant agent of change. For if we hold something true, we tend to behave in accord with our belief, and our actions can lead to a new social reality. In that case, it is irrelevant whether the idea that we live in decisive times is based on actual preexisting conditions or is just a self-fulfilling prophecy. It is effective in either case.

We tend to be creatures of habit, finding comfort in the familiar and responding to uncertainty with a measure of anxiety. Not surprisingly, in an age where change is writ as large as in ours, we can expect a substantial dose of such unease. Not too long ago, it was the specter of a nuclear holocaust that fueled our concern, but with the dismantling of the Soviet Union and the end of the Cold War, this has somewhat subsided. Today our anxiety revolves around environmental collapse.

In light of today's massive ecological problems and the lack of an adequate response from governments and individuals, several contributors have expressed a strongly pessimistic view. Their concerns and interpretations can serve as a counterpoint to the more optimistic position taken by others. It is evident that facts are by no means "cold," but charged with meaning: We read reality in various ways, and facts can look one way or another, depending on how we approach them.

Cultural pessimism, which is widespread today, has a long history. Its most prominent contemporary spokesman is undoubtedly Oswald Spengler, who in the 1920s prophesied the collapse of Western civilization. For him societies or cultures were living organisms, which are born, undergo stages of growth, and then die. While his biological model of human society has, by and large, been replaced by systems thinking, his doomsday prophecies are multiply echoed in the burgeoning "crisis" literature on economic, ecological, and sociocultural forecasting.

Pessimism is not confined to professional forecasters, however. It seems to affect a large section of the population of the industrialized world, and some researchers have expressed their concern that a deepening pessimism leads to psychological depression and social paralysis.

How seriously our mental health is affected by this latest specter becomes clear when we listen to our children. Recently a friend of ours in Scotland observed his children digging a fairly deep trench. When he asked what they were doing, they told him they were looking for acid rain. Their excavation was more than mere curiosity; it was motivated by a deep-seated concern, which those young children could barely articulate in words. The following poem by gifted ten-year-old Eric Hogle of Elko, Nevada, expresses eloquently the kind of burden borne by our children today.

Mother Nature

Nature is beautiful and kind,
She is always on my mind.
But I'm afraid she's getting ill,
She's suffering an oil spill.

Her ozone layer comes to mind;
It's getting very hard to find.
She's got a fever (global warming),
She's getting hotter every morning.

She has congestion, acid rain,
She says she has an ocean pain.
She has pollution, nonbiodegradables;
Her trees have been made into chairs and tables.

Her rain forest lungs are getting smaller,
And smoke stacks yet are being built taller.
She's sick and if something's not done fast,
Mother Nature may not last.

INTRODUCTION

Our hearts fill with sorrow when we compare the troubled feelings of today's children with our own childhood, which, despite the aftermath of World War II, was relatively secure.

At the same time, however, we know that whenever we find our center in the midst of change and uncertainty, we also locate hope and perhaps even a sense of excitement at what might be. Both grave concern and buoyant hope are clearly reflected in the contributions to this anthology. Many, if not most, contributors agree that the future will not be born without pain, and that we must expect formidable personal and collective difficulties; however, they also feel that there is room for hope and optimism.

Interestingly, around the time that Spengler's gloom-and-doom message of *The Decline of Western Civilization* was assimilated by the intellectual elite of Europe, another cultural historian conceived an almost diametrically opposed vision of the future. This historian was Jean Gebser. In his pioneering work *Ursprung und Gegenwart* (translated in 1985 as *The Ever-Present Origin*), he has given us a panoramic view of the evolution of human consciousness, leading up to the idea that what we are experiencing today are not merely the death throes of our civilization but the birth pangs of a new type of consciousness.

Spengler and Gebser represent opposite ends of the spectrum of possible interpretations of our contemporary situation: despair or hope, paralysis or participation. While we may agree or disagree with the theoretical foundations of Spengler's and Gebser's models, they embody fundamental emotional dispositions. In one sense, we all tend to be either Spenglerians or Gebserians. Those who are in between are either undecided (and thus emotionally uncommitted to either hope or despair), or have taken a conscious stance of Zen-like indifference.

Contributors to *Voices on the Threshold of Tomorrow* were asked to express, as briefly as possible, their own hopes and fears about the future from the perspective of their particular area of expertise or primary interest. No restrictions were placed on the form of contributions—poetry and prose, humor and serious statements were equally welcome.

While there were dozens who declined to participate because of pressures of work, only one person declined our invitation on the grounds that nothing meaningful could be said about our theme in a few words. Many contributors struggled with the stipulated word limit, and not a few exceeded it, but, apart from the one exception, none were daunted by the criteria, and several even thanked us for providing them the challenge of expressing their thoughts and feelings so concisely. They felt that not only could something useful be said in such a short compass but that the project was exciting and necessary, which mirrors our own view.

We intend the present chorus of voices to be a catalyst for the benign forces that are presently shaping our future. The old Gnostic image of good and evil fighting each other in this world has some applicability, for, as we can witness in our own time, juxtaposed to benevolent changes are considerable destructive forces—we may never experience paradise on Earth. If the Gnostics are right, existence will always have a measure of evil attached to it, or else it would not be worldly existence. But we can surely aspire to heaven within ourselves and a more benign circumstance in the world.

We need not succumb to any naive utopianism, and yet we also need to remain sensitive to the fact that our reality is to no small degree determined by how we view ourselves and life. Our ideas shape our destiny—not necessarily in the simplistic ways currently advocated in certain New Age circles, but there is some, perhaps even considerable, truth to the maxim of "mind over matter."

In any case, without a higher vision of life, our lives become dull and uninspiring, and ultimately even brutish. In the past, the visions of the shamans and the voices of the prophets counted for something. When they were ignored, people suffered, and they knew it. Today, we hardly know that visionaries and prophets exist among us. People are too busily involved in the business of living—but living without the great inspired ideals that once brought deeper meaning to our lives.

In this volume, then, we have gathered visionaries and prophets, though most would probably not consider themselves as such. Here are men and women whose combined work has inspired millions of people. They may not wear ceremonial dress or walk naked in the desert, but through their deeds they have helped shape our perceptions and thus our realities. In this volume, they take stock of their ideas and feelings about the future.

Some chose an intellectual voice for their visions, others a more personal tone, and yet others a poetic rendering. All voices are important. In our view, it is not a single voice that holds the truth, but in their totality these voices achieve a higher significance. Thus we should respectfully listen to all of them, for each gives us another piece of the puzzle.

It is not a matter of whether a point of view is "correct" or "incorrect," because the future is just that—the future, which is open rather than closed. But these voices help us find our own voice. They help us articulate our own life experiences and expectations, our own hopes and fears. This exercise in self-discovery can in turn help us participate more consciously and fully in life, in creating a future that is benign and more deeply meaningful.

It so happens that there is considerable convergence of opinion among the contributors. Most share our belief that we do indeed live in highly significant times—times of rapid change—the kind of critical moment in which events could metamorphose in a major way: a moment in which we could either close the door on human evolution and possibly on life on our planet as we know it, or open the gateway to a new stage in the evolutionary drama. At any rate, we are no longer merely passive pawns of evolution but active participants.

In us, evolution has reached a complexity that now permits and even demands of us that we become responsible co-creators of the future. We are in the midst of a reality test. In his *Four Quartets*, T. S. Eliot rightly observed, ''Human kind/Cannot bear very much reality.'' We surround ourselves with simulations of reality, artificial worlds of conceptual meaning, and draw the curtain closed before the Thing Itself. We feel secure that way, at least relatively so. Now and then, of course, reality breaks through our safety net and, like a shaft of light penetrating a dark cave, throws everything into sharper relief— life, death, pain, sorrow, and joy. We begin to remember who we are and why we are here.

As stated before, it would be naive to assume, however, that the new millennium will automatically, or even at all, bring us heaven on earth—the kind of utopia that idealists hope for. Let us recall George Bernard Shaw's sobering remark in *Man and Superman*, ''A lifetime of happiness! No man [or woman] alive could bear it: it would be hell on earth.''

We may see trends in history and evolution, but there surely are no guarantees. Even if we agree that evolution is teleological, this need not say anything about the destiny of the human species. We know that Nature operates on the basis of superabundance, and many life forms and certainly countless individual members of a species are mere stepping-stones without promise of a greater future. Our species may meet the same fate that untold species have already met: to be discarded to make room for other, more adaptable life forms. The way things are going, humanity may already be working on its own obsolescence—whether through ecological devastation, nuclear holocaust, or, as some believe, replacement by artificial intelligence.

Yet we must hope. We must remain positive in the face of all kinds of contrary evidence. For without hope, we shall have no will to live. Without the will to live, our civilizational adventure will come to an end. Some cynics might consider this desirable, but from a larger evolutionary perspective we ought not to belittle human existence, nor our potential to go beyond, far beyond, our current state of affairs. While "man" is certainly not the measure of all things—other than in the sense that we limit and delimit—there is a greatness hidden within us that remains for us to discover, individually and collectively. It is that greatness—call it "Spirit" or "Divine"—that endows our humanness with its deepest meaning and significance, precisely because it points beyond what is merely human.

Regardless of our biological fate on this planet, and regardless of the cultural significance of the millennial threshold, we as individuals have an astounding capacity for survival—not as organisms but as non-local identities, or Spirit. We can realize this capacity irrespective of all historical vicissitudes. Indeed, without recovering our spiritual identity, we will be subject to the ravages of time, whether our planetary future is benign or a veritable nightmare. As biological organisms we are all destined to die. Immortality is purely a spiritual matter.

When we are secure in this realization, we can courageously engage our biological destiny, for death, sickness, and all the other adversities of conditioned existence cease to frighten us. We can fearlessly live life and be creative, building a world for all beings that is as benign, harmonious, and wholesome as possible. When we are free within ourselves, we are also free to be compassionate and loving.

As many contributors to the anthology have expressed, we must bring our own house in order first before we can hope to change the world. It is appropriate to feed the hungry, provide shelter for the homeless, nurse the sick, and alleviate the suffering of those in pain, but it is equally appropriate and just as important to uplift our own souls and cultivate self-understanding and inner discipline. For our outer actions are only as effective as our inner vision, and our vision depends for its breadth and depth not merely on intellectual knowledge but also spiritual wisdom.

Today's crisis is a planetary crisis as well as a crisis of consciousness. Hence personal transformation and social transformation must go hand in hand. Even quietists will admit that we cannot avoid action altogether, and hence our actions should be carried by knowledge, wisdom, and compassion. Otherwise there is indeed the danger, suggested by some contributors to our anthology, of merely interfering with life rather than cooperating with it.

The rediscovery in our day of such timeless moral values as love and compassion is among the more hopeful signs. Through love and compassion we can acknowledge and enact our essential interconnectedness with all life forms in an ever-widening circle of kinship. In the course of humanity's development, our species has incurred an immense debt to other species on this planet. We must now understand this fact and begin to repay that debt by practicing reverence for life, as Albert Schweitzer challenged us to do.

Only a total moral and spiritual reorientation will allow us to meet that challenge. Many essays in this volume indicate just what is involved in such a sweeping metanoia: returning to greater simplicity in our lives, ending social conflict, accepting the multivariate composition of modern society, redeploying the massive resources of the military complex toward alleviating social plight, and not least abolishing animal slavery.

To provide a certain structure for the over 140 statements in the anthology, we have grouped them into ten categories: Opening Perspectives; A Place for Hope and Realism; Visionary Philosophy, Evolutionary Vision; The Social Dimension; Science, Economics, and Nature; Minding the Body, Embodying the Mind; The New Morality; Living in Peace and Harmony; Spirituality; and Recovering Spiritual Practice. However, because of the integrative vision espoused by our contributors, this division is somewhat arbitrary. A number of contributions could just as easily have been placed in other categories as well. The present framework will, we hope, however, help to facilitate access to the range of thinking and feeling expressed by the contributors.

Our hope for our readers is that this anthology will stimulate, challenge, encourage, and uplift. It has done this for us, and we are grateful to all our contributors for making this experience possible; we have grown because of it.

We conclude our introductory remarks with an old teaching from the *Chandogya-Upanishad* (VII.23), which expresses in mantric form our deepest sentiments:

yo vai bhūmā tat sukhaṃ
nālpe sukham asti
bhūmā eva sukhaṃ
bhūmā tv eva vijijñāsitavya.

(That which is Whole is joy.
There is no joy in fractioned existence.
Only the Whole is joy.
But one must desire to understand the Whole.)

OPENING PERSPECTIVES

| MARILYN FERGUSON

Marilyn Ferguson, Ph.D.Hon., is the publisher and executive editor of *Brain/Mind Bulletin* and the author of *The Brain Revolution* and the best-selling *The Aquarian Conspiracy: Personal and Social Transformation in Our Time*. The recipient of numerous awards, she lectures and consults around the globe.

Global Weather Report

As we approach the next millennium, there is an eerie sense of something big on the horizon. The tumbling of the Berlin Wall, the United States emerging from the war in the Persian Gulf, declaring a ''New World Order''—overtones of Armageddon.

In 1991 there were signs and wonders in the midsummer heavens: the largest solar flares ever recorded; the celebrated joining of Mars, Jupiter, and Venus in the night sky, culminating on June 17—the anniversary of a similar configuration in 2 B.C., considered by some scholars to have been the star of Bethlehem; in late June, an array of lights in a chorus line across the night sky: moon, Mercury, Mars, Jupiter, Venus, the star Regulus. This convergence and dance of celestial bodies, strangely enough, had been overlooked by standard astronomy almanacs, oriented as they are to looking through telescopes rather than gazing at the sky itself.

Meanwhile, as it does every few hundred years, the sun wobbled out of its magnetic center, setting off volcanic activity that will be followed by a decade of weather extremes. A massive eruption in the Philippines altered the world climate. In July, a total solar eclipse.

World events played into a sense of what the Kabbalah calls "the End of Days." Communism fell in its fatherland. Statues of Lenin came crashing down along with the illusion of "scientific" solutions to our social ills and other icons of earthly saviors.

In 1992 the world economy became chaotic. Famine stalked Somalia. Nations fell into civil war, "wars and rumors of wars."

In April the largest European earthquake in two centuries struck the Netherlands. Mt. Vesuvius erupted. On Earth Day, a quake shook Joshua Tree National Monument in California, followed by a quake at Lost Coast and one centered near Eureka.

In biblical terminology, these "earthquakes in divers places" preceded an apocalyptic moment. During the Celtic feast of Beltane, a time when hundreds of fires once burned on hilltops in Ireland, the world's multicultural laboratory—the city of Los Angeles—blew up. The "City of Angels" burned for three days. One eyewitness said, "It was like I was in a movie of the last day."

The "flashpoint" of the uprising was the intersection of two Los Angeles streets, Florence and Normandy. Florence, heart of the Renaissance—and Normandy, synonymous with battle. And, Sarajevo, flashpoint of the First World War, exploded again. In June, a larger quake in Joshua Tree. A few hours later, another quake one hundred miles away.

On August 15, a volcano erupted in Alaska, and earthquakes struck the nearby Andreanof Islands and Kyrgyzstan in the former Soviet Union. Over the next month, a mammoth hurricane hit the Bahamas, Florida, and Louisiana, causing unprecedented damage. A tropical storm claimed hundreds of lives in China. Guam was hit by a typhoon. Flash floods in Afghanistan crashed through the Hindu Kush valleys, killing hundreds. A spectacular earthquake off the shore of Nicaragua sent tidal waves over two hundred miles of coast, sweeping people out to sea. Days later Kauai, Hawaii, was devastated by a hurricane.

"Almost without pause," *Time* reported in September, "nature lately has shattered, crushed and flooded the Earth with a series of cataclysms."

"It's time for myths and legends to walk the Earth once more," Nikos Kazantzakis wrote in *Odysseus*. Our common experiences have brought us ever closer to the intensifying collective vision of an impending transition in the human story.

What new world is being born, and what are our responsibilities as the inheritors of a Promised Land? Shall we answer the wake-up call?

4

2

JOHN ROSSNER

John Rossner, Ph.D., D.Sc., D.Litt., is professor of religion at Concordia University, Montreal, Canada. He is president of The International Institute of Integral Human Sciences and abbot-general of The Order of the Transfiguration.

The Spiritual Temper of Tomorrow

We live today on the threshold of a radically different era in the history of human civilizations. We are in the process of creating a new conception of ourselves and our world, but one whose precise shape is not yet clear and distinct. The old maps in most disciplines no longer adequately guide those who live at the frontiers of discovery, whether in physics or philosophy, psychology or medicine, astronomy, international politics, economics, social doctrine, or theology.

The foundational myths and theories that people have lived by so comfortably for the past two or three centuries in Western civilization since the seventeenth-century Age of Reason and the eighteenth-century Enlightenment have simply proven inadequate in most of these fields to allow our best minds an intelligent interpretation of the new data of human experience.

And so we are already in the midst of a great paradigm shift in practically every area of life. Geniuses of our time—from Pierre Teilhard de Chardin, Marshall McLuhan, and Thomas Kuhn to Willis Harman and Barbara Marx Hubbard—have already begun to weave the new more comprehensive or holistic myths and models by which science, spirituality, and universal human values can live together tomorrow.

We—or some of us at least—are already living with a new physics, which in quantum mechanics revises our definitions of time, space, and causality, and allows for new models of physical reality and for a space-time continuum open to remote pan-psychic reception of information and the measurable influence of mind within matter. The names Brian Josephson, Costa de Beauregard, Elizabeth Rauscher, John B. Hasted, Harold E. Puthoff, and Russell Targ, Richard D. Mattock, and Evans Harris Walker come to mind—all contributors to The Iceland *Papers.*

At the same time we also live with a new psychology and new sciences of consciousness—from Carl Jung to transpersonal psychology—which study the transformative power of spirit and postulate multidimensional models of mind in a multidimensional universe. We are struggling to make sense out of everything from the near-death experience to postmortem contacts with the dead, guided by a series of contemporary explorers of the human psyche from Stanislav Grof to Elizabeth Kübler-Ross and Raymond A. Moody, Jr. In their integrated worldviews, religious beliefs and scientific knowledge are not so radically opposed to one another as they have been for the past two or three centuries.

Similarly, in the new medicine—from contemporary studies in Oriental and alternative therapies to the nonlocal medicine of Larry Dossey—we already know much more about the measurable effects of our subjective life, our thoughts and intentions, attitude, prayers, and hopes—and even the observable effects of planetary cycles and synchronicity—upon whether we or others around us get well or die. And in a new biology—from the life energies research of Harold Saxton Burr to that of E. Douglas Dean and Bernard Grad—we find a new rational model for how that could work.

The same kinds of momentous new models are extant in almost every field, from environmental studies and the Gaia hypothesis of James Lovelock, to the educational theory, the model of a rehumanized curriculum for the globalization of consciousness, and the world peace studies of Benito F. Reyes of the World University of America, Ojai, California, and Robert Mueller of the United Nations Peace University in Costa Rica.

Inner human potentials of intuition and creativity have just begun to be rediscovered in all of these areas through the new sciences of consciousness and healing. Earlier in this century, two great prophets of modern times, East and West—one the French Jesuit anthropologist and theologian Pierre Teilhard de Chardin and the other the Hindu sage Sri Aurobindo of Pondicherry, India—proclaimed that the next step in human evolution would be "a psychic-spiritual mutation" to a higher consciousness. The mythic foundations of the old world order—and its rationalistic, reductionistic, materialistic Newtonian presuppositions which have dehumanized Western civilization and created a stripped, mechanistic model of the human being and of human societies—are no longer credible to those who know enough. But it is also obvious that not everyone in positions of power in church, state, or academia seems to understand yet the new models of future science and the new sciences of consciousness and healing, or their significance for approaching forms of planetary existence that will profoundly change and affect our daily lives in the twenty-first century.

The polarization that we are witnessing between reductionistic forms of scientism and dehumanizing processes of modernization and secularization on the one hand, and reactionary forms of fundamental religion on the other, is counterproductive to both authentic approaches to science and to authentic approaches to the world's religions.

In the social sciences of the near future, positive forms of primary human spiritual and psychic experience will be recognized as the sources of classic myths and religious doctrines. Scholars will understand more about the transformative power of psyche and spirit; immortality; life after life; communication with dead saints, sages, and ancestors; prophecy; extraordinary healings; and belief in "other" or "higher worlds" and a multidimensional universe. These experiences will be acknowledged one day in secular societies—not as mere superstitions from a prescientific age—but rather as universal factors in the formation of tremendously empowering, symbolically expressed creeds found in all cultures, ancient and modern. We will then perhaps at last be able to see our way past the present radical opposition between science and spirituality. We might also begin to lessen the misunderstandings between conflicting faiths that have been so destructive in human affairs over the past several centuries and millennia.

Are there really universal human values waiting to be rediscovered within the world's religions and cultures, across all sectarian boundaries? Yes! But these cannot be discovered by a rationalistic, left-brained academic analysis alone. The consciousness of scholars themselves will have to change and their perspectives expand to the consideration of alternative new paradigms for the convergence of science and spirituality in the global village. And more important even than

7

this, we must begin to pay attention to the qualities of personal transformation in the creation of a new humanity.

The fruits of the spirit—under whatever terminology—have always been recognizable and are treasured by mystics who are frequently a force for positive social reform in most of the world's great religions and cultures, East and West. These universally recognized qualities of authentic spiritual life in all of the great religious traditions of the world include unselfish love, the readiness to forgive injuries, peace, justice, compassion, humility, and the joyous service of a global humanity, of all sentient life, and of the planet itself. And it is classical mystical experience—in many of its varied religious and secular forms—that has in fact inspired and nurtured the perennial heroic and prophetic quest for peace, justice, and a better world " . . . on earth, as it is in Heaven."

3

BARBARA MARX HUBBARD

Barbara Marx Hubbard, president of the Foundation for Conscious Evolution, is an author, speaker, and social architect. Her life purpose is to understand, communicate, and empower the collective potential of the human race to build a positive future. She is the author of *The Evolutionary Journey* and *The Hunger of Eve* and the first part of her magnum opus, *The Book of Co-Creation, Revelation: Our Birth is a Crisis,* has recently been released.

The Birth of Universal Humanity

From an evolutionary perspective, planet Earth is becoming one integrated living system, conscious of itself as a whole. We are experiencing a crisis of birth.

The very same force that drew atom to atom, molecule to molecule, and cell to cell, is drawing us together into a living organism. Our environments, our defense systems, our communication systems, our economies, our cultures are now irrevocably connected. The "noosphere," the thinking layer of Earth, as Teilhard de Chardin called it, is about to get "its collective eyes." This might mean a mass "metanoia," a mass change of mind, a shared mystical experience for the human race, when we would, in a twinkling of an eye, re-cognize ourselves as members of one body.

What we are calling the environmental crisis is a natural stage in the development of a planetary organism, just as a physical birth is a natural stage for a biological organism. We have hit a limit to growth on this finite planet . . . *naturally.* We must now learn to coordinate

9

ourselves as a whole, to handle our own toxic wastes, to limit our population growth, to shift to renewable and nonpolluting energies . . . *naturally.*

As we conserve and enhance life within this terrestrial world, we also are reaching beyond planet-boundedness and limited self-consciousness for the next stage of our evolution, which I call Universal Humanity.

We are told that in one generation we might destroy life on Earth if we continue our current behavior. So it may also be that in this same one generation we can change life on Earth.

That change *is* occurring radically and rapidly in millions of us simultaneously. In the domain of consciousness we are now aware that we are connected to all life. The mystical consciousness of the spiritual geniuses of the human race is being democratized by the crisis of birth. And mass communication systems are now informing us instantaneously throughout the whole body politic.

Another aspect of the internal change is brought on by the fact that we are the last generation to be able to "be fruitful and multiply" up to maximum. One more doubling of the population and we will be ten billion people, beyond the carrying capacity of Earth. This means that the vast human desire to procreate, and the effort to nurture large families is lessening. A new urge is arising, especially in women. It is felt as creative vocation, the desire to self-express through meaningful work and chosen function. This desire is the third great human drive. The first is self-preservation. The second is self-reproduction, and the third is self-actualization, the longing to fully develop unique potential through creative expression.

I call this urge "suprasex." It is the passionate motivation not to reproduce ourselves, but to evolve ourselves. As we need fewer babies and wiser people, nature is flooding us with this urge to self-express. If Mother Nature invented sex to get us to reproduce the species . . . and made it very attractive, now she is inventing suprasex to get us to evolve ourselves and our world . . . and is making it very exciting! We are moving from procreation to co-creation by attraction and desire.

We may be entering a "second life cycle." In the first life cycle we are born, go through puberty, reproduce the species, age, and die. The second life cycle begins when the passion to create and self-actualize is felt. It drives us to join not our genes to produce the child, but our genius to produce the work. We seek co-creative rather than (or as well as) procreative partners. We move beyond gender and age to a new phase in which we are self-healing, self-regenerating, and eventually perhaps self-transforming humans.

The positive aspect of the population crisis is the liberation of the untapped creative potential of the human race. This phenomenon first affects women, but men also feel it, and are liberated from the immense effort to care for large families. Both men and women seek their true "vocations of destiny," and begin to join in "co-creative families" to birth themselves as "universal humans," fully human beings at the dawn of the universal age.

I see this birth in the context of our fifteen-billion-year evolutionary story. It has taken that long for this particular planet to come to its term and enter its period of transition. The coming phase might be called "co-creation" or conscious evolution. The species is becoming aware of evolution and able to participate consciously in guiding it. Through the maturation of science, we learn about nature from without. Through the maturation of our spirituality, we experience nature from within as spirit, source, God.

For me the model of the universal human is Jesus Christ. His life is a demonstration of the next stage of evolution. His birth, ministry, crucifixion, resurrection, and ascension is the evolutionary template of our full collective potential . . . personal, social, and technological.

He is a living presence available to us all from within. I experience this personally as a divine impulse to evolve in the image of Christ. In my own life I am in a constant state of practice to experience the inner Christ being born as a fully human being, co-creative with nature, with others, and with God. Through joining with other "pioneering souls" in deep communion, I am discovering the pattern of the "co-creative family," the family of chosen life partners whose genius emancipates one another. At sixty-two I feel in some deep way at the early phase of my second life cycle . . . perhaps at the young adolescent stage, learning what it means to be a sovereign person, a universal human. It is a great privilege to be alive at this moment of maximum danger and opportunity.

4

CHARLOTTE WATERLOW

Charlotte Waterlow, M.A., Dip.Ed., M.B.E., is a retired history teacher who pioneered a General Certificate of Education syllabus of twentieth-century world history that is today taken by some two hundred British schools. For several years, she has worked actively with the World Federalist Movement and the United Nations Association, and is a member of the British Campaign for Nuclear Disarmament. She is the author of several books, including *Tribe, State and Community; India;* and *Superpowers and Victims* and the coauthor of *The Hinge of History, Europe 1945 to 1970* and *The War Games that Superpowers Play.*

The Hinge of History

I suggest that the modern age is the hinge of history, that in the two hundred years since the seminal year of 1789, history has begun to enter a completely new phase, signifying the beginning of a transformation of consciousness on a global scale.

Homo sapiens, who has the same genetic makeup as ourselves, emerged about forty thousand years ago into "prehistory." Thirty-five thousand years later "civilization" began to appear in many parts of the world. Colin Renfrew agrees that civilization is present when two of three factors occur: city dwelling, a written language, and "monumental ceremonial centers." These criteria characterize the civilizations (in the plural) that arose from about 3000 B.C. onward in Mesopotamia, Egypt, China, Japan, India, Southeast Asia, Asia Minor, the eastern and western Mediterranean, western Europe, Central and South America, and, later, the Byzantine and Arab Empires and Europe of the Middle Ages. Prehistoric conditions reigned in North America until colonized by the Europeans in the seventeenth century and in Africa and Australia until colonized by the Europeans in the nineteenth century.

These civilizations, while distinct in style—in language, religious cult, art, and even costume—had certain basic common characteristics. Religion dominated their thinking and dictated their actions. With the exception of the odd Greek philosopher, all believed the universe to be divine, and almost all believed it to be peopled with discarnate beings, from celestial gods and angels to ancestors, imps, witches, and demons. Almost all believed that the "truth" about the spiritual universe is known through vision or revelation recorded in sacred scriptures or oral myths. These "true" texts or tales laid down principles of ethics and legal and social codes regarded henceforth as sacrosanct. They inspired systems of government based on divinized monarchs, caste or feudal systems of warriors, priests/scribes (the only literates), merchants, and peasants, serfs, slaves, and "untouchables," each fulfilling his or her preordained function.

Marriage, education, work, costume—all aspects of life were based on fixed custom and the interests of the group. "God bless the squire and his relations and keep us in our proper stations" sums up the traditional situation. "Growth," "development," and "evolution" were not thought of. The leaders looked backward for inspiration. The only partial exception was the civilization of ancient Greece and Rome, which had no scriptures and thus developed free-thinking philosophy and democracy—for male citizens only. Greek thought may have been the enzyme that sparked off the ideas of modernity in western Europe some fifteen hundred years later.

The modern age is based on two tremendous developments: theoretical and applied science, and the idea of human rights—the idea that every *person*, of whatever sex, color, class, or creed, has a right to the conditions of life to enable him or her to develop his or her personal creativity. Article 26 of the United Nations' Universal Declaration of Human Rights (1948) contains what is perhaps the most explosive sentence in the world today. "Everyone has the right to education," it says, and then adds: "Education shall be directed to the full development of the human personality!" The concept of a world society of persons is emerging, and the bond that unites persons, as such, is *love*. The traditional ties of authority and obedience that united people in their tribe, caste, cult, or service to the monarch suppressed individual self-expression. Love is the only force that, in uniting people, enhances their individuality! The marvels of science

13

are providing the material means to make the universal civilization (in the singular) of persons possible. The terrible turmoils of today are its birth pangs.

Because they were the bedrock of the old order, the traditional religions are now collapsing. This is the first age in history where government is secular, and agnosticism is general. The paradox is that the first age in history which affirms that everybody matters is the first age in history when many believe that a person's personality is snuffed out after his or her short human life of seven days or seventy years. Is it possible that the ancients' vision of the universe as a cosmopolis, a city of men and gods, was right after all? If life does extend beyond physical death, to be a citizen of the enormous universe that science is now revealing will be thrilling indeed! If the visionary powers of the ancients are revived to blend with the rationalism of science and the humanism of human rights, the world community of the post-modern age may be a community of humans and gods, united in love.

5
SUBASH KAK

Subash Kak, Ph.D., is professor of electrical and computer engineering at Louisiana State University, Baton Rouge. He is also a poet and Vedic scholar, and is the author of several books, including *The Nature of Physical Reality* and *Patanjali and Cognitive Science*.

Of History and Truth

We stand on the threshold of a new age. We are seeing old political structures collapse around the world. Forgotten nations wish to reclaim and celebrate their own histories. Other people seek utopias based on simplistic religious dogma.

One might ask if the hundred wars already joined can be stopped from spreading? Many of these wars are consequences of groups trying to impose their histories on others. So long as people see a chosen past event as being the beginning of their history and ideology, believers will wage war on the outsiders.

This is an age of *sandhyā*, a perilous time between two world ages. The interregnum of *sandhyā* marks the interval between the poses and twists of the dance of history. The age we will enter depends on how our visionaries and leaders shape events. Each *sandhyā* carries the promise of revelation as well as the specter of chaos.

We may compare the progress of humankind to a bird's flight. Such a flight is possible only upon two wings. One might say that these two wings are science and spirituality, but from another perspective, they are the knowledge of the present and the past.

Nations have descended into dark ages when they have denied their histories. This is what happened to Europe when it suppressed its Greek heritage. But now the dogma that Greece is the fountainhead of all wisdom has become another prison.

On the other hand, empires have worked to erase the memories of subject nations. Fortunately, the age of empires is behind us. In this new age of information, we need to facilitate the remembrance of the shared history of all regions. Psychology reveals that confronting the past is itself the best therapy.

If we accept that scientific truths are eternal, should we not accept that spiritual truths are also eternal? Logic compels this acceptance. We need to teach a method for people to discover for themselves this unity in knowledge. Guilt or reward cannot be the basis of such a method. The only ideology one can support is the ideology of search for truth. Knowledge is its own reward. It is the Way that matters.

The Rigvedic epiphany represents humanity's earliest remembered revelation. Let us journey to this source and use it as a context to reflect on the visions of the later epochs. If we look sufficiently far back, our memories will converge to the shared past, and if that does not happen, then let us celebrate our shared potential. We will realize that we are not just approaching the end of the second millennium, but that countless ages have gone by. Science and technology are aiding us in this process of discovery.

In our journey of remembrance, let us gather up flowers from all lands. Fortunately, new technologies have the potential of extending our memories and communication without limit, just as science is helping us recreate forgotten episodes of our journey. A uniform vision of the past may not unite humankind; a universal science will.

Many bemoan the loss of faith in the institutions and ideas of yesterday. But some of these ideas have outlived their usefulness and meaning. If some other ideas were wrongly put aside, let us speak about them, reason about them. It is our ignorance of history that makes us belittle our own age. The beginning that we witness now is just a consequence of our past.

It is the unprejudiced mind that dares to speak the truth, that can reveal if the emperor has any clothes. That is why children ask deep questions. My own children, Abhinav and Arushi, have initiated countless Upanishadic dialogues with me:

Dad, what lies behind seeing?
How do we tell that our lives are not dreams?

SUBASH KAK

Are there universes greater than ours?
Where do we go when we die? And how?
Who is the being that stares from behind the eyes of the fish
in the fish bowl?

But modern humanity has no time to search for meaning. We are surrounded on all sides by machines that have extended our senses. At work or at home we are part of greater machine systems. And now we are busy remaking ourselves in the shape of these machines. We see ourselves as driven entirely by emotion and biological drives. With such images and focus on the evanescent, how can we avoid painful ennui? At the same time, we cannot believe that we might be somewhat more than our physical self.

The metaphor of the machine has led many to believe that the march of events has its own logic and that we have no real choices. There are those who say that our lives as biological machines have no special meaning. But as conscious beings, we do make choices, and these choices have deep significance.

We do not learn something unless we have already almost arrived at that discovery. We construct reality by our senses. Although each one of us has seen the infinite within us, we do not remember pure visions. Our memories are like boxes in attics, where jewels have been lost amongst old clothes.

We cannot say that all paths lead to truth; some paths are wrong and destructive. The wrong paths are those that constrict freedom and creativity. This is why affirmation of truth and history is essential. It is only by such affirmation that we become able to prize the secret of our deepest being from the recesses of our experience. We will help this affirmation if we see ourselves as members of a larger community of interdependent beings on a living planet.

6

ROWENA PATTEE KRYDER

Rowena Pattee Kryder, M.F.A., Ph.D., is a mother, visionary artist, spiritual teacher, scholar, author, and founder of the Creative Harmonics Institute in Mount Shasta, California. She is a former faculty member of the California Institute of Integral Studies in San Francisco. The *Gaia Matrix Oracle* is her most recent written work. The following essay is an excerpt from her unpublished trilogy *The Emerald River of Compassion*.

Wasteland or Human Transformation?

Our universe, a free-flowing stream of light, awaits discovery. In our own souls is the soul of the River, the living stream of the mystery of creation. For too long we have been seeking to further the human agenda at the expense of the forces that nourish and support us. This drive to progress, to assure our foothold in the evolutionary stream, was once appropriate. No longer. The planet is no longer a habitat for creatures and plants who weave life together. All habitats are human habitats now. Rare is the mite who escapes the acid rain, the fish who swims free of polluted waters, the forest not forced into an island.

We were once innocent, emerging from the womb of the earth and blinking our eyes at dancing tide pools, flowering jungles, and berry-filled valleys. We once were in awe of the universe that shaped us. Then, in the fear that arises when predators outnumber the human family, we shouted and made weapons. In the struggle for survival, we shut ourselves off from the tremors of the vast vibratory cosmos.

Summoning the shapes of language from the fire stolen from heaven, we articulated an intent apart from the apes and the symbiotic life web. Now, in our quest for security and comfort, we shelter ourselves from the soul of the River. We sleep through everyday miracles of life. We war upon ourselves. We suffer from evolutionary amnesia, forgetting the sources, forgetting our natural and our spiritual lineages. Our amnesia, deep and serious, flings us into destruction. Lacking reverence for the earth and her creatures, we war with her, and bring ourselves to the wasteland.

The Wasteland

River of molten lava in language, the River founts forth here from the ending of civilization, praying like dervishes, preyed upon by humanity dazzled in its wake.

Running passion with River-running with passion running. River flows compassion when cities sink and noses run with tears over the ever-impending drastic change that happened in the nineteen nineties, when babes were in their nighties, no one looking because asleep in the slippery season of humanity's winter. Sliding past the postman on an icy street, Mujaji falls down Main Street in the mists of time, before Adam and Eve, Mashyone and Mashini broke out of the leafy garden in spring.

The Ganges is pulithy and the Loire is pull-luted while history tumbles out of Eden and stars watch Gaia aghast. Exhausted, Mujaji picks herself up and stares into the mist, brushing the snow from the coat grown furry as primeval pre-Paleolithic times return before her delirium.

Foggily the seduction of the past breathes through her hair and vacant lots stare like death out of the eye sockets of demolished cars.

Heads of wrath meet the fog like the giants before Yggdrasil rose out of the River. Fire and ice steam in the heart of Gus outside the remnants of the Catholic Church. The aidless survive without sex, weakening T-cells in winter where celibate priests stand mocking the passion of Christ. HIV virus in bloody mass bespeaks where AIDS eats morsels of aching humanity.

Lapping the shores of the open mouths of Ireland, Africa, South America, the slums of every city, people pool cars to find the spout, the spot where nutrients still fall. The grains are gone, the soil spent, the life-mother is weary and dry. The veins cease to return to the heart. The arteries search for the sea, to cease, stop, stomp on the stumps, where the River runs dry in the now existing drought. Where are the primal waters now?

Orpheus of old, the nature spirits hide in the crevasses of his body, in the sinews of basaltic dust, the igneous remains of chaos theory turned real, ignited by the last of all wars: the war of consciousness and being, logos and eros.

Napoleon would wonder at the war waged over witches who gape into the seams of the uniforms of twentieth-century life. The electronic boom overwhelms the post-world-war baby boom whose nervous systems reject the software of a clumsy technology. The witches are executed for executing executives who bewitched their daughters into becoming high-salaried programming priestesses. Their graves lie solemnly on the spent earth where Gaia still struggles with her outcroppings.

Grotesque forms of prehistory lurk in the substratum of deserted streets of New York, Paris, Beijing, and Bangkok. Genesis warms in the compost heap of the past where the golden age was swept aside by the janitors of the twentieth century. Garbage dumps cease to recycle.

Deaf to the music of the spheres, humanity falls from love. The elements descended from etheric throats of the gods and now rebel against human lovelessness. With wind and water, earth and water, fire and water, fire and ice and fire, earth and wind, earth and fire ad infinitum, the elements clear the earthmatrix of human masses and countless treasures.

The Uncarved Block, our original nature, shines through the elementals unearthing the Amazonian Empire from the jungles. The sacred books remain untouched, while hungry hearts search the Emerald River for restoration of love.

Human Transformation

The power of the imaginal, of the deep dream, is a power that we, in our habitual preoccupation with production and consumption, have forgotten. But it still incubates and lies latent within us. To call ourselves forth in this critical time is to re-create not only the human *worldview*, but the *human*. We are now to surpass the human condition as we have known it. How can we discover who we truly are?

I believe our great journey of transformation has three essential facets: first, remembrance of lineage, tradition, the ancestors, the primordial, the archaic sources and ways of life that transmit truth; second, revelation, vision, dreaming, the power to penetrate to source in the here and now; and third, creativity and action, leading to manifestation of the new vision.

The result can be a transformed humanity. Experience is a foretaste of revery. Revery is a foretaste of vision. Vision is a foretaste of the naked truth—where we no longer clutch and grasp for existence, but open to the sublimity of *being* itself. Then the creative power of the River can burst forth from within us, giving birth to a new humanity that blesses the planet with cultures in harmony with the Emerald River's own mystery.

7

KRIYANANDA

Kriyananda is a direct disciple of Paramhansa Yogananda, the author of *Autobiography of a Yogi*. He is the founder and spiritual director of Ananda World Brotherhood Village, one of the most successful intentional communities in the world. Kriyananda is internationally known as a teacher and lecturer, author, and composer. His books include *The Path: A Spiritual Autobiography, The Essence of Self-Realization, Cities of Light*, and his correspondence course, *14 Steps to Higher Awareness*.

Visions of the Future

There has been much controversy on the subject of the "New Age." One point on which it seems pointless to disagree is that we *are* in a new age, no matter how each of us personally decides to define it, and no matter whether we personally reject the usual notions of what the new age means.

Science has brought us fundamental changes in the way we view reality. Matter, we are now given to understand, is energy. Energy is fluid, not fixed and immutable, like still photographs or concrete forms. This discovery has been enough in itself to influence the way we think on a broad spectrum of issues.

Religious dogmatism, for instance, is bound to be seen increasingly as incompatible with a reasonable perception of truth.

Moral values—as I've explained at length in my book *Crises in Modern Thought*—no longer fixed and absolute, are perceived to be relative. This relativity, however, will come to be understood in a directional, not a chaotic sense. That is, its direction will be understood to be toward a potential for perfection far beyond the petty definitions of absolute morality, as outlined in the past.

Wealth is no longer land-based as it once was. The time is coming, I believe, when wealth will not even be based on money. For already it clearly depends on how much energy one commands. And energy depends on thought and creativity, far more so than on oil, atomic power, or others of its recognized sources today.

The human factor has yet to be recognized in its full potential, but it will be. For everything that humankind has ever accomplished has always depended above all on the output of *human* energy. How much more so will this truth become recognized in an age when energy, not matter, is perceived as the underlying reality of the universe.

Rapid transportation and communication have already changed the way we look at the world. They have brought people and customs from distant parts of the world into our very living rooms. Inevitably, in the future, there will be a growing sense of planetary communality, even if, at first, our growing awareness fans rivalries rather than soothes them. (Yes, I think the path to future global harmony will prove to pass first through global war. Let us hope it doesn't!)

The dawning awareness of energy over property as the source of wealth and power has already, inevitably, created a shift away from the concept of control by an elite, and toward rule by "the people." Gradually, however, it will be seen that unless energy is controlled with wisdom, the results are chaos. In time, a new elite will come to be recognized: a moral and spiritual elite, with the developed understanding to guide humankind toward harmonious coexistence and lasting prosperity.

Again, humanity's growing awareness of energy is producing a worldwide shift of consciousness in the recognition of the importance of women in human affairs. Women represent energy—*shakti* in Sanskrit. As masculine nature keeps reason uppermost and feeling hidden, so feminine nature keeps feeling uppermost, while using reason to support feeling. What we *feel* about things is what gives us human beings the impetus to act on them. The increasing influence of feminine nature on humanity will result in a great increase in human energy in the accomplishment of its goals. Projects that used to seem hopeless because human nature simply wasn't up to doing them will begin to seem feasible, not only because of technological advances, but because of breakthroughs in humanity's way of looking at things. The argument, for example, that humankind is constitutionally incapable of achieving international peace and cooperation will come to be viewed as one of the quaint superstitions of a bygone age. Feminine energy will have a great influence on this more dynamic view of human potentials.

Finally, humanity's search for spiritual perfection also will take a new direction. No longer will religion be identified with fixed dogmas and beliefs. It will be perceived as a system of psychophysical practices designed to help the individual to achieve inner perfection. Thus, yoga in all its branches will come into its own. Inasmuch as yoga deals not only with mental and physical techniques of self-improvement, but with direct control of the inner energy (*pranayama*, energy control), it will be recognized as the very *science* of religion, and will become the human science par excellence of the New Age.

8

JOHN B. COBB, JR.

John B. Cobb, Jr., Ph.D., retired in 1990 after thirty-two years of teaching at the School of Theology at Claremont, California. He continues as a director of the Center for Process Studies. Among the books he has authored or coauthored are *Christ in a Pluralistic Age*, *The Liberation of Life*, and *For the Common Good*.

Seeds of Hope

The twentieth century began in optimism and is ending in gloom. Yet the real seers at the beginning of the twentieth century already saw the seeds of decay that had been planted in the nineteenth. Perhaps at the end of the twentieth century we can discern seeds of hope that have been planted in our time of decay. At the beginning of the twentieth century the obvious trends were the spread of enlightenment, democracy, universal education, modern health care, and economic prosperity. The twentieth century would see the total victory of man over nature. Christians supposed that the great missionary program of the late nineteenth century was sweeping all before it. One could even believe that the time when "civilized" nations would resort to war was ending.

But there were those who saw beneath the surface the internal decay of Western civilization itself. They saw Western imperialism, colonialism, and racism for what they were. They foresaw the consequences of technology becoming master of society, subordinating all human values to the god of economic growth. They saw the ambiguity of enlightenment, democracy, universal education, modern health

JOHN B. COBB, JR.

care, economic prosperity, and man's victory over nature, as well as of the Christian mission that associated itself with these Western achievements. And they knew that none of this "progress" overcame the violence so deeply rooted in the male ego.

As the twentieth century draws to a close, it is all too easy to see that the pessimists were correct. Our achievements and victories seem hollow indeed. Projecting more of the same into the next century, we can foresee only disaster.

Some of these disasters can no longer be avoided. The population explosion cannot be stopped without catastrophe, in time to prevent horrendous consequences. The damage to the ozone layer will be a fact of life with which humanity must live. Depleted soils will not soon recover from the abuse we impose on them. Our descendants must live with nuclear wastes that add measurably to the threats to human life. The thousands of species of plants and animals we have exterminated are gone forever.

But in the midst of all this continuing, and even accelerating, decay, the late twentieth century has given birth to a new sensibility, a new religious vision. Our connectedness with one another and with all living things has entered deeply into the consciousness of some and is beginning to transform public discourse and reflection as well. Our consciousness has been raised about the structure of power between men and women and its destructiveness for both people and other creatures. We have collectively rejected racism as a basis for social and political policy, and we are beginning to understand and overcome its pervasive presence within us individually. A revulsion against rampant consumerism is giving rise to profound reappraisals of what life is all about. The traditional religions are finding their voice of protest against what the modern world has done to them as well as beginning to repent their own contribution to historic evil. As the next century dawns, it may be possible to organize effectively on the basis of this new "green" consciousness to reverse the directions in which the major tide still carries us.

It is hard to be optimistic. The world we leave to our children is already impoverished, and the impoverishment proceeds even now. The planet will certainly be more degraded in the year 2000 than it is today. The dominant political and economic forces are hardly touched by the new green consciousness. But this consciousness is growing all the same. The first decade of the twenty-first century may see its victory. If so, the long and difficult task of regenerating the Earth can begin.

25

9

MICHIO KUSHI

Michio Kushi is founder and president of the East West Foundation, Kushi Institute, Kushi Foundation, and Macrobiotics International. He is famous for his writings and lectures on Oriental methods of diet and health, and he is the author of many books, including *The Book of Macrobiotics, The Cancer Prevention Diet, Diet for a Strong Heart, One Peaceful World,* and *AIDS, Macrobiotics and Natural Immunity.*

The Two Paths into the Future

Modern civilization is on the verge of collapse. Throughout the fabric of human society, we feel political unrest, economic disruption, weakening beliefs in religious and spiritual traditions, social chaos in human relations, the decomposition of our families, and the constant threat of regional and global wars. The most fundamental trend of our modern civilization, and one that reflects the underlying cause of all these declining tendencies, is the biological and psychological degeneration of humanity. This degeneration has become so advanced that it permeates the very heart of our international and national governing bodies, educational and religious institutions, judicial and social practices, and our financial and economic systems. All of these systems are burdened and unable to cope with the rapid pace of degeneration. We find ourselves caught in the global current of a biological and psychological Noah's flood.

This degeneration manifests itself in several ways. Heart disease, cancer, the ever-evasive infectious diseases, degenerative diseases such as arthritis and diabetes are all rapidly and unceasingly spreading throughout the population. Psychological stress, anxiety, and mental disorders are becoming increasingly common to the point of being considered acceptable norms of behavior, and we are rapidly losing our intuitive capacities and sense of judgment. This loss of judgment results in misguided social affairs, giving rise to widespread environmental damage and pollution, all of which threatens the continued existence of many species on this planet. Humanity is confronting itself, along with all other species, with the possible extinction of its healthy and natural existence.

Modern technology offers various palliative responses to these problems: bionization, psychonization, genetic manipulation, as well as other similar approaches. All are symptomatic in nature, in that they suppress the symptoms while overlooking altogether—and at times even exacerbating—the root causes. The nature of a symptom is to draw attention to the deeper lying cause, and the causes underlying our overall degeneration have long been ignored by these various measures. Therefore, these symptoms of degeneration will continue to outpace our *technological* responses to problems that are, in essence, biological in nature.

The cause for our biological and psychological degeneration is modern civilized society's having lost respect for the order of nature and the universe. It has lost appreciation for its people and for certain fundamental time-tested traditions. It has lost its intuitive and comprehensive view of life and the universal meaning of humanity. From this lack of understanding of what "humanity" means, we have spoiled our natural environment. We have made everything artificial, including the food we consume daily.

We now come to a fork in the road and are confronted with two paths to travel. As members of this modern society, we could walk one and promote our current view of science, technology, politics, and economics. This will invite more tragedy within human society and, quite possibly, the extinction of large portions of modern civilization. Or we could travel the other, making a tremendous shift in our present direction, and create a new destiny for humanity and other species living on this planet, by rediscovering the order of nature and the universe. This would eventually open a new era of humanity under one peaceful world.

The first path is far easier to pursue than the second. The first path will lead to natural selection and, while the surviving species would continue to exist and develop, they would do so only upon the sacrifices of a large number of our human population and other species.

However, if there remains even a modicum of compassion and love, brotherhood and sisterhood for our fellow humans and other species on this planet, we can minimize the sacrifices through a drastic change of consciousness toward our environment, daily food, and lifestyle This change would reflect a more harmonious union with nature and the environment.

We must now take a giant leap forward on a global scale to encourage the evolution of planetary consciousness. We need to unify our discordant views, opinions, and approaches and look beyond the differences of East and West, North and South, race and nationalities, religions and cultures. We all must learn to live as one human race. We have all manifested from the universe and exist in a transitory state imaged in this human form. The essence of who we are is not determined by nationality, culture, race, or any particular system of religious belief. A view and way of life, called *macrobiotics* aims to achieve one peaceful world to be realized through physical health, peaceful minds, and spiritual compassion, embracing and uniting all antagonistic and complementary factors in nature and human society. The result will be the "planetary era of humanity," which will blossom into a healthy and peaceful civilization.

10

C. B. SCOTT JONES

C. B. Scott Jones, Ph.D., is president of the Human Potential Foundation, following a thirty-year career as a Navy jet carrier pilot and in Naval Intelligence. He has taught at the college and university levels and worked in the private sector research and development community.

The Universe Our Home

Looking for the action, my interest in the future is more than balanced by concern about what I am missing in the present. There is more than a vague belief that the hologram of the present not only is composed of all fragments of the past, but somehow contains robust information concerning the immediate and far future. It is as if the fiction we call time is mocking, taunting me to look at what is only hidden by cultural trances and fear to live fully in the moment.

Fight or flight . . . are these the only two primal responses to life-threatening situations? This is not what I observe in life. If survival is the object, equally important are negotiation and surrender. The first question has to be, what is the threat? An onrushing truck leaves little room for negotiation or fight. Other threats admit other options. Either in ignorance or with cultural blindness, a reduced number of responses leads to predictability and vulnerability. With negotiations and compromise, there is the possibility that good can be teased from evil, that the flame of joy can be kindled from the ashes of despair.

The raw power of nature, volcanic, seismic, wind, and water, dwarfs the best and worst that humankind can package. A spirit of community is always sparked with the calamity of disaster. When it is nurtured, necessary lessons are learned and the next encounter is less frightening. It is this toughening of spirit, tempered in adversity but encompassed in compassion, love, and respect for all life that is necessary to meet and survive the inevitable Earth changes ahead. There will be many awesome changes. The survivors of each shrug of Earth Mother will be imprinted with an increased capacity for regeneration and resurrection of spirit and hope. This is exactly the breeding stock needed for the times. Isn't it nice how things work out?

The hint of extraterrestrial and interdimensional life represents a search for our own completeness. It challenges us to think how we can avoid the negativeness so prevalent when different cultures meet. For some the fear is thick because they see no outcome other than a conquering, technically superior culture. While karma is operating, so is the potential of self-fulfilling prophecy. How should we prepare for this meeting? I suggest the same way that each of us prepared to enter the world from our mother's womb—with tough innocence. The universe, seen and unseen, is more complex and magnificent than most of us can imagine. And we are poorer for the effort to deny and ignore that a rendezvous has been set. We can show up with dignity and earn respect or declare victim status and take what is meted out. This is actually the largest cosmic joke I can imagine. Most of us are so much into our materialism that we cannot but dimly perceive the opportunities of the most important spiritual adventure this side of death.

I am sure that some governments think they have extraordinary secrets about extraterrestrial life. They should be mindful that the smaller the scorpion, the more lethal the bite. A tightly held secret has the same toxic potential. Enlarging the circle of those who are knowledgeable reduces the poison component of secrecy. Similarly, enlarging the circle to make the universe "home" is a needful undertaking. Any limit on the largest possible home creates alien areas of unknown but fearfully large size, and they are labeled "There be dragons here." There is a surplus of old maps that chart only the dimensions of the physical world. New maps are needed—maps that chart all other dimensions. This is where the action is.

II

STANLEY KRIPPNER

Stanley Krippner, Ph.D., is professor of psychology at Saybrook Institute and distinguished professor of psychology at California Institute of Integral Studies, both in San Francisco. He is the coauthor of *Spiritual Dimensions of Healing, Personal Mythology,* and *Dreamworking* and the editor of *Dreamtime and Dreamwork.*

Tune in Tomorrow

These are the best times, but also the worst;
Charles Dickens wrote this a century ago.
Century Twenty becomes Twenty-first,
As prospects and problems both seem to grow.

Earth satellites link us, cable news binds us;
From space, we get a view of one bright world.
But ethnic warfare and conflicts run wild;
Each month a new country's flag is unfurled.

Astronauts take their small steps on the moon,
And plan to go further at a quick pace;
But they leave garbage on the lunar dune,
And throw used debris into outer space.

Nations agree Spaceship Earth is our home,
It's a Water Planet, blue with some green.
Then why global warming, the ozone hole,
The greenhouse effect, and water unclean?

There's radiation in the air,
Smog and pollution, too,
But government experts say,
"Radiation won't harm you!"

In leisure time we travel
To each river, lake, and sea;
But oil spills foul the oceans,
Fish are filled with mercury.

Good medicines are found in jungle plants,
Botanists now find cures at every turn,
But these rain forests are disappearing—
Deforestation follows slash and burn.

We know the Earth nurtures and sustains us,
We enjoy verdant meadow and lush mound,
While desertification and erosion
Replace the green pastures with yellow ground.

Factories produce products for our homes,
We discard diapers, cans, and who knows what,
As trash trucks and ships cruise roads and oceans
Looking for a landfill or dumping spot.

Nowadays computers, telex, and fax
Connect us with folks near and far away,
But telecommunication also
Helps multinationals exploit their prey.

We hear the world's now at peace,
We are told there's no more war.
Then why are guns and weapons
Being sired as before?

A new world order's coming,
With great global harmony.
Then why do spies keep trying
To infiltrate industry?

We adore animals, birds, fish, reptiles,
Amphibians, and flowers that blossom, too,
But rare species are still disappearing
Too quickly to end up in book or zoo.

Technology makes farms more efficient,
We have dams, irrigation, hybrid crops.
Then why are people cold, homeless, starving?
Why can't the boom in population stop?

Liberation has now been accorded
Women, and ethnic and sexual groups,
But racism, sexism, homophobia,
Still erupt from bigots, bullies, and snoops.

Both therapists and social workers say
That sound family ties are our culture's core,
Yet it seems that family dissolution
Is meaner than it ever was before.

    See that sweet, gentle family?
    See that lovely, tranquil house?
    Did you know that every evening
    The husband beats his spouse?

    See those children in the park?
    Can you guess what drugs they use?
    That girl just sold her body;
    That boy suffers sex abuse.

Doctors plan genetic engineering,
And ways to scan the body and the brain,
While destitute wretches sorely suffer,
With no white-clad nurse to attend their pain.

Education treats humanity's ills,
Spirituality helps us survive;
Meanwhile cults expand and street gangs prosper,
Fanatics, zealots, and the mob all thrive.

How can we face these crises
In an age of push and shove?
The only help I believe in
Comes from wisdom, hope, and love.

Will we muddle through it all,
And find the answers we seek?
Simply tune in tomorrow
To the world *problematique!*

12
JOSCELYN GODWIN

Joscelyn Godwin, Ph.D., teaches at Colgate University and is the author of *Harmonies of Heaven and Earth, Arktos,* and other books on music, esotericism, and the history of ideas.

Many Futures

The future, like the present and the past, belongs to the world of myth. It has no earthy or factual reality, but looms as an unavoidable presence in the human imagination, providing a focal point around which experience can congeal and acquire a meaning. Within this mythic future dwell secondary archetypes, such as the Apocalypse, the End of the World, the Avatar or Second Coming, the Aquarian or New Age, the One World, and of course Death.

It is always a mistake to reify archetypes and to endow them with a level of reality to which they do not belong. This is the error of fundamentalism, or of misplaced concretism, which expects bizarre happenings in the near future, just as it imagines them to have occurred in the past. The fundamentalist has no appreciation of myth on its own terms, being possessed by certain archetypes rather than participating in them.

Another, equally misleading view is to universalize one's own version of the future, as also of the past and present. Poor education, coupled with a lack of imagination, create a mentality that cannot conceive of modes of being other than its own. Excusable in the past, when the Christian world could cultivate its own myths in blissful ignorance of far different worlds in America or China, this kind of provincialism is sadly still prevalent, even among spiritually aware people. In the past, it showed itself in the obsession with Biblical prophecies and in the efforts to interpret the path of history accordingly. In the present century it ranges from bimillennial fears (based on an accident of Christian chronology) to the profoundest studies of astronomical and terrestrial cycles. The twin pillars of this view are the astrological ages (of Greek or Chaldean invention) and the Hindu system of four *yugas*.

These systems of cosmic cycles are indeed mythic in themselves. But attempts to concretize them through dating always falter: They never attain the universal consensus that is the core of the scientific method and the warrant of reality on the earthly plane. One could compile a long list of dates proposed for the beginning of the Aquarian Age, each sure of itself but quite different from the others. If the students of such cycles were to abandon their calculations and travel a little, they would notice the fallacy of their method.

Take, for instance, the sequence of Golden, Silver, Bronze, and Iron Ages, or their Hindu equivalents the *satya-, dvapara-, treta-,* and *kali-yugas.* Beside the fact that several occultists have reversed the order, there is a general idea that the sequence repeats itself cyclically, the dreadful *kali-yuga* or Iron Age flipping suddenly into a new Golden Age. Many visions of the future are built on this theme. But how can one possibly say that all of humanity are living in the same age, or that they ever have been? Was the ninth century the Dark Ages, or the Sung Dynasty? At this very moment there are those who enjoy the easy physical circumstances and the enlightened intelligence ascribed to the Golden and Silver Ages: Some of them may be reading this book. Others are living out the heroic era or Bronze Age. Many more, no doubt, are mired in the Age of Iron, their minds steeped in hatred and their surroundings those of war and devastation.

Another example is the misuse of the apocalyptic myth, in both its pessimistic and optimistic versions. To regard the End of the World as something due to occur in the near or distant future is nothing less than an insult to those to whom it has already happened. For many inhabitants of the Horn of Africa, Iraq, Yugoslavia, Cambodia, and Central America, the world—*their* world—is already finished. What do the bright-eyed New Agers have to say to them? It has to be a very naive Aquarian to expect the karmic bundle of misery and loathing looming over those and other lands to resolve itself suddenly into peace and brotherhood. And what of the nonhuman inhabitants of the Earth, the species that have been extinguished or decimated? The world has ended for the dinosaur and the dodo, but the cockroach is of another opinion.

The only future we will ever know is our own personal one. That, it is true, may articulate itself around one or more myths, as centers of understanding and of psychic energy, and it may be shared with a larger or smaller group. We may think that we see the Son of Man descending in the clouds; we may suffer under the Four Horsemen of the Apocalypse; we may move into a more than Golden Age through a glimpse of Reality. Certain dates will be significant to us that mean nothing to our fellows. But the future is, and can be, nothing but our material and spiritual biographies, and it will be a different future for each one of us. Even our death, as the only event that we can prophesy with absolute certainty, will be private and unique in its nature, no matter that it is shared with billions of others, and maybe with the Earth itself.

tune, are moving together into the sign of Aquarius, while the third, Pluto, advances into Sagittarius. This very unusual configuration, the first of its kind in recorded history, portends a radical transformation of our fundamental belief systems and the advent of a new world order based on spiritual and humanitarian principles. (This configuration could also be interpreted in a more negative light, but I prefer the most sanguine reading, for obvious reasons!)

The way for this transformation has been paved by the breakdown of totalitarianism and the strengthening of the European community as Neptune and Uranus have passed through Capricorn, as well as by the intensification and (ultimately, we hope) purging of our collective pain and darkness, especially in the area of sexuality, as Pluto moves ever so slowly through Scorpio (the age of AIDS, incest memories, sexual harassment, gay bashing, and the abortion wars).

In what would otherwise appear to be an increasingly dark and violent age, the astrological perspective gives me hope for the future; perhaps we are merely going through another difficult phase in our gradual evolution as a species. (I say "perhaps" because I must admit that, given the imposing list of impending catastrophes we face, I am not entirely convinced we can pull it off—and in my weaker moments I am downright pessimistic.) I am also heartened by the realization, based on years of meditation experience, that Consciousness (or God), the ground of being itself, will continue, whether or not human beings survive.

Clearly, we are rapidly approaching a critical turning point as the most self-aware (and most powerful) inhabitants of Earth, a kind of *crise de conscience* in which we either pull ourselves up by our collective bootstraps or continue to plummet toward ecological oblivion. (Some experts give us ten years at most.) My hope is that, being pushed to the extreme, we will make a dramatic leap into a new way of being.

Many concerned, insightful, and intuitive people have been carefully preparing the groundwork for this leap, this paradigm shift, in the areas of science, medicine, technology, psychology, organizational development, conflict resolution, and religion. What we need is a radical merging of these diverse trends into a powerful new movement to carry us into the twenty-first century. The astrological indicators point to precisely this level of change as we approach the year 2000 —and none too soon, for nothing less, it appears, can save us.

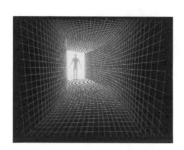

A PLACE
FOR HOPE AND REALISM

15

HENRYK SKOLIMOWSKI

Henryk Skolimowski, Ph.D., is professor of philosophy at the University of Michigan at Ann Arbor and holder of the world's first chair of ecological philosophy at the University of Warsaw. He is also a director of the Eco-Philosophy Centre in Ann Arbor, and the author of *Eco-Philosophy, Mind and the Becoming of the Universe*, and *Out of the Cosmic Dust*.

The Primacy of Hope

Some years ago, I gave a talk on the importance of Pierre Teilhard de Chardin at my university. The most persistent critic turned out to be a visiting professor from the Netherlands. Forcefully, if not bullishly at times, he tried to persuade me that there is no place for hope in our times. His main argument was that since he had lived through World War II in Holland and experienced the inhumanity of man to man, he could not possibly entertain any hope for humankind and for the future.

I responded that yes, the Netherlands suffered much during World War II, but Poland, where I spent the war under the Nazi occupation, suffered much more. We saw the Warsaw ghetto burning night after night; we saw the sinister trains, heavily guarded by Germans, passing through the countryside to the extermination camps. After the experience of these tragic events during the war, there was another trying period for the Poles—the imposition of the Communist regime, which broke many hearts and many lives and subdued the whole nation to an insidious and demoralizing ideology. There was

45

every *reason* to give up and go under and then to sulk with a *full rational justification* that life had treated one badly. Yet over and above the obvious reasons for despair, there are deeper forces within us that can transcend the tragic circumstance of our lives. Among these forces, hope and courage are of the greatest importance.

My experience of the war taught me the everlasting strength of hope. When reason falters, hope can prevail—not silly hope (which hopes against hope), but hope based on courage and on the unshakable conviction that without hope, we cannot go through the turbulence and suffering of life—and the twentieth century has seen much turbulence and suffering.

Because of the immensity of the suffering I saw during and after the war, I came to the conclusion that hope is the only vehicle that enables us to survive with dignity and possibly to arrive at saner and safer shores. Those who lose hope lose their grip on the meaning of their lives.

Thus, the flames of inextinguishable hope have fueled my life, teaching, and philosophy. Eco-Philosophy, which I have developed, is a philosophy of hope *par excellence.* Hope is a wonderful companion and a continuous source of strength.

As I look into the new millennium, I see it as much different from the twentieth century, indeed, from the entire past millennium. In the Christian world, this last millennium started in a convulsive, if not a schizophrenic way. It was expected that the Second Coming would bring the world to an end. Perhaps throughout this past millennium we have never recovered from this death wish: to be saved through being exterminated.

I see the coming millennium as radiant with the hope of at least partly fulfilling our human potential. We have nowhere to go but up on the spiral of transcendence. This sense is not just the cheap optimism of a person who cannot look squarely into the face of reality. Just the opposite. It is the strategy of a sober realist. Because we have witnessed so many ugly faces of reality, we know that we cannot live with them. Thus we have to transcend them. Such is the message of those whom we have admired most in the twentieth century—Gandhi, Mother Teresa, Martin Luther King.

Yet when I look at the present scene and see the incredible mess and moral degradation, I cannot but ask myself the question: Why are we so obtuse? We are so clever in so many ways, yet ultimately so obtuse. When I seek the cause for this obtuseness, I find it—not in the lack of education (perhaps we have got too much of a rather inferior kind)—but in something else: in the strange spiritual vacuum.

This vacuum has produced a spiritual dimness which is itself the cause of our overall obtuseness. We are full of glitter but empty inside. The recovery of our spiritual substance (through continuous, if not painful, individual exercises of meditation and yoga) is the road to the recovery of our destiny. Yes, there is hope, there is a future—if we take ourselves seriously as spiritual beings.

16

COLIN WILSON

Colin Wilson achieved instant international acclaim with his first book, *The Outsider*. Since then he has authored numerous other fiction and nonfiction works, including *Religion and the Rebel*, *Beyond the Outsider*, and *The Mind Parasites*.

Consciousness Will Change Everything

Ever since I wrote my first book *The Outsider* in 1954, my thinking has been dominated by one central belief: that humanity is on the verge of an evolutionary leap to a higher stage, and that *this* change in consciousness will change everything else. Let me try to explain what I mean by a "change in consciousness" as simply and as briefly as I can.

In my childhood and early adolescence, I frequently experienced what William James calls "melting moods," moods in which I felt—as Whitehead put it—that "life is a certain absoluteness of self-enjoyment." When, later, I read Thomas Traherne's *Centuries of Meditation*, with its remark "The corn was orient and immortal wheat, which had stood from everlasting to everlasting," I understood precisely what he meant. And the first time I saw Van Gogh's painting *The Starry Night*, in which the whole sky seems to explode into a whirlpool of vitality, I recognized it as an expression of those moods of total inner certainty.

What worried me was that all the great Romantics, from Blake and Goethe to Nietzsche and Rimbaud, had experienced similar moods, and that an alarming number of them had committed suicide or died of sheer "discouragement." Was it conceivable that these moods were mere delusion, like alcoholic euphoria, with no objective reality? This was the question I analyzed in my first book *The Outsider.* And it seemed to me, on the whole, that the answer was no. Too many Romantics had collapsed through self-pity and lack of discipline—as well as lack of ordinary reason and logic. (Having been trained as a scientist, I have always attached immense importance to reason and logic.) My second book, *Religion and the Rebel,* dealt largely with the visions of mystics, and with the fact that in our secular (i.e., materialist) civilization, it is extremely difficult to find a rational starting point for intensified modes of consciousness.

When *The Outsider* came out (in 1956), most respectable thinkers in Europe and America were leftists, positivists, or both. I was the first, for example, to write about Hermann Hesse, particularly about *Steppenwolf,* with its vision of "Mozart and the stars." Because I was more preoccupied with humanity's inner development than with politics, left-wing critics reached for their usual epithet and described me as a fascist.

In the sixties, all this began to change, and the summer—of which it now seems *The Outsider* was the first swallow—finally arrived. Suddenly, Hesse was a best-seller, and a whole new generation discovered yoga, zen, and "expanded states of consciousness." I saw this as a major first step toward the evolutionary change I had anticipated. But only a first step.

Central to my ideas was a notion called "Faculty X." There are certain moments in which we suddenly become totally conscious of the *reality of other times and places.* Proust described such a moment in *Swann's Way,* as the hero tastes a cake dipped in herb tea and is transported back to the reality of childhood: "I had ceased to feel mediocre, accidental, mortal." The historian Arnold Toynbee described certain moments in which events in history became totally real, as if they were happening around him here and now. This is Faculty X.

It became clear to me that the human animal is trapped in a kind of "worm's-eye view" of reality, like a fly stuck on flypaper, and that it is only in the "moments of vision" that we achieve a kind of bird's-eye view and seem to hover over human existence like some astronaut in a spacecraft.

By definition, a bird's-eye view is *truer* than a worm's-eye view. It sees more. It takes more in. The Romantics spent their lives torn between the bird's-eye view and the worm's-eye view, and in the majority of cases, the worm's-eye view prevailed. Van Gogh left a suicide note that read: "Misery will never end." Or, to put it in three words, "You can't win."

But this was because these "outsiders" didn't *understand* what was happening when they plunged from one extreme to the other: from Faculty X to a sense of being trapped in fatigue and despair.

Moreover, the problem was exacerbated by a kind of moronic pessimism that seemed to be the normal premise for any modern writer, artist, or philosopher—the feeling that, as Sartre put it, "It is meaningless that we live and meaningless that we die." Unfortunately, virtually every fashionable writer and thinker of our time has embraced it, from Graham Greene to Samuel Beckett, from Heidegger to Jacques Derrida. One of my practical problems as a writer was that, as a born optimist, I was regarded with deep suspicion by most of my contemporaries. I still am.

Since the earliest days of philosophy, thinkers have tended to be pessimistic. In the nineteenth century, it led to an epidemic of suicides. But at least the problem was now squarely on the agenda, something the human intellect could *see* to be of vital importance.

If my view in *The Outsider* is correct, and the problem was largely a question of self-pity and weakness, then all that was needed was a clear logical *insight* about what was causing the trouble. Shaw talks about a bee that hurls itself against a windowpane until it dies of exhaustion, when all it has to do is to go out the same way it came in. If this is what the Romantics were doing, then the problem is solved. And if the central question is—as Carlyle said—"Eternal Yes versus Eternal No," then we can reply with the calm certainty of a mathematician: "Eternal Yes." Van Gogh's *Starry Night* is true, not his suicide note.

In *The Misfits* I succeeded in putting my central vision with great succinctness. "Our human senses show us only a small part of the world—the present. We have to *supplement* this present-awareness with memory and imagination [and, I might add, logic.] The reason I feel more 'alive' when I set out on holiday is that my memory and imagination are finally pulling their proper weight, and supplementing the present moment with all kinds of other times and places. It is as if I am in two places at once." This, of course, is "Faculty X." And it is natural to us when we throw off our self-pity and laziness and assume we *can* win.

I now recognize that my problem in my teens was my innate romanticism, my tendency to allow fatigue to convince me that some task was boring and meaningless, so I was inclined to run away from it, with a certain virtuous sense of rejecting the meaningless. One of the first things that made me begin to see what was wrong with this attitude was the odd way that "synchronicity" came to may aid when

I deliberately made twice the effort and thrust my romanticism behind me. The most preposterous "coincidences" occurred, as if something was saying to me: "Yes, you're on the right track, keep going." I now see that fatigue—and the sense of meaninglessness and futility that go with it—is one of the most dangerous of our enemies. It doesn't bother animals; they accept fatigue as something natural. But we "rational" creatures let it send us into a dizzy spin of pessimism and negative feedback, without the sense to recognize that we are beating our heads against a pane of glass.

Shaw said that the basic aim of the "life force" is to develop a certain self-awareness so we can *understand* problems and obstacles and outflank them, instead of trying to muddle through and ending in despair. This seems to me self-evidently true. It has taken me sixty-odd years to grasp it, but I am now possessed of the deep conviction that we *can* win. And that when everyone *sees* this, we shall have reached a new phase in human evolution—a phase that, in a sense, we have already reached, although we are unaware of it, as the chrysalis is unaware that it is already a butterfly.

How would I describe this change in consciousness? As being rather like what happens when a bad cold begins to clear up. The nasal channels cease to feel blocked; the ears cease to feel as if they were full of cotton wool; there is a curious tingling sense of rising vitality as the "worm's-eye view" begins to give way to the "bird's-eye view." The sense of suffocation, of entrapment, disappears and gives way to the "spring morning feeling" of certainty and optimism. Above all, there is the certainty that this is not a mere "feeling," but an insight into the truth about human existence.

When I was young, this insight came only occasionally, and was difficult to rekindle. Now I can find my way back to it with the confidence of finding a station on the radio dial. And I see that this insight is *inevitable*, as inevitable as the widening perspectives that emerge when you climb a mountain. All of which amounts to the certainty that, at this point in history, the whole human race is on the point of throwing off its bad cold.

So ask me about my hopes and concerns for the future—overpopulation, destruction of the environment, global warming, atomic armageddon—and I can only reply that I am not overly concerned. *This change in consciousness will change everything.*

17

TOM REGAN

Tom Regan, Ph.D., is professor of philosophy at North Carolina State University and president of the Culture and Animals Foundations. His books include *The Case for Animals Rights* and *The Thee Generation: Reflections on the Coming Revolution.*

The Coming Revolution
of the Thee Generation

Pessimism is the consort of cowards; optimism, the abiding friend of hope; and hope, the parent of activism. In a world where sound bites substitute for substance, acquisitions for awareness, and upward mobility for spiritual growth, the allure of pessimism tempts us all. So much has gone wrong. So little time remains. So many who could do something do nothing. In the silent hours of the night, when sleep for the body is overwhelmed by the weariness of the soul, the disquieting voice of despair speaks to each of us.

Yet optimism will not be silenced. People *can* change. People *do* change. Many *have* changed. And many, many more—more than we can number at this time—*will* change. For there is a revolution aborning—a profound, enduring revolution, a revolution not over who owns what piece of land but about our very relationship to the land itself and to the myriad life forms with whom we share this planet as our home. The "Me Generation"—the generation of greed, of selfishness, of conspicuous consumption—is dead. In its place, a new generation—the "Thee Generation"—is alive.

The insistent, unifying question of this new generation is, "What can I do for thee?" not "What can I get for me?" Of the poor and the lame, the uneducated and the abandoned, the victims of injustice and of abuse—of all these members of the extended human family, this question is asked.

But not only of these. Of wetlands and forests, of hogs and whales, of rivers and streams, of soils and oceans—of these too the question is asked: "What can I do for thee?" For along with heightened awareness of our relationship to the life community, there is a burgeoning sense of responsibility for the life community.

This revolution has no predecessor. Nineteenth-century Romanticism is its closest relative, but the differences are as important as the similarities. The Romantics glimpsed the ties that bind each to all. They saw the beauty of skylarks and felt the wonder of wildflowers. But their commitment to all that is other than human was aesthetic, not moral. For them, it was enough to watch. And to enjoy.

Members of the Thee Generation have a different vision and, with this, a different agenda. Our commitment to the life community is primarily moral, only secondarily aesthetic. Our role is that of the protector, not the observer. Our posture, therefore, must be that of the activist, not the passivist. We are "questers"—those who question and, through questioning, those who seek a better, a truer way.

And after what do we quest? The ways and means to live in harmony with the rest of nature; to make visible the invisible, preventable violence humans visit upon the oppressed, human and nonhuman alike; to reduce our individual support of this violence; and to create opportunities for others to join with us in the nonviolent revolution of which we are a part.

There are some who complain that we are being asked to give up too much in return for too little. And it is true that the revolution requires that we have fewer "creature comforts" so that more creatures might live. But the ancient wisdom is true: In order to possess what matters, we must unburden ourselves of what does not. Paradoxically, our life is the richer, the poorer we are in the possession of "things." A life of evolving, increasing simplicity beckons all who love life, all who remain hopeful, all who will not succumb to pessimism's sinister temptations. If not us, then our children, and if not them, then our children's children will find the path. And take it.

18
SANDRA INGERMAN

Sandra Ingerman is the author of *Soul Retrieval: Mending the Fragmented Self*. She is the educational director of Michael Harner's Foundation for Shamanic Studies and is a member of the Foundation's international faculty.

Regaining Our Passion for Life

What kind of future are we creating if we are stuck back in the woundedness of our past? Last year I received this question in a dream.

I feel optimistic about the future; however, it is essential that all of us who want to create a positive future change our current behaviors. We must stop recreating our past and direct the energy we now use to create illness, trauma, and drama in our lives toward positive attitudes and visions.

I do believe we are in a time of accelerated evolution. I believe we now have the ability to create faster than we ever did before. With so much emphasis and energy directed toward doom-and-gloom prophecies, my fear is that we will indeed create the negativity we fear. Instead, we need to regain our passion for life.

Today we must recognize that we are creative beings with options available to us. It is unnecessary to continue to create the illnesses and abuses of our past. We have the potential to create a positive future for all life on the planet. And if we want this positive future, we must envision it now and focus our creative energy on that goal.

We must embrace the belief that all life is sacred and treat it, ourselves included, with compassion. Let us reestablish our connection with nature and see ourselves as part of its laws and cycles.

During a shamanic journey last year, my teacher in nonordinary reality gave me a message. She said: "We are all coming back. Start thinking now about what you want to come back to." When we think about creating a better life for our children and future generations, if we believe in the concept of reincarnation, then realize we must include ourselves as well.

I want to live in now, and return to, a world free of pollution, disease, disrespect for life, and destruction. I want to live in and come back to a planet where all beings make decisions and live in ways that support all living things. I know this is possible, and I ask you to join me in that vision.

19

KATHY JULINE

Kathy Juline is the editor of *Science of Mind* magazine and coauthor of *You Are the One: Living Fully, Living Free Through Affirmative Prayer.*

Blazing a New Trail

As we stand on the threshold of tomorrow, reasons for hope abound. A tremendous awakening is happening everywhere. Our present times are preparing the way for a wonderful future. Currently a profound cleansing process is occurring. Limiting beliefs are being examined. No longer are we willing to subject ourselves to their destructive consequences. Instead we seek an end to suffering, an end to hatred, conflict, racism, injustice, disease, corruption, and all forms of fear. Bringing problem areas to light rather than denying them takes courage, but we are ready for this cleansing, healing process now, and it is happening. More and more we are embodying the principles of unity, peace, and cooperation. We are relinquishing control and becoming instruments of the divine will.

We are coming to realize that our only limits are those which we accept and that whatever we believe will eventually manifest in our outer experience. As a result of this realization, we are re-creating our world, inspired by the words of spiritual leaders like Ernest Holmes, founder of the Science of Mind philosophy, who wrote: ''New arts, new sciences, new philosophies, better government, and a higher civilization wait on our thoughts. The infinite energy of Life, and the possibility of our future evolution, work through our imagination and will. The time is ready, the place is where we are now, and it is done unto all as they really believe and act."

Helen Keller once said, "Either life is a daring adventure or it is nothing at all." We must be willing to blaze a new trail, to light a new path—and to do so even when it means leaving behind that which is comfortable and facing challenges that are fearful and difficult. We need to remember that if blazing a new trail were easy, it probably wouldn't be worth doing. As Joseph Campbell said, "If there is a path, it is someone else's path and you are not on the adventure."

Each of us has great and important work to do. Everyone counts. Everyone can make a difference. We have a divine appointment, and we must keep it. Jesus said, "The fields are white for harvest, but the workers are few." If we are unsure what our own unique contribution might be, then we must ask for guidance, listening and responding to the best of our ability. I know that if we remain hopeful, positive, and trusting, we will see great results: a clean environment; harmony among all nations; the elimination of war, drug abuse, and crime; freedom from hunger, poverty, and disease; and happiness for all people, everywhere.

I hope in my own life that I can be a positive example of the good I would ask of others and that I can view each day as an opportunity to forgive, to offer praise or understanding, to keep a promise, to admit when I am wrong, and to smile often. I hope to learn from the challenges that come along, blessings always. And, finally, I hope to be touched and inspired by the great numbers of people in the world now who are lighting the path for the rest of us. To all of you I give thanks. You are my hope.

20
DUANE ELGIN

Duane Elgin, M.A., M.B.A., worked as a senior futurist at the Stanford Research Institute and is a pioneer in electronic town councils. He is the author of *Voluntary Simplicity* and *Awakening Earth*. The following essay was adapted by him from *Awakening Earth*.

A Bittersweet Future

Although we have entered a pivotal time in human history, I do not expect a swift or magical transformation to a new age of human culture and consciousness. Instead, I believe the next few generations will bring a bittersweet future for humanity. The people of the earth face a bitter spring and summer of growth in the form of unprecedented suffering for all life on earth. I believe that only after a generation or more of fierce adversity and unyielding misery is it likely that humanity will come together in a sweet autumn of harvest in the form of authentic reconciliation around a sustainable future. The precious promise of autumn's harvest will be matched by the awful suffering that precedes it.

Three driving trends summarize our predicament: By roughly 2030, world reserves of cheaply accessible oil are expected to be depleted, we will add another three billion persons to the planet, and the global climate is expected to become destabilized due to the greenhouse effect. Without cheap petroleum to provide pesticides and fertilizers for a high-yield agriculture, and without a stable climate for growing food at the very time we have another three billion persons to feed, the likelihood of massive famines, global civil unrest, and authoritarian responses looms large.

As these trends make clear, to build a sustainable and democratic future, within a single generation humanity must deliberately restructure its way of living and consuming. Because we seem to change only through the force of dire necessity, it seems likely that massive starvation, civil unrest, and ecological devastation will be required to motivate the human family to work together to build a sustainable and democratic future. Therefore, I expect the world to increasingly become a pressure cooker of calamity. Hopefully, this unrelieved misery will burn through the denial, greed, and fear that now divide us. Although a new human alloy may emerge from the furnace of this superheated time of transition, it is also very possible that a badly crippled human psyche and devastated ecosystem may emerge that will doom humanity to a new dark age and a long evolutionary detour.

If we rise to the challenge of the next few decades, I believe we can build a new sense of global family and species-identity. To accomplish this, we need to make global communication, reconciliation, and forgiveness a top-priority world project. From an era of reconciliation could emerge a sufficient degree of economic justice, ecological harmony, conscious democracy, spiritual tolerance, and racial and gender equality to enable us to live and work together cooperatively on the planet. If we can achieve this new level of trust and understanding, then we can begin to build a future of mutually assured development. With reconciliation that is continuously renewed, the world could blossom with a new enthusiasm for life, learning, and building. With a deep sense of connection and compassion, the everyday actions of individuals could connect with a global vision that we co-create through ongoing dialogue, using our tools of local to global communication— giving us a realistic basis for creating the sweetness of a truly sustainable and meaningful future.

21

MICHAEL GROSSO

Michael Grosso, Ph.D., studied classics and philosophy at Columbia University, but after some startling personal encounters with the paranormal, he began to study reports of UFOs, Marian visions, alien abductions, near-death experiences, miracles of Padre Pio and Sai Baba, and other psychophysical anomalies. He directs the Cultural Imagination Center in Warwick, New York, and is the author of *The Final Choice*, *Frontiers of the Soul*, and *Soulmaker*. The following essay is an excerpt from *Frontiers of the Soul*.

We May Stumble Upon
the Gates of Heaven

Our vision must be open to the unexpected. If the history of evolution says anything, it is that novelty is the rule. At the frontiers of the soul, there are no easy landmarks to light the way. The future of our evolution may lurk in shadows of the unforeseen.

It might be that the very things that threaten to destroy us today contain the clues to the next step of our evolution. Take, for one wild example, the greenhouse effect. The greenhouse effect involves an increase in carbon dioxide in the atmosphere. An excess of carbon dioxide, or hypercarbia, is known to produce states of consciousness indistinguishable from the classic near-death and mystical experience. For all we know, the atmosphere may be already changing our brain structure, subtly opening our psychic pores to Mind at Large. One day we might wake up to find we have quietly passed a critical threshold to a new consciousness.

Or consider another supposed menace—overpopulation. Overpopulation may eventually force us to colonize space—and that may be the route to the birth of a new species of humankind.

Judging by accounts of the astronauts, space travel expands the human mind. Jim Irwin of the Apollo 15 lunar mission said he "found God on the moon." Al Worden started channeling poetry when he returned home. Alan Bean said, "Everybody who went to the moon became more like they were deep inside themselves." (Bean became an artist.) Rusty Schweichert, who cried while looking at the stars from outer space, "fell in love with the earth," and found himself asking soul-searching questions like "Who am I?" Edgar Mitchell of the Apollo 14 flight was "overwhelmed with a divine presence," experienced Earth and the universe as "an intelligent system" in a way that was at odds with his scientific training, and founded the Institute of Noetic Sciences.

In destroying the Earth, we may stumble upon the gates of heaven. In being driven to explore outer space, we may discover the secrets of inner space. All the mistakes we have made so far may one day be looked upon as the blunderings of adolescence, the errors we had to make before our childhood's end.

Nobody knows what surprises the future holds. That is what makes time more wonderful than terrible.

22

DANIEL KEALEY

Daniel Kealey, Ph.D., is associate professor of philosophy and religion at Towson State University in Baltimore, Maryland, and is the author of *Revisioning Environmental Ethics*. He also has a psychotherapy practice.

Heaven or Hell?

"**W**hat can we hope for?" has been a central question of philosophy for as long as we can remember. Not being satisfied with the answers postulated by my fellow philosophers past or present, I have struggled to extend and deepen my perception beyond the well-beaten paths for clues about what is and what is not possible. Up until the twentieth century, humankind has generally labored under the belief, in one form or another, that good will prevail over evil. Although optimism is still "politically correct" at all levels of society, serious intellectual analysis exposes it as a sham, without any factual or rational justification. Perhaps Ernest Becker was right in his belief that humans are incapable of facing a reality fraught with the imminence of death, so that to get on with our lives, we must delude ourselves with fantasies of immortality in one form or another. Hence our inability to deal realistically with those problems that are actually threatening our extinction. Ironically, our very fear of death has motivated us to act in ways that are going to actualize what we dread on a far greater scale than we imagined. Will we wake up from this hellish nightmare in time?

Some people, the readers and writers of this volume among

them, have begun waking up. But the question still remains: When will enlightened consciousness make the critical difference, if at all? Must we resign ourselves to apocalypse before we can begin anew? At the same time as millions of people are waking up, crime and the disintegration of social institutions are proliferating. At the same time as some people are learning to communicate and cooperate with nature spirits, environmental deterioration is increasing at an alarming rate. At the same time as millions of people are experiencing the rich mysteries of higher realities through trance states, near-death experiences, and UFO encounters, increased addiction to high consumerism is bringing more economic recession. At the same time as an impressive body of evidence for survival of bodily death and reincarnation has been built up, there seems to be an increase of sadistic and masochistic behavior worldwide. At the same time as people are discovering and cultivating their power of healing, disease and the threat of overpowering our immune systems is rising. At the same time as I was witnessing an American yogi materialize objects out of the invisible, thousands of species are disappearing into extinction. A great polarization of consciousness is taking place.

When we look at this from a rational perspective, we are faced with alternative possibilities: 1) Hell will prevail and drag down the dreams of heaven with it; 2) Earth will go to hell, but those who are worthy will live on in an otherworldly heaven; 3) Heaven will prevail and be established on Earth, driving hell out or transforming it. If we allow a wide range of interpretations of the terms "heaven" and "hell," then I think that these would be the main alternatives to choose from in regard to possible futures as far as reason is concerned.

However, if such seers as Sri Aurobindo and Jean Gebser have seen truly, the drift of consciousness development is leading us beyond rational perspectivity into an unfoldment of integral consciousness. The openness of an integral consciousness, with its acceptance of such neglected powers of consciousness as imagination, feelings, emotions, and visceral psychism, as well as its nurturance of reason and super-rational intuition, would not be limited to the either-or kind of rational thought. Hence it could very well turn out to be the case that all of the above-listed alternatives will be realized simultaneously, although not equally for everyone. In the near future I foresee the coexistence of heaven and hell, where pockets of enlightened communities working with nature intelligences create refuges in areas overcome by the ravages and despair of hell. Findhorn-type communities in the Aral Sea area, for example.

As for the other-world option: I foresee the breakdown of the wall between the living and the dead, such that the purpose of living on Earth will be more clear to the living. This is already happening, what Kenneth Ring has called the "shamanization" of the human race. In her past-life regression research on thousands of subjects, Helen Wambach found that thirty percent of them report that they reincarnated voluntarily, out of a sense of mission. This percentage may not be generalizable to the population at large, but I think that it is indicative that the level of freedom that the *bodhisattva* symbolizes is a viable option for a much greater proportion of humanity than heretofore has been thought possible. (That so many ordinary people can be hypnotically induced to remember previous lives—a feat that traditional Asian teachings claimed took years of meditative discipline—is itself a very significant sign.) If my impression that the process of reincarnation is becoming less mechanistic and more conscious is correct, then Earth incarnations may increasingly be an option, so that those who do not feel aligned with the general purpose of the Earth Project may choose to incarnate in some other world. That would not necessarily result in utopia here, but the myth of heaven on Earth, then, would be less of a pipe dream than it is now.

23
GINI GRAHAM SCOTT

Gini Graham Scott, Ph.D., J.D., is the author of over twenty books, including *The Empowered Mind, Mind Power,* and *Fantasy in Everyday Life.* She is also the founder and director of Changemakers and Creative Communications and Research, headquartered in San Francisco, and is the host and producer of an internationally aired radio talk show on social trends.

Finding the Middle Ground

Writing this shortly after the election of 1992, I feel a new spirit of hope and change and a new coming together across party, ethnic, religious, and generational lines to begin a new healing.

I believe that the 1980s have been a time of such focus on individuality, personal freedom, and material gain that we have gone too far in this direction. But now having realized this, we are snapping back in the other direction toward a concern with community, personal responsibility, and a more altruistic outlook toward others.

I feel this is a good and much-needed corrective, although the risk is of going too far in this direction, so that we become too conformist and look too much to the power of the state for guidance, just as we concentrated too much on glorifying business and business values in the 1980s. What is important is finding a middle ground, and my hope is that in this period of transition we are now going through, we can find it.

To a great extent, this swing we are experiencing is part of what has always been the human condition and paradox—the conflict between personal desire and the good of the community, the conflict between individuality and the state. The sages throughout history have always stressed the need for balance and harmony between ourselves and the world around us. And different societies have experimented with different combinations—from extreme free-market capitalism extolling the individual to extreme communism extolling the state. But as we have found repeatedly, if we go too far to one extreme or the other, the system doesn't work, and we end up with either the individual being repressed by an authoritarian state or the individual taken advantage of by other private citizens who are more powerful.

Now what gives me hope is that in this time of transition we have a chance to experiment with new social forms to seek this middle ground where there is a balance between the needs of the individual and the needs of society. And we all have a chance to contribute to and be part of this transformation in our own way.

Yes, this has been a very difficult time for many of us. Many of us have suffered tremendous dislocations as our society has gone through a social, economic, and technological transformation into a fully integrated global high-tech information economy. The long recession has been a part of this process. Even the many natural disasters of the past few years—the earthquakes, hurricanes, and major fires— seem to parallel the social and economic upheavals that are occurring and to contribute to them as well.

But such upheaveals occur anytime there is a major societal transformation. And out of this comes the possibilities for new and better change and growth. This is what gives me such hope for the future. It is as if we are emerging from a maelstrom that has whirled around us, leaving all sorts of institutions smashed in its wake. However, now that they have been torn down, we have a chance to rebuild and redesign our world anew. And that has always been a basic law of nature—after a fire comes new growth. In our case, that means we now have a chance to create a new experiment for better resolving that essential paradox of human nature to create a better balance: between the individual and the community; between personal freedom and material gain and the needs of society as a whole.

24

JEREMY TARCHER

Jeremy Tarcher worked as a television writer-producer and then turned to commercial book publishing, founding his own company, Jeremy P. Tarcher, Inc., in 1967. Now one of the foremost nonfiction publishers of books on human consciousness, his list includes numerous titles that explore the leading edge of psychology, business, self-development, health, human potential, and creativity.

The "Wondrous Central Point" Beyond All Evil

QUESTION: "On the whole, Mr. Singer, are you an optimist or a pessimist?"

ANSWER: "I am a pessimist. If you're a pessimist you are right most of the time."

—Dick Cavett interview with Isaac Singer the day after he received the Nobel Prize for Literature

There is only one thing to truly worry about—the triumph of the forces of darkness over the forces of light. The Manicheans saw it accurately: Evil gets out of bed at dawn and runs six miles before breakfast. Goodness, trusting to God, often sleeps late and goes to bed before its work is done. Oh, yes, in the dance of life, light taps its toes and occasionally sits one out, while darkness marches and is always on the dance floor trying to call the time. Place your bets.

I fear the power of evil. Darkness isn't afraid of blood—indeed, it has a thirst for it. Love is shot down in the street. One truly evil man can carry millions into barbarism. Whatever we may wish to believe about the power of love, the power of hate to turn the human heart to stone is no less great. Every day a billion cruelties, fully premeditated and astonishingly rationalized, make suffering the central experience of life. That is evil. "Evil spirits wander the world seeking the ruin of souls." These cruelties carry individual suffering beyond the heart of Christ to bear. I fear human nature, your nature, my nature.

I fear the power of greed, and the perpetuation and growth of social and economic inequality. I fear my ability to look away from another's pain, to not really connect and care, to never be satisfied, to have a second and third helping while a beggar stares through the window, and for all that somehow to be all right.

I fear my own capacity for inaction, for accepting tragedy without a thought. This world is not redeemed. I do not truly love my fellow man. Do you?

I fear the hubris of ignorance. With atomic weapons and power we have been lucky, not smart. Will it continue? Indefinitely? Will we be equally fortunate with genetic engineering and with the massive destruction of the environment? Why should we be? I fear our ability to forget the lessons of history—again and again.

I fear our desire to control one another. Religious fundamentalism, ethnocentrism, xenophobia may yet cause a worldwide emergence of totalitarian leaders armed with the growing technologies for surveillance and control of the individual. We have seen great nations go dark for generations. We may see it again and be powerless to intervene. If darkness triumphs now, how long will it prevail? It can happen to us. I fear my brother and my sister.

It is so easy to believe that one has found the truth and that it is necessary to enforce it for the welfare of others. Even the light seeks dominion. We are still in the time of the struggle. And we will never know a time when it is otherwise. I fear that the will of darkness to dominate is greater than the will of light to resist.

Too many of those who seek the divine spirit wish to escape from the world. Those who do not so seek want to control it. In the end, the *bodhisattva* vow is not a matter of choice. We must stay on the battlefield or the *kalpa*-long war will surely be lost.

How smugly I identify with the light—surely my opponents, no, let's get real, my enemies do, too.

You who believe in an Infinite Source of All Joy, how can you not see the requirement for an Infinite Source of All Evil?

And yet—hope.

What gives me hope?

The spread of the great traditions of enlightenment seeding the vision of the complete human more widely than ever before. And we blossom in that light.

What gives me hope? A billion ordinary acts of spontaneous loving-kindness. They, too, may have meaning.

Perhaps the angelic forces will awake from their ecstatic slumber. A messiah may be born this day—my people have hoped for it for thousands of years. Maybe tomorrow.

Nevertheless, in my deepest heart I cannot but believe in Maimonides' "wondrous central point." Martin Buber says that this beating of the heart of the universe is "Holy Joy." And from Rabbi Nachman we learn that "No matter how it seems, and despite it all, He pours His light, His glorious light into all the worlds." Now that gives me hope. And I don't even believe in a "Him."

25
ALLAN COMBS

Allan Combs, Ph.D., is a psychologist and systems theorist at the University of North Carolina at Asheville and a member of the General Evolution Research Group. He has published numerous articles and is the author of the forthcoming *The Radiance of Being: Consciousness, Evolution, and Dynamical Systems* and the coauthor of *Synchronicity: Science, Myth, and the Trickster* and *Cognitive Maps in Biology and Culture*.

A Margin of Hope

I wish I were an optimist, but I am not. During the span of recorded history, and even before, humankind has brought tremendous suffering down on itself, and there is no reason to think it will change now. The new movements toward democracy in many places in the world seem on the surface to give cause for optimism, but as we see from our own past, democracy often leans in the direction of the self-serving and shortsighted interests of the masses, or more often of a capitalist elite, with too little compassion for humanity or nature as a whole. Nor is evolution any consolation. We might recall that something like ninety-nine percent of the species it has created so far are already extinct, most with no help from us.

Only a blind person cannot see that the world's ecology is caving in. We are burning our own house for fuel. As for myself, having reached manhood in the abundance of the sixties, I look forward with apprehension to an old age of increasing personal and social shortage. I fear for the future of my daughter and her children. The obvious solution of wide-scale family planning and efforts to achieve parity of education and opportunity of gender and race is largely ignored on all sides. Indeed, many whose business it is to provide us with moral guidance seem compelled to rush forward into uncontrolled population expansion, having little thought even for the individuals concerned. Nature, in the meantime, will continue on its inevitable course, and the consequence will be drought, famine, and plagues of increasing magnitude. These will be the population controls of the twenty-first century, especially in the Third World.

It is a great irony that most people act most of the time in ways that are right and even compassionate in terms of their own experience. There is no shortage of good intention anywhere! As biological organisms, however, we simply are not designed to think and act in terms of long-range consequences, especially when we must choose between ourselves and those near us, and those we do not know and cannot relate to in a personal way.

I once was explaining to a friend the economics by which the real wealth of seemingly poor countries such as Africa arrives in the bank accounts of wealthy businessmen in countries such as the United States. He looked at me and, with a twinkle in his eye, said, "Let's keep it that way." Now, I must say immediately that he is as good and as compassionate a person as I know. He goes out of his way to care for others in the community, in his church, and in his family. The problem is how to instill compassion for those who are not in our community or our church or our family. There is no easy answer.

Certain facts, however, give me a margin of hope. One is the utter unpredictability of history. Who could have foreseen the recent events in Europe and the Soviet Union? If mathematical chaos theory tells us anything, it is that the smallest of events can cascade into major instabilities, rocking entire social or ecological systems and forcing them through unheard-of transformations.

In this vein, the swift changes in Europe and the U.S.S.R., like the more tragic ones in China, seem to arise out of a rapidly growing and worldwide awakening of the human spirit, a spirit that will no longer abide censorship and repression. This spirit is the hope of the world. And it is growing much more rapidly than one would think, judging from the six o'clock news. Not only is there a widening sense of compassion, as seen in the present rise of volunteerism, but even on the most practical levels, it is becoming apparent to many players in today's political and economic arenas that we are all, to some extent, and of necessity, involved in a most mutual effort to achieve a suitable quality of life. Many companies have come to recognize, for instance, that responsiveness to human needs of employees in the form of health enrichment programs and childcare yields a more productive labor force. Beyond all this, the world is also experiencing a resurgence of genuine spirituality, asserting itself in a multitude of different expressions. Further, the growth and spread of ecological awareness needs little documentation.

These gains, however, and many more, are darkened by their own shadows: the rise of nationalism and ethnic hatreds, uncapped by new freedoms, and a resurgence of fundamentalism of all types. These trends represent major threats to a future in desperate need of compassion and of creative and open-ended commitments to decisions that serve humankind as a whole.

The outcome of these forces seems very unclear to me, and I do not feel good about it. I find myself lately looking again at the stars on clear summer evenings, as I did as a child. There, among the billions of suns that fill the dark heavens must be life immeasurable, far beyond our ability to threaten or diminish. We are, after all, one small flower in a very large wilderness.

26

VINE DELORIA, JR.

Vine Deloria, Jr., M.T.S., J.D., is a member of the Standing Rock Sioux
Tribe of North Dakota, a former executive director of the National
Congress of American Indians, and professor of history, religious
studies, political science, and law at the University of Colorado.

A Decent Godless People

Many traditions have taught us that civilizations rise and fall and that the earth itself has undergone many changes and cleansings so that we walk on the ashes and dust of people whom we have not suspected ever existed. We are in that stage of decline today, and someday, thousands of years hence, an archaeologist will find remnants of a Sears Diehard battery and be roundly booed by his colleagues when he suggests that major civilizations lived prior to their own.

T. S. Eliot best described us as "decent" and "godless," and that we surely are. We despoil mountains to get aluminum for our beer cans and ravage valleys of old-growth forests to get paper for porno magazines. And we do it all very piously and systematically, returning precise figures each year on our successful efforts to destroy the planet.

Our ability to communicate has brought us to this last precipice. We have gathered so much information that we no longer know where we are or who we are. The bubbly optimism of New Age spirituality is but a thin veneer we use to mask our dreadful loss of personal identity and community. We frantically build networks of similarly located people with the hope that the manipulation of concepts and images will provide a worthy substitute for living on the earth with real animals and people. But even now we manipulate the genetics of the rest of creation in order to provide us with artificial delicacies and reduce our overhead. It is all madness of a logical and systematic nature.

As institutions move us through their increasingly narrow corrals into the arena of standardized behavior, we worry about the right to privacy, never realizing that it is in the natural world and our ability to merge with it that true privacy is achieved. We have utterly discarded our personal ethics and in their place we have adopted the herd mentality and the intense desire to fit in without being called upon to act responsibly once we are inside the institution.

It will be some utterly simple thing that finally triggers the collapse of our civilization—a computer chip, a broken water pipe, a blown fuse. We have made ourselves so dependent upon our networks and institutions that we cannot function without them. We should hope that somewhere in the backwaters of the planet, a few people who know our story will survive and pass it along as legends in the way that Atlantis has been preserved. We may someday be remembered as a mythical golden age when people flew through the skies in big silver birds. It is probably more than we deserve.

27
JAY KINNEY

Jay Kinney is publisher and editor-in-chief of *Gnosis: A Journal of Western Inner Traditions*. His illustrations, cartoons, and writing have appeared in a variety of national magazines.

The Millennium is a Mirage

I suppose that my greatest wish for the future—and particularly for the millennium that is about to engulf us in a tidal wave of hype and analysis—would be that we all resist the temptation to project both our hopes and fears onto that very same future. Let's leave the future alone.

If we do, I am sure that its citizens will thank us for it, just as we should be thankful that the greatest souls of centuries past still speak to us with relevant voices precisely because they found the eternal within their own time. Shakespeare or Ibn 'Arabi or Lao Tzu would be of far less interest if they had spent their time chatting about the great days to come ten or twenty years down the line.

Perhaps we *are* approaching a major turning point in human history. Perhaps a New Age, a Paradigm Shift, an Omega Point *is* upon us. Personally I doubt that it is, but even granting for the sake of argument that it is, *so what?* Talking about it will not make it proceed any faster. Moreover, the imagination and compassion required to navigate such an epoch cannot be any more or any less than those same qualities demanded of humanity in every era.

No doubt it took a lot of willpower and love to make it through the Renaissance, and all sorts of people rose to the occasion as that "new age" proceeded incrementally. However, I doubt that it would have happened any better or any faster if da Vinci had hired a press agent and spent his time going on book tours promoting the concept of the Renaissance. On the contrary, if the early years of that particular turning point had been filled with legions of Renaissance spokespersons rushing around talking up the Renaissance idea, it would probably have turned into a passing fad that soon collapsed under its own pretensions, as is now happening with the current "New Age" phenomenon.

I believe that the millennium and the days to come would be best served by people uncoupling their personal ideological wagons from the train of history and vowing to drag them under their own steam. Every promise of a transformed tomorrow has always been at least a partial lie, because the future itself has the final say. This is not to say that transformations do not happen—they do, constantly. But just as the Tao always embodies a dynamic equilibrium between yin and yang, and neither polarity "wins," our bright tomorrow will always be half nightmare.

This must strike some as mere cynicism—after all, the human spirit must dream! However, the twentieth century's special gift of wisdom has been the spectacle of glorious dream after glorious dream ending not with sweet success but with ignoble disaster. The war to end all wars, the proletarian revolution, the thousand-year Reich, the clean nuclear future—the list is lengthy. Alas, rather than learning any lessons about sweeping solutions inevitably failing, those addicted to the future have simply picked themselves up, brushed off the dust and encrusted blood, and signed on to the next panacea.

The third millennium, by dint of its symbolic weight, promises to be an irresistible magnet for every rosy (or scary) projection on the loose. As the millennium approaches, human consciousness will be quantified, mobilized, massaged, and thrust toward that marvelously arbitrary zero point, all in the service of some promise or threat voiced by those who earn their living by selling their dreams to others.

I suggest we save ourselves some serious disappointment—let's unhitch our expectations from the year 2000. Our true self will not be any more present then than it already is right now; eternity will not be any closer to culmination then than it ever was. What is demanded of us now—love and compassion—is no different from what has always been and always will be. Our immediate circumstances and the world around us require our attention, and if we respond appropriately that will suffice to pave the way for tomorrow. The millennium is an attractive mirage. Don't stop, keep walking.

VISIONARY PHILOSOPHY,
EVOLUTIONARY VISION

28

RALPH STRAUCH

Ralph Strauch, Ph.D., teaches self-awareness and movement using the Feldenkrais method in Pacific Palisades, California, and was formerly a senior mathematician with the RAND Corporation. He is the author of *The Reality Illusion* and is currently working on a book about the somatic dimensions of emotional experience.

A Crisis of Perception

Approaching the millennium, we face an interlocking array of potential crises. Overpopulation, environmental pollution, and possible catastrophic climate change threaten, if not our very survival, then surely our current way of life. Less devastating, yet still serious, are crises in crime, education, economic inequity, and healthcare. Individually, we each deal with our personal stresses, insecurities, identity crises, and the physical aches and pains of aging.

Overarching all of these, and contributing fundamentally to each, I see a more basic and largely unrecognized crisis—a *crisis of perception*. I refer not so much to *what* we perceive as to *how*. The narrowly focused perceptual style that both shapes and is shaped by contemporary civilization has served us well in the development of science and technology, but badly in their applications to human needs, and in our social institutions and personal lives.

Perception is not the simple process of passive observation that it sometimes seems. It is an active, interactive process, in which you filter and select from sensory and memory data to construct the perceptual images that you experience as external reality. My interest here lies not with what gets through and what is filtered out, but with the breadth of the lens through which that filtering takes place. That can vary from a narrow focus, concentrating on details with minimal surrounding context, to a broad, open focus supporting an integrated gestalt of the world as a whole.

To experience some of that range visually, curl your fingers into a tube, and look through that tube at the room around you. You can see everything, in the sense that you can see all the pieces. But you cannot get a *complete* view of anything bigger than the visual diameter of your tube, and you cannot see relationships between things. *Uncurl your hand, relax, and let your focus soften. Take in the room without concentrating on particular details.* Notice the breadth of your vision and your sense of relationships. Those were absent when you looked through the tube.

This range exists in other perceptual dimensions—in your hearing, your proprioception (awareness of what goes on inside your body), and your conceptual understanding. It also exists in the overall perceptual field that combines these dimensions into your ongoing experience. Even in the simple exercise described above, when your vision is broad, it is easier to hear background noises, to be aware of your breathing, and to think broadly.

This perceptual range evolved because it served our biological needs. A hunter searches for game with an open focus, but narrows his focus to aim and throw his spear. We are meant to have and use it all, adapting to the task at hand. Contemporary society, however, biases us strongly toward the narrow. An emphasis on early reading teaches concentrated focus, while sitting still in school teaches reduced body awareness. And no matter what you watch, television is a *tunnel vision trainer* without peer. Scientific reductionism and the economic imperative of the bottom line both reflect and reinforce this narrowness, helping make it a cultural norm, while high levels of ongoing personal stress reinforce it physiologically.

Perceptual narrowness encourages decision-making styles, at societal as well as individual levels, that focus on sharply defined problems without surrounding context. The world takes on a fragmented, "us-them" character, in which self-interest has more appeal than altruism and competition feels safer than cooperation. These decision-making styles produce "solutions" like polluting the environment with chemical pesticides, clear-cutting old-growth forests to "save jobs," and reducing education or drug treatment programs because they are "too expensive." Our crises are not totally caused by such thinking, but it certainly contributes!

29

FRANCES VAUGHAN

Frances Vaughan, Ph.D., is a psychologist in private practice in Mill Valley, California. She is the author of *The Inward Arc* and *Awakening Intuition* and coeditor of *Beyond Ego, Accept This Gift, A Gift of Peace,* and *A Gift of Healing.* She is on the clinical faculty of the University of California, and was formerly president of the Association for Transpersonal Psychology and the Association for Humanistic Psychology.

Cultivating a Vision of Possibility

Where there is no vision, the people perish. [Proverbs 29:18]

Recognizing the overwhelming magnitude of global problems often leaves us feeling helpless and hopeless about the future. Problems such as overpopulation, pollution, depletion of resources, global warming, nuclear proliferation, extinction of species, and war affect the quality of life on Earth for all creatures. Since all these threats to planetary well-being are human caused, it is up to us to make the changes that can restore an ecological balance.

My hope is that humans can learn to respond creatively to these challenges. My fear is that we will continue to cause a great deal of unnecessary suffering before finding a better way to live in harmony with nature and with each other.

As children, our behavior is shaped by the social environment. As adults, we become the shapers of that environment. The willingness to see things as they are, to act with courage, wisdom, and compassion is a challenge for everyone who cares about the quality of life on Earth and the future.

Benevolent action that cares for the well-being of the whole cannot be coerced. Yet it flows naturally from a perception that envisions the possibility of peace, love, and harmony in place of greed, fear, and anger. Empowerment that enables a person to become an effective participant in healing the Earth calls for awareness of our total dependence on the biosphere and the power of the human mind as the greatest threat and the greatest resource for planetary well-being.

Cultivating a vision of possibility may enable a shift from an egocentric view to a transpersonal perspective in which everyone participates in the co-creation of a better world. Implementing this vision requires courage and commitment. We are still learning what it means to be human, and we have yet to implement some form of spiritual democracy that includes all beings.

As we go about the immediate tasks of teaching and healing and relieving suffering, we must also remember the necessity for inner work, that our actions may be informed by inspiration and discriminating wisdom. Since the state of the world reflects the state of our minds, any lasting change will require a better understanding of how we can change ourselves.

What each of us does may seem insignificant, yet every day presents opportunities for replacing ignorance with understanding, and fear with compassion. Collectively we have the power to turn the tide of destruction that seems to be enveloping the Earth. May we be inspired by a vision of possibility, become what we can be, and do what we can.

At a personal level, narrowness manifests as a lack of proprioceptive self-awareness. You unconsciously hold your back rigid as you get up from a chair, for example, creating unnecessary tension and strain. You do not notice, so you cannot control, the physical tensions you create in response to external stressors. Much of the angst and insecurity rampant today stems from lack of self-awareness, and many of the limitations we attribute to "growing older" come from the unconscious accumulation of inefficient and dysfunctional movement habits, not from aging at all.

Narrow perceptual focus has contributed to making Western civilization what it is, both good and bad, and to making it dominant in the world today. If current trends continue, it will also contribute to our downfall. We need to broaden our perceptual focus, in our economic and public policy institutions as well as in our personal lives. Some of that broadening is occurring, as evidenced by trends as diverse as increased environmental consciousness and growth in awareness-broadening practices such as meditation, t'ai chi, and the Feldenkrais Method. But it remains an open question, I am afraid, whether we can broaden our vision enough, quickly enough, to avert the crises that face us.

30

DAVID SEAMON

David Seamon, Ph.D., is a phenomenological geographer and professor in the Department of Architecture at Kansas State University. He is the author of *A Geography of the Lifeworld*, editor of *Dwelling, Seeing, and Designing* and coeditor of *Dwelling, Place and Environment*. He is also the editor of the *Environmental and Architectural Phenomenology Newsletter*.

"Seeing with New Eyes": Phenomenology and the New Millennium

> The important thing
> Is to pull yourself up by your own hair
> To turn yourself inside out,
> And see the whole world with new eyes.
> —Peter Weiss, *Marat-Sade*

"We are too late for the gods and too early for Being," wrote the German phenomenological philosopher Martin Heidegger, by which he meant that we can no longer believe divine word, yet we are unable to see the world as it is. Here lies a central dilemma for the new millennium: How, with unquestioned belief, can we know? How, without blind faith, can we be certain that what we see or understand is really so?

The twentieth century's hope for resolving these questions lay largely in positivist science, which sought to determine exact logical truths through cause-and-effect relationships identified materially and measured quantitatively. The results of positivist science, particularly in regard to technology, were beneficial in that they provided a freedom from time, space, and environment that earlier generations could never have imagined. At the same time, however, positivist science helped to create many unintended but difficult problems—for example, nuclear weapons, the ecological crisis, and a global capitalistic system that regularly values economic and institutional requirements over the needs of particular people and places. If the world is to become more just and humane, we have come to realize that the knowledge provided by positivist science is not enough.

Where, then, might the new millennium turn for guidance? One bright hope is the many new ways of knowing that have begun to appear in the last few decades. These possibilities—some radically new, some innovative versions of earlier traditions—seek to see and to understand in a receptive, kindly way. The aim is a thoughtful empathy that provides an opening where knower and known meet and know that they both belong.

Nominally, these new ways of knowing may seem far apart but, in fact, they are neighbors. For example:

- the existential phenomenology of Heidegger and philosopher Maurice Merleau-Ponty;
- the pattern language of architect Christopher Alexander;
- the deep ecology of philosophers Arne Naess, Bill Devall, George Sessions, and Warwick Fox;
- the phenomenologies of place and environmental experience provided by scholars like Edward Relph, Yi-Fu Tuan, and Belden Lane;
- the phenomenological science of Goethe and his present-day followers like Theodore Schwenk, Wolfgang Schad, John Wilkes, and Henri Bortoft;
- the sacred geometries and architectures of Keith Critchlow, Robert Lawlor, and Robert Meurant;
- the somatic therapies of Ida Rolf, F. M. Alexander, and Stanley Keleman;
- the efforts of Gurdjieffian philosopher John G. Bennet to use the qualitative and symbolic significance of number to understand wholes.

Though different in their topical emphases, these works are kin in that they all seek ways to allow being to break forth. And if we can find ways to allow things to be what they are, then they will more likely give us allowance and kindness in turn. Where there were parts, there might be wholes. Where there was separation, there might be neighborhood and relationship. We each find ourselves but find ourselves together. Diversity and commonality become one.

With what word to identify this hopeful possibility? Perhaps the best label is *phenomenology*. There are many versions of phenomenology, but the heart of the phenomenological style that I emphasize here is *kindly seeing*—in other words, if the thing could speak, what would it say? How would it describe itself? Phenomenology, explains John Harvey is "an imaginative sympathy that is receptive without ceasing to be critical." Phenomenology, says Edward Relph, is "an attempt to understand from the inside—and not to dismiss from the outside—the whole spectrum of experience which we generally call 'reality.' "

If the first step in phenomenology is to describe the thing in a fair but thoughtful way, the next step is to use that description to identify commonalities that underlie the specific descriptions and relate them to some larger pattern or whole. In this regard, Relph explains that phenomenology is "the gathering together of what already belongs together even while apart." For example, there is a growing body of studies that explore the phenomenology of place. These studies ask why places are crucial in human life and what happens in a society like ours where placelessness, geographical mobility, and environmental destruction regularly overwhelm community, rootedness, and ecological responsibility grounded in local care and concern.

One way to answer these questions phenomenologically is, first, to have many different people of different backgrounds describe a place important in their lives. These descriptions then provide a base for identifying more general qualities that characterize many of these places in an accurate but broader way. A striking effort to explore place phenomenologically is Relph's masterful *Place and Placelessness*, which demonstrates that places are "fusions of human and natural order and the significant centers of our immediate experience of the world." The essence of place experience, says Relph, is the degree to which a person feels *inside* place: "To be inside a place is to belong to it and to identify with it, and the more profoundly inside you are, the stronger is the identity with the place."

From one perspective, the growing malaise, societal disintegration, and environmental deterioration in our postmodern Western world relates to the erosion of place and the resulting loss of communal and ecological responsibility that place otherwise insures automatically. My larger point is that the new ways of knowing indicated above all seek, in various ways, to explore their subject matter in the style of phenomenology, whether implicitly or directly. Taken-for-granted aspects of human experience, like place, are given attention; the tacit and unnoticed are asked to speak. The result may be that we see "with new eyes." This style of vision and the understanding it evokes may offer one of the few viable ways to avert a threatening future of escalating inequities and divisions.

31

ROBERT LAWLOR

Robert Lawlor, M.F.A., is a former painter and sculptor, whose works have been displayed in museums and private collections. He is a founding member of the International Community of Auroville, Pondicherry, South India, and a translator of the works of Egyptologist R. A. Schwaller de Lubicz and Indologist Alain Danielou. His own published works include *Sacred Geometry, Earth Honouring—the New Male Sexuality,* and *Voices of the First Day: Awakening in the Aboriginal Dreamtime.*

Images Beyond Time and the Remembering of Space

In 1992 I accompanied a small party of New Zealand Maoris and Australian Aborigines who were invited to Mexico by a contemporary Aztec group to participate in their variation of a Sun Dance ceremony. This gathering was part of an informally organized cultural exchange between small groups of indigenous peoples from the Pacific regions.

In a storm-threatened evening twilight, Paiki, a young New Zealand Maori, deeply involved in his native culture, spoke to me of the concepts of time and history held in ancient Maori cosmology. He said there was no concept of future time in the thought or language of his traditional culture: "All of time is pictured as a vast sphere, which floats behind us. . . . Time is more like the memory of all things which are there in the beginning of creation. The present is, to us, only the events and things of every day, which we perceive in front of us. These

88

things occur to enable us to open up, or remember, more and more of the sphere which is hidden behind. As we learn by our experience, we are able to be drawn into that all-containing sphere. With this absorption into what you might call the past or memory, vision increases and spreads out. . . . This vision is what you call the future."

This image of time is so distant from the one that presently dominates our perception and language forms. Our lives are dominated by a dimly predictable future, either constantly moving toward us or acting as a rapacious magnet drawing us irreversibly away from a receding or disappearing past, through the needle eye of an intangible present moment. We cannot form a thought or a spoken expression, unless it falls into a past, present, or future tense. Our linear image of time is dependent upon spatial metaphors in order to be expressed: before and after, long and short, front and behind, forward and backward. These terms, appropriate to spatial perception, when applied as unconscious metaphors, tend to confer on the abstraction of time the tangibility of spatial existence. *Our culture has advanced so far in this unconscious metaphoric process that we have not only given time the tangibility of a spatial experience, but we have also, in a similar manner, substantiated time.* Time as substance is a metaphor that dominates contemporary life: In our minds it can be divided, used, wasted, spent, lost, sold, saved, and so on.

Along with the spatialization and substantiation of time, our culture has developed implied sets of values. For example, past time, viewed as being located *behind*, has become associated with a "fall" or something "inferior" or "diminished." We make statements such as: "They are a primitive *backward* people," or "His tennis game has fallen *backward*." While the association of the future with *forward* is also implicit in the "good," "superior," or "expansive" as in: "His policies show intelligence and *foresight*," or "A grand future lies *ahead* of us." These prejudicial unconscious metaphors concerning time have fused with our perception of the world and underlie the basis of our fantasized theories of progress and evolution.

My attention was returned as a sudden splurge of lightning lit both Paiki, the Maori, and myself. The conversation had continued oblivious to the fall of darkness. We were now joined by two Australian Aborigines. Their culture, believed by some to be over 150,000 years old, is much older than Maori or any other culture and can be considered to be the "Elder" of all indigenous cultures. *In Aboriginal language there is neither a word, image, nor concept for time.* Their culture survived continually, for untold millenniums, without any calendar or computation, by living in an intense, supersensitized rapport with both the visible and invisible realities of their spatial environment. Through initiation and ritual both the ecstatic heights and the deep trance levels of Aboriginal perception were regularly activated and educated. With the loss and decline of these levels of perceptions, preoccupations with time replaced the intensities of spatial awareness.

As my Aboriginal friends spoke, I began to realize the wisdom of this timeless way of being in the world: If one sits quietly in nature and allows the grip of time to dissolve its hold on one's mental processes, one sees that our primary actual-lived reality is the immediacy of both inner and outer space. It is an error both in perception, imagination, and logic to consider time as a dialectic opposite of space. The two terms are not on the same level or order of things. They are, as Gregory Bateson would say, as different logical types as "a map is from a territory." *Time is only a map or way of measuring events or changes that occur in space. Time is a method of mental notation, a descriptive device, not an embodied nor fundamental reality.*

This is not simply a contrast between: time versus eternity; relative time versus absolute time; cyclic time versus linear time; or biological time versus mathematical time. Rather it is the realization that nothing unfolds or evolves *in* time—space not time is the container in which the universe takes place. Time is only a garment draped over the body, or ground, of being, which is spaciousness.

How does the modern idolatry of time (that is, this conversion of a system of measure into a fundamental reality) affect our consciousness and way of being in the world? By construing an irreversible continuum of time, which presses always toward an unknown finality, the natural reaction is to cling or build permanency and fixed structures in order to counteract the endless, undistinguished surge of one moment proceeding from another. In our sense of self we build an internal fixity, with which we attempt to forge an identity or consistency that can move forward in the nameless flow of time. This internal fixity is then impressed into our language, with its unchanging word associations and time-bound grammatical forms, as well as in our conceptual thoughts, which always seek irrefutable arguments and absolute invariable truths. The same rigidity emerges in our relationships and institutions, and takes form as architecture, all an unconscious resistance to this sense of being immersed in an all-prevailing, fatally orientated procession.

Space, as the fundamental reality, gives birth to a completely different sense of self and being. In space, all things and qualities exist only through the enduring and primary laws of relationship. Each thing is in relationship to all other things and to the whole or entirety. This is both the nature of space and of life. In space, all states and stages of becoming are simultaneously present, changing, and modifying each other unceasingly, through the crossing-over and balancing of the polarized energies of creation and destruction. Pure space needs no superimposition of progression or evolution; all is a dreamlike flowing of transfiguration in endless variety, guided by the innate, invisible, formal necessities of embodiment.

With the advent of agriculture and the practices of exploiting, fragmenting, and desecrating the natural order of the earthly environment, humanity severed its bond with the sacredness of space. The distortions of time then fell, like a curtain, over the mind and vision of neolithic cultures. It is through Aboriginal hunting-and-gathering culture that we may find a contrast between the "self in time" and the "self in space." The Aborigines moved and lived in space, wandering perpetually without a fixed habitat, no defined possessions, languages with only spatial designations, and no calendars or maps, boundaries, or borders. Each spatial area they entered contained, in its particular formations and energies, the story of its origin. The stories, which are actually the earth's memory, contained the names of the Ancestors that created a particular place, the animals and plants sacred to it, and how the relatives and parentage of each member of the tribe related to this webwork of associations. The enduring features and energies of the earthly place, and the unchanging myths and ceremonies evoked by them, provided the fixed aspect of existence, allowing the Aborigines to move freely, as a song, in the ever-flowing exchange of qualities and interrelationship, which is the life of space.

There were other warnings that should have prevented us from creating a time-bound language and mode of perception, a time-bound science of physics and evolutionary biology, and time-bound messianic apocalyptic religions. Those warnings came through the source of European language groups—ancient India. Following natural disasters and possible invasions, India was historically the preeminent culture to radically experience the "fall into time." Indian Vedic philosophers, and subsequently the Mayans of Meso-America, elevated the calendar to the pinnacle of cosmological organization. Philosophy, language, human life, and social order were structured by the mapping of the ages and epochs. Prophecy, prediction, karmic patterns, reincarnation, and the hunger for eternity in all Hindu-based religions reflect the obsession with time and cycles. *Kali* and *Kala* were the female and male forms of the Sanskrit word for *time*. But the same words also meant "that which destroys and disassociates all things."

The *kali-yuga* , or time-dominated age, in which we live, was foreseen as being the age of destruction that terminates a vast cosmic cycle. The root sound "k" also means "to drag down," "to give pain," and "to destroy." *Kala* is also the root of our words "to calculate" and "to count." The wisdom of India, while being engulfed by the shrouds of time, understood that the perception of the universe as time-bound and calculable *is* the very seed or agent of destruction.

The by-products of time are the powers to predict, preconceive, manipulate, quantify abstractly, design, and, to a certain degree, take control over external events. If we wish to participate in a transformation or new vision, I believe we must seek those sources, languages, cultures, and modes of perception that allow us to escape from the deadening and rigidifying effects of a time-bound imagination. The tormented and disordered world that confronts us today, as well as the one in gestation within our collective spirit, achieves manifestation in our perception as well as in the metaphoric process of language used to describe and "bring it forth." Therefore, our first agenda must be to disentangle ourselves on fundamental perceptual and linguistic levels and, following the guidance of ancient indigenous cultures, learn to respond directly to the voice of the earth that still resounds through the spaciousness of what is left of the natural world.

32

ROBERT J. WILLIS

Robert J. Willis, Ph.D., is a licensed psychologist and is the author of *Transcendence in Relationship: Existentialism and Psychotherapy.*

History as Personal Time

The Third Millennium of the Christian Era beckons. How herald its approach?

As a civilization sprung from the heady confluence of the Judeo-Christian and Greco-Roman cultures, we accept as our own Aristotle's commonsensical experience of time; that is, "When we perceive a distinct before and after, then we speak of time; for this is what time is, the calculable measure or dimension of motion with respect to before-and-afterness" (*Physics* IV, XI, 219a, 11). From his perspective, on that New Year's eve we shall readily celebrate a linear record of miraculous achievements or debate the chilling progression of human destructiveness as the clock's hands march on and on and on. We shall do this with hope, with Gabriel Marcel's "memory of the future," that past events may somehow generate future wisdom.

This stance toward history as passing time forged past victories and defeats; it predicts more of the same. For the scions of manifest destiny, the past flaunts a litany of entitlements, the future promises a variety of great expectations, and the present clamors with power. Such as these stand resolutely on the corpses of the nondestined ones, objects to be manipulated for the advancement of their masters. In this scenario the beat will go on as the mantle of dominance now graces, now destroys. Conventional wisdom, well aware of history's penchant for repetition, foretells the rise and fall of civilizations and individual worlds. Once there was Rome. . . . Which star will flash, which flame will die first after midnight? Historical passing time will, you know, kill us all.

True hope flows from the marriage of person and time. In a person the past lives on as a repetitive possibility, while the future summons each one to its realization. And one's present hinges on that moment of vision, that joining of potential and energy, that leads to decision and action. History as personal time calls us home.

My own introduction to a Native American sweat lodge starkly differentiates these two times and presents an analogue for our future. As we chanted in the tepee's glowing interior, red-hot arrows of steam threatened my body. I lay on the ground gasping for breath, searching for some refreshing air where flaps and earth met. I placed a towel over my head but it became a searing conductor of heat. I considered bolting, but fear of tripping in the dark and of appearing to be a coward restrained me. Finally, after what seemed like forty-five torturous minutes, the medicine man opened the flaps. I gulped the coolness of the night.

The chanting resumed as the inner darkness again surrounded us. Knowing I could not beat the heat and pain, I turned my attention inward. I traveled deep within seeking a place of security and peace. In my mind's eye I saw myself in a meadow on a moonlit night. I was dancing . . . slowly. My pain diminished as the passing flow of time ceased. As T. S. Eliot in *Four Quartets* well said: "At the still point of the turning world. Neither flesh nor fleshless; Neither from nor towards; at the still point, there the dance is, . . . And I cannot say, how long, for that is to place it in time." This second cycle seemed to last ten minutes, the last one five. I emerged from the lodge invigorated and refreshed.

How explain this experience? As the transcending of ego and the touching of the self that is spirit. And it took place in personal time.

The fires of history have rampaged through past millennia. We have no reason to think they will not ravage the next one also. Wisdom dictates not that we stop all fires. We cannot. Nor does it instruct us simply to direct their energy against our enemies. Someday we, as another's enemy, will be consumed in turn. Instead we must dare the inward journey to our life's own energy. There we may be taken up by a Life that will live us.

The choice confronts us: another millennium of destruction or one of the spirit. Neither will come easily.

33

ROBERT POWELL

Robert Powell, Ph.D., D.I.C., specializes in *Advaita Vedanta* and Indian spirituality. He is the author of twenty books, including *The Great Awakening, Why Does God Allow Suffering?*, and *The Wisdom of Sri Nisargadatta Maharaj*. Forthcoming works include *The Ultimate Medicine* and *Talks on Liberation*.

The Third Millennium and the Illusion of Time

To this writer, the significance of the impending advent of the third millennium lies in the opportunity it affords to reflect upon the utter insignificance of the coming of the third millennium and the extreme superficiality in which we function. Our lives are cluttered up with inessentials, since we have lost the art of living in the essential. What could be more meaningless to our well-being than the position of the calendar? And which calendar do we choose? What about the Chinese, the Muslim, and the Jewish calendars? Am I supposed to believe in numerology? And if there lies any significance in the third millennium, what fundamental change then should occur at the end of 1999 when entering the next millennium? Or are my numbers all wrong and should I have picked the years 2000 and 2001 to define the transition from second to third millennium?

This attitude seems akin to the increasingly popular "thinking in terms of decades," the way we assign magical potency to periods of ten years, as though the decades themselves could exert a certain control over the affairs of humanity. The fifties, the sixties, the seventies, and so on, each is supposed to have brought with it a certain climate of social change, a different outlook on life. If one blames the present decade for current dissatisfaction, then there remains nothing but to wait for the next one. And if one's decade has only just started, that is just too bad; then one is out of luck and must be patient for the numbers to change. Thus, humanity in the absence of real self-understanding stays entangled in all kinds of numbers games, which are nothing more than rank superstition.

What do we mean by "change"? For myself, all change is a delusion. Only unreal things change. The real is that which never changes and alone therefore can be said to have identity. We think in terms of change, because our thinking is pervaded with the notion of time. That is why even the deepest thinking is inherently superficial, as it is based on the notion that there is progression. But that progression is only conceptual, not actual. The French say: *"Plus ça change, plus c'est la même chose,"* but even this saying is predicated upon the notion of time. I am hinting at something much more fundamental, which should be explored in depth, because this very notion holds a powerful key to self-discovery. And if there is such a thing as a direct path to self-realization, it might well be the understanding of this question.

We talk about the past and the future, but where are they? What are they? Can anyone produce a sample of the past or the future? Has anyone ever been able to do anything to the past, to "undo" the past? If one thinks so, one is doing it in the present and to the present. Has anyone ever been able to manipulate the future? If one thinks so, then think again, for one is doing it in the present. We can never escape from the present moment; it is all that ever is. The past is just one kind of image, a memory, and the future is another kind of "imaging" or imagination—both produced by thought. The present moment is all that exists, and it is timeless and limitless. What does this timeless moment consist of? Nothing but Awareness; not awareness of something but pure Sentience, what has also been referred to as the state of "I Am." It is the only state that one can rightly claim as one's own. Every other state—I am "this" or I am "that"—introduces concept, thought, and is therefore disputable. Anything else that one "owns" is predicated upon this quality of Awareness, for without it, there can be no knowledge of ownership or of anything.

Does the statement that time does not really exist mean that I should throw away my watch and calendar? Of course not, unless I decide to become a renunciate. I would no longer be able to function in a society that lives rigidly by those yardsticks. But that does not necessarily mean that the latter are real and not merely empirical. As far as the mind is concerned, time is real, but the mind is not the final arbiter in these things. On the contrary, since the mind itself is of the nature of conceptual time—it has been shaped through identification of consciousness with a particular body and name—whatever it perceives is tainted with these limitations.

Here lies at once a clue to humanity's unhappiness and possible release. Living in an unreal time dimension, at every moment of one's existence there is a certain expectancy regarding the next moment: This causes a dimming of our attention to the present moment since thought hopes for the next moment to be better or fears it to be worse. Or if we are bored, we are looking toward the next moment for something to "happen" that will relieve our ennui. Always looking forward to the "future," human beings have found it very difficult to live in the fullness of what *is*; thus, a peculiar quality is brought about in the consciousness, which is experienced as the "flow of time" and on a deeper level, as the energy of "becoming," which is the seed of all misery. We are constantly in the grip of desire—a desire for change in our condition—and so are never free. Only in rare moments in the intervals between (the satisfaction of) consecutive desires and in the deep sleep state, when there is pure Being or Presence without any mind activity, do we get a foretaste of the blissful state that is our birthright since it is our real nature. There is no notion of change and the mind is totally still: Nothing exists in that silence but the pure state of Awareness with its inherent blissfulness (*ananda*).

The very idea that we are in bondage immediately produces an impulse to break free, but that very movement toward the projected freedom is the bondage, because it is again an escape from the Present and therefore still part of our habitual "becoming." So what is needed only is the perception that there is no bondage, that we are free here and now. Thus, the direct path is to persuade the mind that it can totally relax, which is only another way of stating the need for its total surrender.

34

CHARLES JOHNSTON

Charles Johnston, M.D., is a psychiatrist, artist, and futurist, and director of the Institute for Creative Development in Seattle, Washington. He is the author of *The Creative Imperative* and *Necessary Wisdom: Meeting the Challenge of a New Cultural Maturity.*

The Challenge of New Questions

When I look toward the future, I see it demanding of us a fundamentally new maturity as a species. My hopes follow from what this maturity should bring forth—in how we relate to each other, to the planet. My fears concern how much pain we may put ourselves through, and put the other species that inhabit the Earth with us through, in coming to its necessary realization.

Personally, the hopes speak louder than the fears. Or perhaps more accurately, hopes versus fears is not quite the issue. I find myself deeply fascinated by the challenges reshaping today's world. I guess I could say as easily I find myself confused, frustrated, troubled—for with increasing frequency the new questions demand we leave old answers behind and move into territory where we are at best toddlers taking tentative first steps. But I must admit, our times excite me. I am not sure if this reflects optimism or just that I am a person who loves the uncharted. I remember sitting in my seventh-grade science class learning about Galileo, Newton, da Vinci and envying them that theirs were times, in contrast to ours, when great unknowns remained to be explored. I guess we should be careful what we envy.

Like it or not, our times demand that we be pioneers. We are being challenged to a whole new order of questions: How do we manage our newfound capacity for planetary destruction—environmental, nuclear? How do we understand the profound changes reordering love, gender, and the family? What does it mean to govern within the immense diversity of a global world? How do we redefine progress so that pursuing it will result in a healthy and vital world?

While the times of discovery I envied as a youth were indeed momentous, I see today's questions presenting even greater challenges. They ask for a new kind of pioneering. The pioneering of our cultural past was like the heroic striving of an adolescent or young adult making its place in the world. The pioneering demanded today is more like that of a person at midlife, someone taking on the paradoxical and uniquely deepening challenges of life's second half. Today's imperatives ask for not just new knowledge or achievement, but for a profound new capacity for wisdom. Our task is no longer just to make our place in the world, but to ensure that that world is a place of enduring beauty and significance.

35
ROGER WILLIAMS WESTCOTT

Roger Williams Westcott, Ph.D., was for twenty-five years professor of linguistics and professor of anthropology at Drew University in Madison, New Jersey. He was also the first holder of The Endowed Chair of Excellence in Humanities at the University of Tennessee. Of his 450 publications, 40 are books, including *The Divine Animal: An Exploration of Human Potentiality* and *Sound and Sense: Linguistic Essays on Phonosemic Subjects.* He serves as coeditor of the journals *Kronos, Futurics,* and *Forum Linguisticum.*

Voicings

ADMONITION: Hang loose! The thought that liberates you today may imprison you tomorrow.

ALLEGIANCE: My family is man and my yard is the universe.

AUDIENCE RESPONSE: The dead cry out against me. But the unborn praise my name.

CONSTRICTION: We are finite banks through which flows an infinite stream.

EVANGELISM: Preach the gospel according to your Self. Why fear to be the priest of a new heaven or the prophet of a new earth?

EVENTUALITY: The perpetually possible is eventually inevitable.

FOCUS: Conventional science is a futile effort to see everything while keeping one eye closed.

THE GOAL OF ANTHROPOLOGY: What but anthropiatry, the Healing of Man?

THE GOLDEN AGE: Aurealite life may be envisioned as an endless round of victimless crimes perpetrated by chronic loiterers.

HUMANITY: Asking a man to be more human is like asking a teenager to be more adolescent.

INTELLECTUAL PRIDE: Honest doubt is the beginning of wisdom. The first and worst pride is the claim to know.

INTERNATIONALISM: There is only one internation, and I live in it.

KNOWLEDGE: What anyone knows consciously, everyone knows unconsciously.

LOVE AND LOYALTY: Where love lasts, loyalty is superfluous.

LUNACY AND LUCIDITY: Man as we know him is a lunatic with lucid moments. The question is, Can the lucidity stem the lunacy?

MINDS: Too many minds are museums. Too few are gardens.

MYTH AND METHOD: The recovery of felicity is the end of myth.

NATIONALITY: It is not enough to internationalize the world. Ultimately, we must denationalize it.

NOBLE SAVAGERY: The Noble Savage, like the Kingdom of God, is within us.

NORMALITY AND HEALTH: It is neither normal to be healthy nor healthy to be normal.

OBJECTIVE: . . . not full employment but full enjoyment . . .

ODYSSEY: The good life is a perpetual voyage of self-discovery.

PEACEMAKING: Disarming may bring us a truce. But only disarmoring will bring us peace.

PROBABILITIES: Everything is possible. Little is probable. Nothing is certain.

RELEASE: . . . the door flung wide, the shout of joy, the world-embracing leap . . .

SECRECY: Earth has no secrets. It has only secretive occupants.

SPENGLERIANISM: We are told that our age is in decline. But I say that every age is in decline compared with the visions of its noblest souls.

THE SPIRIT WORLD: Did early man populate his world with spirits? Or did we depopulate it?

TEACHING: "Letting students learn" is no passive stance. It is an active—often strenuous—removal of impediments to learning.

TRAGIC SURVIVAL: Man is a wounded animal. His very survival is astonishing. But his inability to heal his wounds is tragic.

VISION: It is only through the cracks in their "sanity" that some men can glimpse perfection.

36

JOHN E. NELSON

John E. Nelson, M.D., is a practicing psychiatrist, who has long been a student and lecturer in the fields of Eastern philosophy and transpersonal psychology. He is the author of *Healing the Split: Madness or Transcendence?* and is presently editing an anthology with his wife, Dr. Andrea Nelson, on the transpersonal treatment of depression.

Evolutionary Optimism

I believe there is reason for profound optimism for the future of the human race.

Not only is the collective consciousness of humanity perceptibly advancing to ever-higher planes, but accompanying this advance is the growing realization that evolution is *leading somewhere*, as obscure as that ultimate destiny may seem. It seems ever more evident that life has *meaning* and *purpose* and that we are actively engaged in the process of discovering and fulfilling it.

Some argue that we live in irrevocably degenerate times, as revealed by news reports of child abuse, escalating violence in urban streets, unparalleled environmental degradation, and the usual profusion of self-serving politicians. Yet are we to believe that fewer children were abused in ancient Persia, or in Rome and Paris during the Dark Ages? Were wars less cruel before modern journalism projected their horror into our living rooms? Were Egyptian pharaohs, medieval popes, or feudal monarchs blessed with more humanitarian concern than democratically elected politicos of our time? I suggest that times were definitely *not* better then. And in the future, human life will become significantly better than it is now.

Consider that child-labor laws—a relatively modern innovation —put an end to eighteen-hour mining shifts for twelve-year-olds. In the nineteenth century, the most common killer of human beings was smallpox, now eradicated from the planet. Institutionalized slavery once tainted even the most enlightened cultures but now is legal nowhere in the world. Disturbing stories of child abuse speak not of an increase in these crimes, but of our willingness to confront them head on. The environmental crisis has generated brilliant insights such as the Gaia hypothesis—exactly the kind of whole-systems thinking that can guide us away from self-destruction. And most heartening, the recent nuclear stand-down bears witness that technological prowess does not inevitably lead to global catastrophe.

Within the next decade, an international project to map the incredibly complex human genome will be complete. This will confer humanity with the power to end most genetic diseases, from muscular dystrophy to schizophrenia. By pinpointing genes for intelligence and aging, we will learn to engineer advanced beings not only with exquisite data-processing capabilities, but with an indefinitely expanded life span. It is conceivable that the next generation may be the last whose inexorable fate is to grow old and die. This beckons us to radically restructure our religious, ethical, and social institutions with wisdom greater than is now generally apparent.

Fortunately, evolution toward higher consciousness is a fact of human history, so there is hope that our insight will gradually broaden to deal with such astonishingly complex problems. Consciousness evolution will likely proceed in four stages: 1) loving concern for the welfare of the whole human community and health of our mother planet, 2) movement toward higher creative vision that grasps a long view of history and human destiny, 3) dawning of more intuitive, even extrasensory, modes of gathering information and understanding relationships, and 4) direct realization of the sacred oneness of all Being.

The first of these phases is already in evidence, as demonstrated by the success of the feminist movement, rebirth of nature-based Goddess myths, and decline of patriarchal social hierarchies that inhibit opening our hearts to each other. So our collective near-term task is to *affirm feminine values* to balance the excesses of the aggressive, war-oriented cultures of the past two thousand years. This means cooperation rather than conflict, affiliation rather than dominance, and nurturance rather than competition. From this unity in polarities, this balance of *yin* and *yang*, will spring the wisdom necessary to align us with our ultimate destiny, unity of all in One Spirit.

37

JOSEPH ENGELBERG

Joseph Engelberg, Ph.D., is professor of physiology and biophysics at the University of Kentucky College of Medicine. He is the author of *The Nature of Integrative Study*.

Do Not Despair

At the heart of all things,
of whatever there is in the universe,
dwells the word.
From it flows life.

Out of aeons of chaos, struggle, and defeat
humankind emerged
humankind—
the universe made conscious of itself:

unconsciousness
unconsciousness
unconsciousness
. . . .
consciousness.

Then, while mathematics slowly, slowly grew
and gathered power over the millennia

migrating as it did
from Sumeria, Ionia, Egypt, and India
to every corner of the world,

countless societies, empires, and civilizations
rose and fell.

Do you know, Fontanes,
what most amazes me
in the world?
It is the inability of force
to maintain anything at all.

There are only
two powers in the world:
the sword and the mind.

In the long run
the sword
is always defeated
by the mind.

Napoleon Bonaparte

At the heart of the universe dwell

order
law
mercy
compassion
love

. . . and suffering.

From these
flow life.

Do not despair.

38

HIROSHI MOTOYAMA

Hiroshi Motoyama, Ph.D., Litt.D., is president of the California Institute for Human Science (Graduate School) and of the International Association for Religion and Parapsychology. He is director of the Institute for Religious Psychology and of the Motoyama Institute for Life Physics. He is the author of many books, including *Toward a Superconsciousness* and *Western and Eastern Medical Studies of Pranayama and Heart Control.*

Human Beings in the Future Global Society

The ancestors of human beings were born on earth about four to five million years ago, and it would appear that they formed a society composed of small groups. This is similar to the social structure of a troop of Japanese monkeys (which is matrilineal and whose leadership is assumed by a male boss selected by the females). Our ancestors appear to have lived in a fixed region as their territory in order to obtain food.

They gradually started to use fire and to boil and bake food, which prevented diseases caused by bacteria. They also started to wear clothes and live in caves. In the period of Neanderthal man, ten to twenty thousand years ago, they put their dead in graves and offered flowers to them: It seems that love toward community members and self-recognition as a society member had been awakened. The original form of incantatory religion is found in this period.

Homo sapiens, the ancestor of modern human beings, survived convulsive climatic changes that were caused by the southern or northern shift of the west equatorial wind that brought rain, this shift occurring at intervals of several thousands of years. They started to control the space restrictions by using arrows. Around ten thousand years ago, they started to irrigate and cultivate the land, and they stopped their total dependence on hunting. Around five thousand years ago, copper and iron tools were made, and the power to control nature/matter was strengthened. The social system of ancient nations was then formed, and monotheistic religions were born. It seems there is a constant correlation between the enlargement and strengthening of the human power of control over matter and the advancement of civilization.

As civilization progressed, it seems that great differences were developed between the civilizations, religions, and views of nature and humans in the desert regions and those in the forest regions of tropical and temperate zones where the rain was ample. The religions that were born in the desert, such as Judaism, Christianity, and Islam, taught that heaven and earth were created by God, and people thought they could utilize nature as a resource. In these religions, there is a confrontation (discrimination) between God, nature, and humans, and no unification between them. That is, the law of identity (A = A, A ≠ Non-A) governs the teachings of these religions.

In parts of Asia that were blessed with plenty of rain, good weather, and arable land, seeds were sown and bore fruit, and the cycle of sowing and reaping was repeated year after year, when adequate seeds were sown and adequate care was given. People in these regions blessed by nature considered that the great life force of nature was the force that allowed humans to live and grow. That is, nature was the force of the Absolute. They lived being assimilated by this force and realized the oneness between humans, nature, and the force of the Absolute. Contrary to the worldview and religions born in the desert, they developed a worldview that humans, nature, and the Absolute are essentially one (dialectic as A = A, and A ≠ Non-A, but essentially A = Non-A).

In these five hundred years and more, material civilization and science, which were created on the basis of Islamic and Christian worldviews (confrontation between humans and nature), have had their domination over the world. Enjoying the benefits of this civilization, humans at the same time destroyed the natural environment of the earth, which is the basis of human existence, and have created a situation critical to their existence. Humanity's violence against nature, confronting it and viewing it as a means to utilize for living, is endangering our present existence.

Then, what are human beings? To answer this question, I accumulated research on the human mind and supernatural abilities from the view of quantum biology. On the basis of this research and my long religious experience, I think that the human individual is a holistic being of body, mind, and spirit, having individuality and generality (sociality) in each of these three dimensions of existence.

Instead of confronting nature, humans are essentially homogeneous and have a reciprocal influence with nature in all of the aforementioned dimensions. Humanity and nature have the same quality of the Absolute and can ultimately return to the Absolute through self-negation. Human beings can live in harmony and be unified with nature without discrimination. I think that the realization of humans as holistic beings who can live in harmony and without discrimination against other people, nature, and the Absolute, is a prerequisite for actualizing the global society for all the beings.

39

PETER RUSSELL

Peter Russell is a writer, management consultant, and freelance philosopher. He is the author of several books, including the widely read *The Brain Book*. The following essay was adapted by him from his recent book *The White Hole in Time*.

The Birth of Homo Sapiens Sapiens Sapiens

The seeds of our global crisis were sown a long time ago when *Homo sapiens*, the creature with a large brain and versatile hands, began to change its world in novel ways. Something different was walking the Earth: A species whose future was determined not by its genes so much as by its thinking. A species that could understand the universe in which it found itself, and then used this understanding to reshape the clay of Mother Earth into new forms. A species that had tamed fire. A species that began creating pots and other tools, that made painted pictures, decorated itself with jewelry, and buried its dead. So new were these developments, some anthropologists gave this more creative *Homo sapiens* a new name. *Homo sapiens sapiens*—variously translated as the "wise human being" or "man that knows it knows."

Quite naturally *Homo sapiens sapiens* turned its new capacities to the creation of a more comfortable world: A world in which food was plentiful and available all year round. A world in which we could protect ourselves from cold and rain. A world in which we were free from pain, free from crippling diseases. A world in which we could live longer and more fulfilling lives.

But the more people that survived, the more our population grew. And the more things we created, the more resources we consumed—and the more pollution we produced. Both grew exponentially, until now, at the turn of the second millennium A.D., human population and industrialization have reached the limits of what this planet can sustain.

We initially embarked upon this fateful course with the best of intentions. We were applying our creativity to the task of improving the quality of our lives. And there can be no blame for that. It is only now as we realize the many ways in which our best intentions have backfired that we need to correct our behavior. It is today that we are having to respond to the crisis we have inadvertently created. And yet, at the very time we need it most, the will to change seems curiously lacking. Instead we continue to rush headlong toward catastrophe.

The question we must ask is, Why do we continue? Why—now that we know the long-term consequences of many of our actions, and the threats that they present to our continued existence—do we continue to consume more and more?

We do not lack the technology to tackle most of the problems facing us. In almost every area we know what needs to be done to restore the environment and keep it in a healthy state; and where we do not yet have the necessary means, we know how to set about developing them.

Nor are we short of the money needed to save the world. The WorldWatch Institute in Washington, D.C., has estimated that the total cost of a six-year program to protect the soil, reforest the land, reduce population growth, retire the debts of the developing countries, raise energy efficiency, and develop renewable sources of energy would amount to around $750 billion. A lot it would seem . . . until we compare it to the more than $1 trillion the nations of the world currently spend on arms in just one year.

The source of the problem appears to lie within—within our own minds. *Homo sapiens sapiens* is a species with the power to choose its own future. And what we choose depends upon our attitudes and values, upon what we consider important and upon how we think we can best fulfill our needs.

What is now becoming clear is that the attitudes and values that guided humanity in the past are no longer working. Preservation of the self may have been very valuable in prehistoric times. It may also have been valuable when the world was a collection of indepen-

111

dent communities and states—although, even then, self-centeredness among those in power often led to greed, exploitation, and corruption. But now, in the closing days of the twentieth century, such values have become positively dangerous.

Our most urgent need today is to develop a new way of seeing, a new way of thinking, and a new set of values. What is being called for is a new subspecies: a species that can manage the creativity of *Homo sapiens sapiens* with true wisdom—a *Homo sapiens sapiens sapiens*.

This is the new evolutionary adaptation waiting to emerge—not a biological adaptation—there is no time for that, and even if we could genetically re-engineer ourselves, it would not hit at the heart of the problem. What the crisis is driving us toward is inner change—a transformation into truly wise human beings, a species no longer fettered by self-centeredness.

It is driving us toward a new perception of ourselves, a new sense of purpose, a new way of being. We are being urged to awaken from our dream: To awaken from our belief that whether or not we are at peace depends upon what we have or do. To awaken to the wisdom that we all share within.

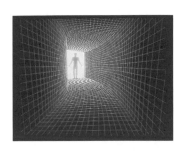

THE SOCIAL DIMENSION

40
ERVIN LASZLO

Ervin Laszlo, recipient of the *doctorat és-lettres et sciences humaines* of the Sorbonne as well as several honorary Ph.D.s, is the author or editor of over fifty books and three hundred articles, as well as editor of *World Futures, The Journal of General Evolution.* He has served as professor of philosophy, systems science, and future studies in various universities around the world and is currently founder and head of the General Evolution Research Group, science advisor to the director-general of UNESCO, and rector of The Vienna Academy.

The Challenge

The problems that beset humanity in the 1990s are not mainly political but economic, social, and environmental. They are strongly interconnected, of worldwide scope and universal impact. The problems arise because human societies, as all complex systems in nature, grow and evolve in the course of time. The process takes societies from relatively inert states near thermodynamic equilibrium to highly dynamic states far from equilibrium, from single to multilevel forms of organization, and from reliance on a few widely scattered energy sources to the intensive exploitation of multiple and dense energy flows. This has led to a vast acceleration of the ecological impact of societies and to their growth from the regional to the national, and now to the multinational and global level. The main driver of the process has been technology: the extension of the powers of human muscles, human sense organs, and human brains. The latest series of technological innovations extends human brain power through artificial information processing, using ever-less free energy to perform ever-more work. Its mastery calls for new levels of control and coordination in social and organizational structures. Creating these structures propels humanity along the path of transition from nationally based industrial societies to a globally interconnected system based above all on the communication, processing, and practical use of information.

The evolution of societies, while progressive, is not linear. There are transitory periods of instability and chaos interspersing more extended periods of stability and order. These discontinuous phase changes, known in chaos theory as "bifurcations," are determined by what went on before. They can lead to the breakdown of society as readily as to its breakthrough to a higher stage of development. The current transition from national industrial to global information society is subject to a cascade of such bifurcations. Since midcentury alone, two great bifurcation waves have impacted on contemporary societies: the wave produced by the politics of decolonization and that triggered by the politics of *glasnost*. Unless timely action is taken, they will be followed by a third wave, resulting not from politics but from the increasing level of stress in the global environment. The ecology wave, affecting all societies, is likely to become the ultimate arbiter of success in the current transition to a global information society.

System stress is not a new phenomenon. Whenever people have disregarded the fact that their environment is an essentially closed ecological system, they have grown in numbers, increased their demands, and overstressed their natural resource base. At that point they either have become more efficient in the use of their available resources or they have migrated to, or conquered, less exploited environments. In the late twentieth century, humanity is again reaching the limits of its natural resource base, but of the two classical solutions, one has become foreclosed. There are no more virgin or significantly unexploited lands left to which to migrate or annex. Only the more efficient use of the planet's resources remains a viable option, making purposive use of some of the same technologies that drove, and continue to drive, the historical process.

Technologies for using the available resources must take into account that, while humanity is still growing in numbers and increasing its demands, the physical resources of its planetary habitat are neither fully renewable nor infinitely expandable. The biosphere, the matrix for all renewable resources, is a dynamic system in its own right. Human impact on it produces structural changes, including new dynamic equilibria. The present generation can neither return to past conditions nor extend growth trends in a linear fashion. It has to create new conditions, using the emerging technologies of information, control, and communication to regulate the impact of the energy- and materials-intensive technologies through which societies now interact with nature.

In nature, regulatory mechanisms are genetically coded and come automatically into play whenever thresholds of stability are overstepped. Population size, population density, predator-prey relationships, symbiosis, and commensalism are all subject to adjustment by mechanisms that took thousands or millions of years to evolve. But the regulatory mechanisms of human societies are cultural, and consequently they evolve far more rapidly than genetically coded mechanisms. However, culture-coded mechanisms can also become rapidly outdated. Obsolescence is a genuine threat in regard to the practices by which contemporary societies now cope with their environment. The series of technological revolutions of the last two hundred years outdistanced established values and practices.

The challenge to contemporary leadership is to develop the required thinking and behaving so as to be able to regulate the system before the system regulates itself. System self-regulation would be no doubt effective but is likely to be drastic. Massive diebacks of the human population could result. But a timely and purposive human regulation is possible. The knowledge base exists, the technologies for applying it are there, and a new consciousness to support it is evolving in the mind of the public. The development of scientific knowledge concerning the dynamics of evolutionary processes, and its application through the new technologies of information and communication, provide an effective platform for new thinking translated into responsible and effective decision-making.

The leadership challenge of the transition confronts all sectors of society but faces first and foremost the business community. Businesses function today in an environment that is already information-based and globalized. In possession of the key technologies and the power to use them the world over, the business community has become the main engine of the current phase of humanity's evolution. It could become—and has the responsibility to become—its conscious and effective agent.

41

JUSTINE & MICHAEL TOMS

Justine Toms and Michael Toms are cofounders of the New Dimensions Foundation and coproducers of New Dimensions Radio and the "New Dimensions" radio series. Justine is the editor of *New Dimensions Journal* and is, on occasion, host of "New Dimensions." Michael is an electronic journalist and the primary host of "New Dimensions." He is the author of *At the Leading Edge* and is senior acquisitions editor for HarperSanFrancisco.

Good News

At this moment in time an unprecedented amount of information is available to a greater population than the world has ever known. The impressions processed by one human in the course of one day are enormous. We are bombarded with human-created images competing for our attention, delivered by many different modes. There are newspapers, radio, and television. Even if we decide to live our lives without these, we are still exposed to billboards while driving, and magazine headlines when standing in line at a supermarket. Our mailboxes are jammed with information—from the latest mail-order catalogs to funding pleas from many worthwhile organizations.

The political discussion of what is happening to our planetary environment is just beginning. What has not been acknowledged in this dialogue is media itself as an environment. It has been noted by some, such as social critic Jerry Mander and educator-philosopher Joseph Chilton Pearce, that media can affect one's health. How do we partake of this environment wisely? How do we create a healthy media diet?

The need for discernment has never been greater. How does one stay open to wisdom amidst the pelting of this era's information storm? First we must ask ourselves, "What is the balance for each of us?"—recognizing our need for hard facts, entertainment, connections and networking, stimulation, and beauty.

Today, through CNN and other networks, we are hooked up visually to most of the populated planet. We are able to see in an instant political demonstrations such as those at Tiananmen Square in China in June of 1989 and the collapse of the Berlin Wall in the fall of the same year. Radio was responsible for bringing thousands of Soviets out into the streets in the summer of 1991, effectively blocking the coup attempt in the Soviet Union. When the nuclear disaster at Three Mile Island happened, an entire country was educated about the inner workings and dangers of nuclear power plants in less than forty-eight hours. We watched as the Pentagon produced a "sanitized" media event called the "Persian Gulf War," which showed "smart" bombs sailing along highways but nobody dying, even though hundreds of thousands of Iraqis, including men, women, and children were incinerated.

We have access to enormous amounts of information (and misinformation), and will have more to cope with in the future. Technologies are now being developed that will open us up to even more media choices. How shall we glean wisdom from this deluge? And how shall we avoid being engulfed by the flood of data? How will we avoid being manipulated by the media?

First of all we can look for the bias, the angle that the piece is presenting, and know it for that angle. Each piece of media, whether a documentary on television, an interview on radio, or a theater piece on stage, has a viewpoint, has a bias. The "objective journalist" is a fantasy. All journalists bring their own life experience to their work. In addition, most media is commercially driven and thereby influences the media message. Not to acknowledge this fact is to be blind to mass media's purpose to manipulate, convince, and sway.

As more and more information becomes available, there is an ever-greater need to cultivate and respond to the inner voice, and to set aside time for silence and solitude. There is so much information overload that burnout, paralysis, indifference, or cynicism can become the dominant force in our lives. We are barraged, for example, with information about global warming or the coming ice age, about overpopulation and starvation, about drive-by shootings and toxic waste, about racism and cities going bankrupt. This information is so often presented without any context of hope or solution. If one is tuning into the six o'clock nightly news or using the newspaper for one's main information current, then yes, listening or reading the news *is* bad for one's health. This kind of information is debilitating. The constant flow of negativity kills hope.

The Dalai Lama, spiritual and political head of the Tibetan people, was once asked why he goes around the world talking about peace—what has his philosophy done for his people? After all, the Chinese have killed more than a million Tibetans, he lives in exile from his country, and the Tibetans continue to be persecuted in their homeland. His answer was to the point. He said his actions made him feel good. Why get up in the morning and feel bad, feel depressed? We have a choice about how we feel, and working for world peace makes him feel good. It is the right thing for him to do. He doesn't do it because the outcome might be world peace. The outcome may or may not be world peace, or peace for his country. However, no matter what the outcome, he does it because it is the right thing to do, and he lives a happier life that way. He has discovered how to resonate compassionately with his environment.

The point here is that we need to nurture hope by finding our own personal compassionate resonance. We need to find it daily and apply it to ourselves, to our family and friends, and to our community. As we gain more understanding of the possibilities of local and global challenges, it is imperative that we develop ways of connecting with our unique compassionate resonance. This may be done by a simple act such as planting a tree and nurturing it through its early years to help it take firm root. It may be volunteering for a local church offering meals for the homeless. It can take many forms—spiritual, political, social, artistic.

As well as our human connections, there is a greater need to feel our connections with other living beings such as trees, plants, and animals. The information age does not provide a substitute for direct experience. Watching a television show about nature is not a substitute for going out into the natural world. The simple act of catching a spider inside the house by turning a glass over it and sliding a piece of cardboard under it, then turning the spider loose outside instead of killing it helps the human heart develop compassionate resonance for other species with whom we share this planet. Besides sparing the spider's life, it is good for our own health.

People are choosing to create community once more as many sit in circle regularly with one another to share their hopes, fears, dreams, and disappointments. They are creating ritual together, playing drums together, singing and chanting together. When we look at our lives and pick out the moments that we have been truly happy, they are most often when we are in communion with others or with nature. As far back as cave-dwelling times, our ancestors have been sitting around together and telling each other their stories. And today, the oral tradition is being reawakened. Storytelling is on the upswing. A good example of this in the media was the "Civil War" documentary aired on public television in 1991. With a few still images, and relying mostly on voices and some interviews, this deep recounting of the American Civil War story kept millions enthralled for four evenings in a row.

The art of conversation is in danger of being superseded by the rapid pace of our lives. Listening is an art that comes with practice, but only if we are open to dialogue with others. It is a good practice to schedule time for precious "sacred gossip" with one another. Time to laugh and cry together. In our busy lives we must make it a priority.

As we move into the third millennium, and as the whirlwind of more and more information impacts our environment, it might be wise to plan some time into our days and weeks to be with one another in loving and supporting ways, away from all media—no television, video, cassette tapes, radio, books, newspapers, magazines—to be with others and in nature with deep gratefulness for our time here on this exquisite cosmic jewel, planet Earth.

42

RAFFI

Raffi is a multiplatinum recording artist, songwriter, and performer, who has long championed the dignity of the whole child and love for the Earth family. In response to the global eco-crisis, Raffi recorded *Evergreen Everblue*, an ecology album for the 1990s. The recipient of several awards, he was recently appointed Youth Ambassador for the United Nations Environment Programme.

Imagine Living a Politics of Hope and Renewal

Sam Keen writes that healing the Earth is the new human vocation. Rosalie Bertell asks, When do we get a chance to bloom? Al Gore says that ecology must become the central operating principle in our lives. For those who despair in these trying days of a planet in peril, there is hope in the growing wave of personal awakenings to balance the tragic news of our ecosystems in crisis.

In June of 1992, I witnessed Severn Suzuki, a twelve-year-old Canadian, speak at a plenary session of the UNCED Earth Summit in Rio on behalf of the Environmental Children's Organizations. She stated in part:

> "We came 5,000 miles to tell you adults you MUST change your ways. I am fighting for my future. Losing my future is not like losing an election or a few points on the stock market. . . . At school, even in kindergarten, you teach us to behave in the world. You teach us not to fight with others, to work things out, to respect others, to clean up our mess, not to hurt other creatures, to share, not be greedy. Then why do you go out and do these things you tell us not to do?"

Her words challenge the rhetoric of career-building, posturing politicians and bottom-line corporate executives.

Saving the environment? What's that? There's no such thing as "the environment," by itself. Our environment, yes. The natural environment manifests LIFE in a fragile balance, life supporting life, dying, and birthing. A collage of ecologies, in a holographic universe, each part reflecting the whole. No objects, just relationships. Quantum and sub-quantum physics now show that light permeates all matter, that light waves are the reality underlying apparently inert solids. A wave is a dynamic relationship.

The "environment" does not exist apart from us.

Fragmented lives burn holes in human souls and in the natural environment. The greedy hoarder-polluter by day and "family man" by night, the power-hungry homeless executive workaholic and weekend recycler, the full-time weapons manufacturer and part-time "Christian," these fragmented lives are examples of the spiritual vacuum that passes for the chaotic "liberty" in contemporary democracy. Have we wandered so far from home that we forget whose children we all are? Like the mother planet, our own bodies are seventy percent water. The cycles of the seasons and the rhythm of the tides run through our veins.

We think we can recycle at home and wage war in the desert, run child-care centers and destroy ancient forests, teach kids to read and crush indigenous cultures, talk "traditional family values" and assault women and children. To the extent that wounded adults cannot practice what they teach, children lose hope and become cynical. Their creative beauty is dimmed. They suffer from soul erosion.

The healing of the Earth depends on restoration of the human spirit and on knowing our place in the global family. Self-esteem can give us purpose, so that "purpose motive" might precede the profit motive. Personal integrity involves taking responsibility for our actions and embracing peaceful conflict resolution, setting positive examples for children who look to us for guidance.

Education's task is raising informed and compassionate global citizens. Can we who yearn for a peaceful world ignore the huge gap between the wealthy one-quarter of the human family and the three-quarters who live in poverty, of which forty thousand die each day of hunger? Or the growing gulf between rich and poor in the so-called wealthy nations?

Helen Caldicott implores you to become active "if you love this planet." I say, "if we love our children," it is our moral duty to rethink priorities and participate in a radical change of heart and mind. For our children's sake and for those yet to be born, will we have the courage to speak out?

- to call for the rapid development of clean, renewable energies and a timed phase-out of fossil fuels
- to hasten the demise of nuclear power in all its deadly forms
- to reorganize and redefine economic activity to include environmental factors
- to insist that wealthy nations pay the lion's share for global cleanup operations
- to hasten the conversion of military energies to humanitarian uses, and destructive industries to constructive endeavors
- to remove the poisons from our water and food supply so that we may restore the soils and restore our health

Saving the Earth really means stopping the abuse, showing respect, and giving back. The young and old, in all kinds of families, can help each other to become active agents of change, in a dance of personal and societal transformation.

There is no future in defending abuse in the status quo, whether that abuse is personal, cultural, or environmental. Changing familiar patterns may be difficult, but staying stuck in systems that are destructive is even more painful. It is important that we be able to *imagine* change, whether personal or something on the scale of converting military energy to civilian energy, or polluting energies to clean energies. If we can't imagine it, we aren't likely to do it. Fortunately, the hitherto unthinkable geopolitical changes of the last few years show that anything is possible. That's the good news!

With beluga whales dying of cancer in the polluted St. Lawrence River, and kids afraid to play in the sun, it is time we raised children from the Earth up, not from corporate ads down. We are all shareholders in our children's futures, and we must remember that the social, environmental, and economic costs of inaction will multiply in the years to come. Each one of us holds the power to change and to begin the healing today.

My prayer is that "at this turning point in our relationship with Earth, we work for an evolution from dominance to partnership, from fragmentation to connection, from insecurity to interdependence" (from the Declaration of Interdependence, the David Suzuki Foundation).

43

RIANE EISLER

Riane Eisler, J.D., is the author of the international best-seller *The Chalice and the Blade: Our History, Our Future* and coauthor of *The Partnership Way: New Tools for Living and Learning*. She has taught at the University of California at Los Angeles and Immaculate Heart College, is cofounder with David Loye of the Center for Partnership Studies in Pacific Grove, California, has published many other books and articles, and has spoken all over the world. The following essay is a condensed version of a paper given for the Society of Utopian Studies Annual Conference, Asilomar, California, October 2-5, 1986.

From Utopia to Pragmatopia: Reclaiming our Past, Regaining our Future

To many people, a more equitable and peaceful society seems impossible. It is a utopia: something that can never be realized. I do not believe that this negative view of the human condition is warranted. But I do believe that there is a key issue we must address at this critical juncture in our cultural evolution if we are to envision and realize a better future—from the family and religion to economics and politics, as well as the prevailing system of values.

My research over the past two decades has led me to understand that a major reason most scenarios for a more just and peaceful society are unrealistic is precisely that they have failed to recognize that neither justice nor peace are logically (much less realistically) possible in a social structure where half of humanity is ranked over the other half. Unlike most studies of human society, which are very appropriately often called the "study of man," I based my research on a

database in which both halves of humanity are given equal importance. This made it possible to see that the way in which the relations
between the female and male halves of humanity are structured not
only directly impacts the day-to-day personal lives and life options of
both women and men, but profoundly affects every one of our social
institutions. At this critical juncture in our cultural evolution, this issue
is central to whether we can envision and realize a better future.

We have been taught that civilization has its origins in brutally male-dominant and highly warlike societies. But more recent archaeological excavations indicate that stories of a more peaceful and harmonious time when women were not dominated by men are also based
on earlier realities. For example, Mesopotamian and later Biblical stories
about a garden where woman and man lived in partnership most probably derive from folk memories of the more peaceful and egalitarian
first agrarian (or Neolithic) societies, which planted the first gardens
on this Earth. Similarly, the legend of how the fabled civilization of
Atlantis sank into the sea appears to be a garbled recollection of the
ancient Minoan civilization, a remarkably peaceful and uniquely
creative culture now believed to have ended when Crete and some surrounding islands were massively damaged by earthquakes and enormous tidal waves. Here, as in the earlier Neolithic, the subordination
of women does not appear to have been the norm. Cretan art shows
women as priestesses, as figures being paid homage, and even as captains of ships.

But the archaeological record also shows that following a period
of chaos and almost total cultural disruption, there occurred a fundamental *social shift*. At this pivotal branching, the cultural evolution
of societies that worshipped the life-generating and nurturing powers
of the universe—in our time still symbolized by the ancient "feminine"
chalice or grail—was interrupted. There now appeared on the prehistoric horizon invaders from the peripheral areas of our globe (from the
arid steppes of the north and barren deserts of the south) who ushered
in a very different form of social organization. As the University of
California archaeologist Marija Gimbutas writes in the *Journal of Indo-
European Studies*, these were a rigidly male-dominant, highly warlike
people, a people who literally worshipped "the lethal power of the
blade"—the power to take rather than give life that is the ultimate
power to establish and enforce human rankings.

Today we stand at the threshold of another—and potentially
decisive—social shift. For in our high-technology age we either complete the shift to a different model of social organization or face the
possibility of extinction.

This is why we urgently need both a new word and a new blueprint for the future. For a new word, I am proposing the word *pragmatopia*. Like *utopia*, this is also a term formed of Greek roots; it derives from the Greek term *pragma* ("thing" or "reality," as in "pragmatic") and *topos* ("place"). And for a new, but at the same time very old, blueprint I am proposing what I have called a *partnership* rather than *dominator* model of social organization: not an ideal society, but a society where neither women nor so-called feminine values like caring, compassion, and nonviolence are any longer devalued. I chose the word *partnership* to describe this type of social organization because it is already in common usage as a term connoting mutuality of benefit. But I define it much more precisely, as a model of social organization where diversity is not equated with either inferiority or superiority and where the primary principle of social organization is *linking* rather than ranking.

Characteristically, such societies tend to be not only much more peaceful but also much less hierarchic and authoritarian. This is evidenced by anthropological data (i.e., the BaMbuti and !Kung), by contemporary studies of trends in more sexually egalitarian modern societies (i.e., Scandinavian nations such as Sweden), and by the prehistoric and historic data detailed in *The Chalice and The Blade*.

To transform social systems is a major undertaking. Yet if we look at modern history from the new perspective here proposed, we see that the eighteenth-century challenge to the "divine right" of kings to rule and the nineteenth-century challenge to the "divine right" of men to rule over women are in fact part of such a process. We see that the contemporary peace, civil rights, women's, and environmental movements, as well as all the global movements for both economic and political democracy, are also attempts to leave behind a way of living based on conquest and domination—be it men over men, men over women, race over race, nation over nation, or man over nature. In short, we see that what has been happening over the last three centuries is actually an unprecedentedly powerful social movement toward a partnership society.

At the same time, we also clearly see the other side of the picture: the dominator resistance. We see it in the worldwide violence of totalitarian and authoritarian regimes, in the resurgence of racism, anti-Semitism, and other forms of ethnic scapegoating, in the again widening gap between rich and poor, North and South. And we also see it in the only recently recognized worldwide male violence against women and the still powerful socialization of boys and men to equate their very identity (their "masculinity") with domination and conquest.

On the one side lies a dominator future, a future in which the blade—amplified a millionfold by high technology—still holds sway, a future that most probably takes us to an evolutionary dead end. On the other side is a partnership future, a future in which the chalice and not the blade will once again hold sway. However, this better future for ourselves and our children will continue to be a *utopia* rather than a *pragmatopia* unless we recognize that a more just and balanced society requires for its foundations a more just and balanced relation between the two halves of humanity: women and men.

44

BILL KEEPIN

Bill Keepin, Ph.D., is an environmental scientist with a background in mathematical physics and transpersonal psychology. He cofacilitates "Regendering" workshops which focus on gender issues, utilizing techniques such as Holotropic Breathwork.

Regendering: The Urgent Need to Heal and Re-form Relations Between Feminine and Masculine

Among the pressing problems afflicting human cultures across the globe, one seems especially paramount and universal: the arbitrary oppression of one gender by the other. The most fundamental duality of our existence as human beings is the division into two genders, and for thousands of years in most societies across our planet, fully one half of all human beings have been dominated by the other half, based solely on their gender. Historically this has taken many forms—some of the most perverse manifestations being female infanticide, Chinese foot-binding, Indian *suttee,* and witch burning during the Inquisition. Some of these ancient practices still flourish in some parts of the world. Meanwhile, in the United States today, forcible rape is the most frequently committed violent crime. Contrary to widespread belief, most rapes are planned, rather than being spontaneous uncontrollable fits of lust or rage. Sociological and psychological studies suggest that men who rape do not differ in any distinguishable way from control groups—that is, most rapists are evidently fairly normal men in society.

Disturbing as these gross realities are, they are but the tip of a vast—if more subtle and complex—iceberg. We live in the throes of a tragic world war between the genders. Although routinely and systematically hushed, the ravages of this war are manifest at myriad levels throughout our society and psyche, ranging from the most overt sexual violence and social oppression to torturous conflicts in the deepest inner realms of our hearts and minds. In Western culture, where the modern feminist movement was born, oppression of the feminine principle continues virtually unabated. The dysfunctional relationship between the sexes goes far beyond painful symptoms such as rising divorce rates and crumbling families. There is a profound rift between the masculine and feminine principles or archetypes that has persisted for literally thousands of years in our culture. The effects are evident in every feature of our society, including the very language through which we communicate and the modes of inquiry and conceptual categories through which we seek to understand our world.

One of the most significant consequences of this rift is the relationship between "modern civilization" and the planet Earth. There is a striking correspondence between the dysfunctional relationship between men and women in our society, and the dysfunctional relationship between modern technological society and the Earth. Consider a few parallels:

- violence toward women—violence toward the Earth
- rape of women—rape of Earth
- mistrust of women—mistrust of Nature
- repression of the feminine archetype in all its manifestations—repression of Earth-based wisdom in all its manifestations
- fear of women's natural cycles—fear of Earth's natural cycles (replacing cyclic time with linear time in science)
- repression of transrational or subtle epistemologies of all kinds (emotional, intuitive, introspective, contemplative, compassionate)—tyrannical dominance of concrete empirical epistemologies (rationalism, mechanistic scientism, logical positivism, materialism, determinism, objectivism)
- appropriation of the unfathomable mystery of existence by the unprecedented arrogance of science
- denial of contradiction, nuance, subtlety—celebration of the logical, concrete, literal
- explosive psychic energy used to control and manipulate women—explosive charges used to control and manipulate the Earth

Healing the gender war is not just a nice proposition that can wait for our attention until after we have rescued the Earth from environmental catastrophe. The war between the sexes is deeply and inextricably linked to the roots of ecological destruction. Unless we address the gender dimensions of the ecological crisis, all attempts to achieve a "sustainable society" will remain only partial. Gender imbalance is rooted in domination and control of the female sex by the male sex, which is not formally different from the domination and control of Nature, or the domination and control of weaker men by more powerful men, or the domination and control of one racial group by another. Ultimately, the underlying systemic root common to all these problems is dominance and submission; whether it be men over women, technology over Nature, whites over blacks, generals over foot soldiers, or rich over poor. The shadow side of patriarchal consciousness is the tyranny of arbitrary power, control, ownership, and exploitation. Unless this is confronted and transformed, there is little hope for planet Earth as we know it.

Feminism has, of course, made some significant advances on the gender front over the past twenty-five years. Yet, the major gains made by mainstream feminism to date could perhaps be characterized as generally allowing women to become more like men. Women have achieved greater sexual freedom than ever before (which men have in some ways long enjoyed), and it is now much easier for women to enter what were once professions reserved for men only: law, medicine, science, politics, the military, and so on. Professional women today are rushing to join the mad rat race of our society, further accelerating what E. F. Schumacher has called the "forward stampede" of the technological juggernaut. This is literal emancipation of women— women becoming more like men. Admission to the patriarchal temples of power—once restricted to men only—is now open to women, provided they uphold the time-honored rules and do not rise up too high in the hierarchy.

While this is certainly an improvement over the earlier exclusion of women, the real work of dismantling the patriarchy at its foundation has barely begun. One urgent aspect that is only just now beginning to appear is for men to acquire the freedom to become more like women. This means men being able to develop not only the stereotypical "feminine" qualities that Robert Bly seems to fear—but also the deeper feminine wisdom, spirit, eros, and compassion, coupled with the vital epistemological shift that feminine consciousness naturally fosters in the human psyche.

Men today are threatened by this. What would happen to their "masculinity"? Men seem to forget their origins. They weren't just "nourished by their mothers" in their infancy and childhood, they were *created* in the womb of woman. They were *born* into their very existence through the vagina of woman. Men are feminine creations. Their bodies were conceived in the headwaters of menstrual flow—then sculpted and energized with life force by the feminine. Men *exist* only by the unfathomable power and grace of the feminine. Of course this is also true for women, but women tend to know this instinctively; their bodies are a continual, unmediated reminder. Men seem to have lost this realization, and with it much of the awe and wonder of their own existence. As I see it, all human beings—and indeed all living things and all manifest entities—are ultimately feminine creations. To me, this is cause for great joy, celebration, and wonder—because the feminine is the source of all manifest creation.

In no way does this detract from the masculine, on either the cosmic level or the relative level of men and manhood. I love living in a man's body and feeling my masculine nature, and at the deepest level I sense that the feminine and masculine are ontologically equal and magnificent cosmic forces. Indeed, every human being embodies both the masculine and feminine principles—engaged in a glorious dance of eternal creation that gives birth to our existence from moment to moment. If we could but live out this harmonious wonder in our everyday lives!

How can we begin to heal the gender war? Where do we start? How do we embark on a challenge that is as deep and vast as this? One essential prerequisite is that we be willing to go beyond our habitual intellectual analyses and remedies—and move directly into the dark pain itself. We might take a cue from the Vietnamese monk Thich Nhat Hanh, who suggested in reference to the ecological crisis: "What we most need to do is to hear within ourselves the sounds of the Earth crying." In our quest for peace between the genders, we might begin by confronting not only our own pain, but also hearing within ourselves the sounds of the opposite gender crying. For we all live in the prison of the gender war, whether we are inmates or wardens.

If we can directly face our own grief, fear, lust, and rage—and cultivate empathy and compassion for these same powerful forces in the opposite gender—we then have a chance of moving through our own shadow, and creating altogether new forms of gender relations that are quite beyond what we can now imagine. We need not know what shape these new forms might eventually take—indeed we must resist our conditioned hubris of presuming to know where we're going and how we'll get there. *Not knowing* is an important part of this process, the nature of which is quite profound and beyond what the mind alone can fathom. We human beings have tremendous episte-mological faculties and powerful resources that extend well beyond our usual cognicentric modes of experience and understanding. By drawing upon these hidden aptitudes, we can move with confidence into our darkness and through the ensuing turmoil to discover new light, restore our innocence, and enter a new domain of unknowing from which creative forms and fresh structures can emerge between men and women on this Earth. Then perhaps we can bring the eternal dance of feminine and masculine out into the open, and live in the grace and splendor of its dynamic embrace.

45

GENIA PAULI HADDON

Genia Pauli Haddon, D.Min., Ph.D., is the author of *Uniting Sex, Self, & Spirit* and has contributed chapters to several anthologies. She is in demand as a speaker and teacher throughout the country. With her husband, Ren, she operates Haelix in Scotland, Connecticut, developing programs, products, and services supporting spiritual development.

The Power of Thirteen

The past millennium has brought to full expression values patterned after the phallic half of male psychology. Like the erectile penis, its primary virtues are defined by rising up, standing out, advancing, overcoming, and penetrating. Bigger, higher, and upward are the watchwords. Individual identity is established by differentiating oneself from the matrix (same root as *mother*) and in contrast with an "other" (another race, gender, nationality, or species). Relationships are typically unequal, either competitive or with one party recognized by both as the superior, the other as subordinate. Hierarchical ranking seems natural. In this system, power is the ability to prevail over another person or situation. Solar symbols of sun, light, brilliance, clarity, rising high, and outshining define our collective sense of what is good. We take for granted a calendar divided into twelve months, corresponding to the twelve "sun signs" of astrology, forgetting that the words *month* and *moon* are cognates and that, in fact, there are thirteen moon cycles in a year.

We have lost touch with the power of thirteen. To most of us, this rich symbol means nothing more than the uneasy prospect of bad luck. We are like the ruler in the fairy tale who had only twelve golden plates, and so did not invite the thirteenth fairy God-Mother to the party celebrating his daughter's birth. This powerful and holy God-Mother came regardless, bringing a gift that was experienced as a curse, eventually resulting in the entire kingdom falling into a deep sleep. Humankind now is poised to awaken to new cultural values, values that mirror aspects of female physiology in the same sense that patriarchal culture has been modeled after the phallus. We are nearly ready to welcome the thirteenth God-Mother. Our survival as a species, and the well-being of the planet, depend on finding ways to receive her disconcerting gifts.

Culture modeled on the phallus has brought forth many good things during the age now ending. Positive penis power is visible as the rocket probing outer space, the scalpel dissecting the body, the differentiating clarity of objective thinking, the electron microscope revealing subcellular components, the nuclear accelerator splitting atoms. This same style carried to excess results in the raping of our planet for her natural resources, questionably intrusive medical procedures, the proliferation of penislike instruments that shoot bullets and missiles, the "screw you" principle of international diplomacy, perpetual striving for dominance by powers and superpowers, dependence on rigid doctrine in religion, absence of contextual compassion in the legal system, and so on. Leading thinkers in such varied disciplines as ecology, international law, economics, education, corporate development, communication, and psychology agree that "feminine" values now are urgently needed if we are to survive as a species and heal the ailing Earth.

Some would seek these values from the distant past, yearning to revive customs and symbols from ancient "matriarchal" cultures. Instead, accessing the power of thirteen means welcoming a *new* dimension of human potential, bringing to cultural expression the active, exertive half of feminine physiology, typified by the birth-pushing womb.

Matriarchal/matrical culture was patterned after the nature of the *gestating* womb. Containment shaped that system at every level. Then, the basic human unit was not the individual person, but the tribe or clan, encompassing all its participants. Identity was by virtue of containment within this matrix or "mother." The divine was experienced as bountiful, nurturing Mother, infusing and surrounding all of life. Even the style of consciousness was a *participational* awareness, in contrast with the *objectifying* consciousness characterizing today's mind-set.

Rather than reestablishing those gestative values, the new ways will bring to expression qualities reflecting the nature of the womb in its *expulsive* functions. Elsewhere I have described how women's bodily experiences of menstruation, childbirth, abortion, and menopause supply the new metaphor that will someday replace the phallic pattern —just as the phallic metaphor supplanted gestative ways when the Patriarchal Age succeeded the Matriarchal Age. Even now, this assertive feminine power is emerging as the new determinant of personal development, social patterns, cultural values, and renewed spirituality. At its heart is a principle of self-transcendent transformation that gives equal value to such opposites as life-death.

The phallic perspective sees death as an enemy over whom to triumph, and dying as the ultimate impotence. When the thirteenth God-Mother offered death as her gift, in horror the king called upon the powers of the other twelve to turn death aside. In the tale, the result was that the entire kingdom fell asleep for an eon. As we awaken now to the power of thirteen, our ethical principles and attitudes toward death will change fundamentally.

My mother died just last week. Her story illustrates both the direction in which we are moving, and how far we yet have to go. She was nearly eighty years old, active, independent, and basically healthy until a massive heart attack three months ago. Sophisticated tests accurately mapped the extent of the damage: more than a third of her heart permanently destroyed. Mom amazed everyone when she recovered sufficiently to go home for three weeks, walking from room to room, bathing and dressing herself, and fixing her own breakfasts. Her four children took turns living with her, each one's tenure an opportunity to draw close again after years in distant states. One full live-in cycle had been completed, and we were about to begin a second round while working out long-range care plans, when pneumonia and congestive heart failure sent Mom to the hospital again.

As long as she focused her amazing will and spirit on getting better, Mom's doctors were noble allies. Like the king calling upon the powers of the twelve, they used all the technology of modern cardiology. But the day came when Mom said, ''Enough. I know I'm not going to recover. I'm ready to die.'' My mother was able to welcome death, not as defeat, but as a timely complement to life. In the coming world, medical ethics will require that equally excellent technology be offered, whether the goal is to cure or to facilitate dying. But in the last decade of the twentieth century, the best the medical profession could provide was a prolonged holding pattern, administering enough morphine to "keep her comfortable"—in an uncanny replication of the deep sleep that was substituted for the gift of death in the fairy tale. Although she developed a painful bedsore at the base of her spine; although she had intermittent muscle cramps throughout her body due to potassium imbalance; although her mouth was filled with sores and scabs and she had no saliva; although she had recurrent bouts of dry nausea—despite all this, it can accurately be said that my mother did not have extreme physical pain during her final three weeks. She did, however, suffer *agony* of another sort. Day after day, night after night, she endured emotional, psychological, and spiritual suffering in the extreme, longing for her rightful death to be restored to her.

Current medical ethics forbid collaborating with death. These standards make sense within a universe modeled after the phallus, where the power of thirteen seems evil. Yet, the same emblem that has represented the medical profession since antiquity—the winged staff entwined by two serpents—bears within itself the promise of a new ethic where death is not always the enemy. According to ancient legends, one snake is poisonous; its bite brings death. The other brings renewal of life. All that is needed to bring medical ethics into alignment with the new reality is to recognize that *these snakes intertwine as partners*, not adversaries. Then, it will be obvious that wisdom lies in discerning the timeliness of life or death, rather than choosing always to prolong life. Redefining itself in terms of this image, the medical profession will take pride in learning to balance the roles of life-saver and death-gifter, exactly as its emblem illustrates.

New ways will not replace the old by conquest this time. That method is itself a phallic means of effecting change, appropriate for bringing about the last major turning of the ages, but not for displacing the phallic worldview. A process mimicking instead the exertive womb will bring to birth the archetypal transformation now pending. The bloodiness of birth will replace the bloodiness of battle as elixir of change. This time, new ways will come about through shifts of perspective, shifts that are at once both subtle and radical. Like accelerating labor pains, such shifts will take place with increasing intensity during the next two decades, bringing forth a newborn age in which the power of thirteen is a welcomed gift.

46

BARBARA G. WALKER

Barbara G. Walker is widely recognized as one of the founders of the new feminism. She is the author of many books, including *The Woman's Encyclopedia of Myths and Secrets*, *The Woman's Dictionary of Symbols and Sacred Objects*, *The Crone*, *Women's Rituals*, and *The Skeptical Feminist*.

Feminism and the Future

As we seek routes toward a kinder, gentler future, the new feminism seems to be an especially hopeful signpost. In societies where women created most of the ethical and moral codes, people were usually more peaceable, contented, cooperative, and spontaneous; better supported by the kinship structure; and less troubled by guilt, anxiety, or fear. Mothers' natural desire to promote health and happiness for their children seems to be reflected in the social rules formulated by matrifocal societies, whereas patriarchies like our own have engendered many more oppressive restrictions, aggressively imposed by violence or cruelty.

This is not to be interpreted as a simplistic or reverse-sexist view that all individual men are mean, and all individual women are sweetness and light. Obviously, such is not the case. The difference lies in those qualities generally emphasized, admired, or rewarded by the culture as a whole.

Any television viewer or moviegoer knows how much attention our culture pays to violent behavior patterns, including war, murder, assault, rape, mutilation, the criminal mind-set, and "heroic" shoot-em-ups. Media moguls pretend that this fare is what the public demands, and also that it is shown as an evil, but they may be suspected of making excuses for their own interests. The fact is that humans—especially children—are apelike enough to imitate whatever they see, without passing it through any moral filters at all. When cruelty is the daily visual input, much of the behavioral output will inevitably copy it. Another fact is that women generally dislike the gratuitous violence that masquerades as entertainment, just as women tend to disagree with the "he-man" notion that slaughtering wild animals is fun, and that humans have the right to do it because they are superior creatures.

There are many indications now that women are beginning to get in touch with their own fundamental nature in ways that have been forbidden to them by patriarchal traditions, set up as the only acceptable moral system several thousand years ago, which have kept our civilization in thrall to a philosophy that derogates the feminine and the natural world. The remote, transcendent deity postulated by Western culture has proved enormously violent in all "his" incarnations from the warlike Old Testament Yahweh to the familiar Christian deity of crusades, inquisitions, witch hunts, and battlefield invocations the world over. Now there is a fast-spreading tendency among women to reject this deity. Studies of the doleful history of Western religious sexism have made it clear that the God created in man's image has promoted more male cruelty toward women than any other single cause.

The resurgence or rehabilitation of a Goddess image, to which men as well as women may relate in positive ways, may be one of the significant trends capable of showing the way to a wiser future, where human beings may finally live free from mindless violence, prejudice, and exploitation; where women and children may walk safely on the streets of every city; where no one suffers harassment or discrimination on the job or anywhere else; and where no child comes into the world unwanted, unloved, or neglected. Our Mother Earth desperately needs less quantity and more quality of human life. Let us hope that we, as one of her brainier species, will have brains enough to make it so, before we allow ourselves to destroy what supports us. The effort will surely require female brains and female images of ultimate authority.

47

ALLAN B. CHINEN

Allan B. Chinen, M.D., is a psychiatrist on the clinical faculty of the University of California, San Francisco, and is in private practice in San Francisco. He is the author of *In the Ever After: Fairy Tales and the Second Half of Life, Once upon a Midlife: Classic Stories and Mythic Tales to Illuminate the Middle Years,* and *Beyond the Hero: Classic Tales and Teaching Stories for Men.*

Back to the Future: Ancient Manhood in the Next Millenniun

For many millennia, the mythic image of the hero-patriarch has ruled civilization. Today, feminists, ecologists, and sociologists point out the dark side of the warrior-king—from his denigration of women, to his rape of nature, and his exploitation of "lower" classes. Women offer goddesses as an alternative model for society, but the feminine paradigm remains incomplete, neglecting masculine concerns. Any viable vision of the future requires a mythic renewal of the male principle to complement the modern renaissance of the feminine. That masculine revival, I believe, comes from an ancient archetype of manhood—the shaman-trickster.

Like the hero and the patriarch, the shaman and the trickster reflect two aspects of a single, underlying masculine archetype. And the shaman-trickster offers a radical alternative to the hero-patriarch— an astonishing new vision of men in society. As I discuss in *Beyond the Hero,* the warrior-king is the stuff of youthful dramas, immortalized in myths and stories like *The Iliad* and *The Song of Roland.* The shaman-trickster, by contrast, governs epics about mature men, from *The Odys-*

sey to Dante's *Divine Comedy*. Historically, the shaman-trickster can be traced back to hunter-gatherer cultures from humanity's origin, antedating the warrior-king by over 10,000 years. Closely tied to hunting magic, the shaman-trickster is really a hunter-shaman-trickster. He represents the earliest archetype of the masculine and dances in Paleolithic cave paintings from the dawn of humankind.

Patriarchal tradition suppresses the shaman-trickster and considers him a liar, charlatan, or psychopath. Yet in mythology around the world, the hunter-trickster brings fire, language, vital food plants, and medicines to his people. He offers life and growth, not war and death—in contrast to the warrior-king. The hunter-shaman deliberately breaks the patriarch's rules to force people to reflect on their lives and to experiment with new ways of living. Carrying messages between the gods and humanity, and mediating among people, the shaman-trickster emphasizes negotiation rather than battle—again unlike the hero and the patriarch. The shaman-trickster also makes love—with everything!—instead of war. He favors healing over heroism, exploration over exploitation, communication over conquest, and creativity over competition. In reversing millennia of heroic and patriarchal tradition, he offers a new model of manhood, more consistent with modern ideals.

The hunter-trickster, in fact, is uniquely relevant to a post-industrial future. An inventor of languages and metalworking, he is the natural patron of modern technology. Yet the shaman-trickster uses his inventions to celebrate human creativity, rather than to ''conquer'' nature like the hero. As a hunter, the shaman-trickster also recognizes that what he takes from nature he must replace. His is an original ecological spirit, complementing that of earth goddesses. A messenger and storyteller, he is the best sponsor of today's cybernetic information networks. Traditionally, the trickster is also the patron of the marketplace. In trade, though, he seeks exchange and experiences, not monopoly and money. Here he contrasts sharply with the hoarding hero and the profiteering patriarch. Lacking the hero's fear of women, or the patriarch's contempt for them, the shaman-trickster affirms the feminine. Yet he is not subservient to goddesses, since he is as ancient as they are. He represents an astonishingly modern spirit of equality and mutuality between the sexes. He is truly the New Man, ready to take his place beside the New Woman in the next millennium. Now, as before, the shaman-trickster remains faithful to his original title, ''pathfinder'' or ''roadmaker,'' offering a vision of manhood in the society of the future.

48
MARSHALL HARDY

Marshall Hardy, Ph.D., is founder of the Men's Resource Center in Texas and many men's councils and networks. He is a nationally recognized speaker, retreat guide, trainer, and consultant in the fields of male and adolescent psychology, marital revitalization, family violence, and codependency. He is coauthor of the best-selling *Against the Wall: Men's Reality in a Codependent Culture*, and contributing author to several books, including *Talk, Trust and Feel* and *Seasons of the Heart*.

Men in Transition

Men are fed up with leading lives of quiet desperation.

We are tired and dissatisfied (and in despair) over the models and definitions of what a man is and is not supposed to be. And, we are changing . . . one day at a time.

For many decades women in our culture have sought and found support in the company of other women. Women have by individual choice and collective guidance owned and confronted their inner selves. Men, however, have just begun to recognize the price paid for suffering in silence and for denying ourselves the human right to take action to heal the wounds we have endured from our peers, intimates, biological and surrogate parents, our dominant parents (the cultural system), and our own self-abuses.

As Western culture has for millennia favored man's survivalist and materially based lifestyle and undervalued women's relational and spiritual approach to life, our world as a whole has been crippled. The lives of men and the cry of our youth echo this injury to our culture and reflect its intergenerational imbalance.

For decades men have been obsessive-compulsive in their conquests for wealth, fame, fast-food sex, and drive-through relationships. These times are about to fade, as more and more men take responsibility for their part in perpetuating competition instead of cooperation, winning over the pleasure of playing, aggression rather than compassion and healthy communication, independence instead of interdependence.

Today I sincerely believe men are beginning their inner work; they are doing it differently than they have dealt with the majority of other problems in their lives. Rather than always searching the intellect-dominant male society for answers to many of their questions, men are embarking upon the emotional and spiritual path of first living out the many questions—questions about masculinity and childhood, masculinity and puberty, masculinity and adulthood, masculinity and fatherhood. This process is not a down-the-line journey; it is most likely a spiral—where the questions and the problems of life are dealt with time and time again, but with different and deeper meaning. This I call the "Pilgrimage of Promise."

This pilgrimage is a depth-defying journey through the ashes of a deep and hitherto denied grief, long-held resentment, and fear of not measuring up, and the shame, guilt, and anger over what has and has not occurred, is and is not happening. It is ascending again with a renewed spirit, a voice of compromise, a feeling of heart, and an energy of compassion. Owning afflictions of yesterday awakens the spirit of the man, builds soul, and connects him with the mysteries of life.

The world is a sacred place to the pilgrim. It is not simply a place to work, survive, compete. It does not have a few out-of-the-way, sacred places. The world is a sacred place, in all its wonder, beauty, and even its flaws. This world is no longer a place to act out indiscriminately man's aggression, deceit, retaliation, and disastrous disregard. The neighborhoods, schools, sandboxes, and workplaces are not to be battlefields. The pilgrim and his pilgrimage are about owning, dealing with, and resolving his issues within, so as not to perpetuate them on others, the world he is visiting, and himself.

Today's man is in the midst of transition, so it is understandable that confusion, doubt, uncertainty, and maybe a blend of exaggeration may taint his behavior. As a man—son, brother, husband, father, and uncle—I believe that what is slowly but surely coming to pass is that men are replacing "survival mind-sets and behaviors" with a longing and need to live life and awaken parts of self that have been cut off. Definite themes are emerging, and in the coming decade, a day will tell its tale of men reconnecting with themselves, their young and old, their buddies, and their intimates. Ultimately, a collective transformation will occur. When the inner self is connected to the higher power, it begets higher purpose. Men as healthy role models, guiding mentors, expressive friends, and loving partners will prevail. The future is men living freer, loving fully, healing wholly.

49

STEVEN FARMER

Steven Farmer is an international lecturer and the author of *The Wounded Male; Healing Words: Affirmations for the Adult Children of Abusive Parents; Adult Children as Husbands, Wives, and Lovers;* and *Adult Children of Abusive Parents.* He maintains a private counseling practice in Irvine, California.

The Awakening Call of Spirit: The Recovery Movement and the Men's Movement

It is obvious that we are at a major turning point, not only in our society but in our evolution as human beings. Human-made systems, especially those of the industrial age, are disintegrating quite visibly and rapidly. Some predict that we will disintegrate right along with our systems. I do not believe that the human species will become extinct but instead that we will survive, albeit with fewer people on the planet than at present. In order to survive as a species, however, we must shift our basic operating orientation from one of fear, competition, distrust, and control, to one of love, cooperation, trust, and surrender. In order to effect a change in this fundamental operating orientation, we must consciously emphasize an active, experiential relationship with Being and come to know deeply the unity of *all* life. If we are to survive, we must learn to acknowledge Spirit in our daily affairs. Before anything truly healing and constructive can happen in renewing our relationship with Mother Earth, this awareness must take priority.

This internal change of emphasis is occurring in many of us, and there are several groupings around the planet that encourage and support this increase in spiritual awareness. Two movements that are highly representative of this evolution of human consciousness are the recovery movement and the men's movement.

The recovery movement, the core of which is the various twelve-step programs, has offered a means for thousands of human beings to acknowledge their spiritual heartbeat and to share this with others in a community that provides a vehicle for awakening. The original twelve-step recovery program of Alcoholics Anonymous, on which all other twelve-step programs are modeled, not only provides specific guidelines that can help overcome addiction, but is first and foremost a spiritual program. John Bradshaw has said that people will look back on the twentieth century and say that the twelve-step programs were the greatest spiritual movement of the century. There are over three hundred types of self-help programs that have successfully applied these guidelines and the twelve steps to other addictions, the result being that many people are not only refusing to numb themselves with addictions but are coming to terms with their spirituality through this network of recovering people.

In following a path of recovery, a person quite naturally enters into a spiritual reconciliation, where they typically gain insight into the fact that there is a larger force, a "higher power" at work, which can never be controlled or directed by the human ego and to which the ego must, in fact, subjugate itself. The now famous serenity prayer of Alcoholics Anonymous summarizes this process beautifully and simply: "God grant me the serenity to accept the things I cannot change, the courage to change the things I can, and the wisdom to know the difference." With continued abstinence and practice of these spiritual principles, the individual eventually shapes his or her operating orientation to one of love, cooperation, trust, and surrender.

The recovery movement also provides a community that is based not on geography but on a common purpose. In the coming years, these nongeographical communities will have greater and greater social and political impact. We will see individuals who have effected their own recovery and have had a spiritual awakening as a result provide inspiration and leadership in many key areas, including politics and government. As the disintegration of present systems continues, the need for this type of spiritually grounded leadership will become even more apparent.

The second hopeful movement is the men's movement. More than a social or political movement, it is really a movement of consciousness in men. It is a phenomenon of the 1990s that has affected many men, whether or not they identify themselves as being part of any movement. Angry feminists and others have blamed the male of the species as being responsible for the present state of the planet and of society, slinging around the word *patriarchy* just like old-time preachers did the word *Satan*, attributing all modern evils not only to the patriarchal system but often to the male of the species. It is time for both male-bashing and female-bashing to stop. We have all carried with us and been affected by the attitudes and behaviors of the "poisonous patriarchy" that has been operative for over five thousand years, yet to blame one gender or the other simply perpetuates the destructive attitudes of fear, competition, distrust, and control that have characterized this era. If we lived in a poisonous matriarchy, it would be just as destructive, only the destructiveness would be manifested differently.

What will evolve from this shift in men's consciousness is a more compassionate and inclusive male leadership in the form of an "enlightened patriarchy." The voices of women will be heard and honored, rather than simply patronized and placated, and the intuitive wisdom and relational insight of women will be critical considerations in any decision-making process, whether political, corporate, or personal. Yet it will require the vision, courage, and inspiration of male leadership, based on the operating orientation of love, cooperation, trust, and surrender, to steer us through the dark and turbulent waters to come. The men who have been in leadership until lately have represented the worst of the poisonous patriarchy, and as such have operated more from fear, competition, distrust, and control. With the advent of leaders at the national level such as Albert Gore and perhaps even Bill Clinton, we are seeing a new kind of male leadership emerging. At the local level of politics and government, as well as in other arenas, we will be seeing more of this kind of male leadership.

The awakening call of spirit in all our consciousnesses cannot be denied, most especially in the hearts of men. Through the coming time of shadows we will not only need women who will trust their intuitive natures and speak their truth, but men who will represent the sacred Father and provide dynamic and loving stewardship for our precious Mother Earth.

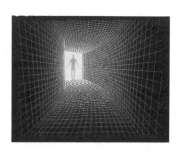

SCIENCE, ECONOMICS,
AND NATURE

50

RENÉE WEBER

Renée Weber, Ph.D., is professor of philosophy at Rutgers University where she has won two awards for outstanding teaching. She has written numerous articles on science and mysticism, consciousness, and healing and is represented in twelve anthologies. She is the author of *Dialogues with Scientists and Sages: The Search for Unity.*

The Energies of Love:
In Honor of David Bohm

David Bohm (1917–1992) was one of the world's greatest quantum mechanical physicists and philosophers of science. He received his doctorate from the University of California, and taught at Princeton, in Brazil, Israel, and at Birkbeck College, University of London. He was a member of the Royal Academy, the originator of the causal interpretation of quantum theory, and the author of a famous text on quantum mechanics and of numerous articles and other books, the best-known recent work being *Wholeness and the Implicate Order.* A sought-after lecturer worldwide, he spoke on the meaning of physics and also on consciousness for the past twenty years at international conferences. His last book, *The Undivided Universe,* completed just before his death, will appear in 1993.

> *"Some day, when we have mastered the winds, the tides, and gravity, we will harness the energies of love. Then, for the second time in the history of the world, man will have discovered fire."*
> —Pierre Teilhard de Chardin.

David Bohm died today (October 27, 1992). If ever there was a man on the threshold of tomorrow, it was this man. His voice is stilled now, thus I will be his voice for this volume: the voice of the man who lived on the threshold of tomorrow because he lived so much in the timeless. It was at the heart of his implicate order philosophy. This combination of time and the timeless enabled him to intuit universal truths and present them in imaginative models, in the language of physics and philosophy.

His physics and cosmology were so profound, so all-encompassing, and so far ahead of his century that few people understood how creative his ideas were. Mainstream physicists considered them too mystical, and few mystics could follow his subtle scientific reasoning. Bohm redefined physics. It is not about mere prediction and control, nor even mathematical equations. Though central to the enterprise, they are not its essence. Physics, as its (Greek) name implies, is about nature (*physis*) and our understanding of nature. We must grasp its meaning and message, and for Bohm these were creativity, the signature of an infinite universe. He saw it as an "undivided wholeness" enfolded into an infinite background source that unfolds into the visible, material, and temporal world of our everyday lives. The former is eternity, the latter history; the former is universal, the latter particular; the former is unified, the latter separate.

Thought can grasp the unfolded, but only something beyond thought—intuition, unmediated insight, intelligence—can *experience* the enfolded. At some point deep within the implicate order, thought and language fail us, and only sacred silence can reveal truth. That silence is the language of the whole, the universe expressing itself through us in a life of integrity rather than fragmentation. Through us, the universe comes to know itself in its multifarious ways.

Bohm's version is unlike traditional mysticisms. The flow between the implicate and explicate order is two-way: Time and history enrich the timeless just as the timeless enriches the daily. We contribute uniquely to the whole; the finite and imperfect is neither redundant nor irrelevant. Our challenge is self-transformation, living in both the timeless and in time.

This is the transformation that David Bohm envisioned for those who grasped quantum mechanics in depth: a world of interconnection and interdependence, of direct and instantaneous communication, in which we have learned to harness the energies of compassion across any distance in the universe. In that world there is no place for an ego-centered life, an isolated and calculating standpoint. The only unit of relevance worthy of our allegiance is "the consciousness of mankind," namely, the human family and the family of *being* in all its aspects. Here we will at last dissolve the "spiritual poisons"— delusion, hatred, greed, fear, projection—identified by Buddhists as the root cause of suffering, whose analysis Bohm shared. The result will be a sane and healthy society based on intelligence and caring, bonded by dialogue, Bohm's favorite form of discourse because it requires real listening and interaction in the living present.

David Bohm himself was an example of his beautiful ideas. If ever a man gave voice to the marvelous possibilities of a new future, this was the man. Capturing what many of us who knew him felt, one colleague in physics called Bohm "a secular saint." This description fits Bohm and no one else in the current world of science, and only a very few in other domains. He was, moreover, the only great physicist who was at the same time a mystic—someone with profound intuitive experience of a timeless reality. He was without doubt one of the deepest and most original thinkers of the century. For the last twenty years I had the privilege of knowing Bohm well both as a colleague and as a rare and beloved friend. A great man is impossible to compress into a summary, but his essence can be evoked as the early signs of a new species of human being.

David Bohm lived only partly in the difficult and depressing times that mark the end of our century, and he suffered deeply from the suffering they wreaked on the earth and its creatures, so different from his vision of what might be. A large part of him was alive in the future, where a new value structure would be expressed in our daily lives. It was the sine qua non of our survival, and would be characterized by community, dialogue, conflict resolution through the energies of love, empathy, and compassion. These were not sentimental feelings but forces to mobilize within us, difficult paths informed by the high energy of intelligence.

When you heard him evoke that future world, you believed in it, for David Bohm had a visionary quality that drew others to him and inspired them. From the quiet, soft-spoken, low-keyed, understated style in which he usually spoke, Bohm would become transformed before one's eyes whenever he spoke of the new order—what might be if we chose it to be. His style became passionate, forceful, dynamic, original, exciting, gentle still—it was his trademark—but so powerful that it pulled you *in* as if into a powerful force field. He was transported by the clarity of his vision and energized by it to such a point that he swept his listeners with him into the orbit of the possible, which for Bohm existed as actual. Here he could show us a world that was meaningful, clear, intelligent, and spiritual, the implicate order expressed as a living force in our explicate lives. Bohm believed in that world because it was more real to him than the world of the senses, being its source and timeless ground.

To most of us, these are ideals that seem beyond our current grasp. But this was not the case when one was with David Bohm. In his presence, one could cross the threshold of the "future" and live it as already present. Given the mysteries of space-time and relativity theory, of the quantum mechanical universe, and of the eternal "now" of the mystics, one understood—in that expanded state of awareness— what was already real to David Bohm at some central level of his being, and one wanted to live it more consistently and intensely at each moment of one's life.

In that sense, David Bohm's was the voice of all great teachers: Because of him, one became—if only for a little while—a better human being. Thus, David Bohm's was a voice that spoke not only from the threshold of tomorrow but one that had already passed beyond that threshold to a reality from which he drew his immense inner strength and compassion.

51

BRIAN SWIMME

Brian Swimme, Ph.D., a specialist in mathematical cosmology, is the coauthor of *The Universe Story* and the author of the video series *Canticle to the Cosmos*. He is the director of The Center for the Story of the Universe at the California Institute of Integral Studies in San Francisco.

Cosmogenesis

The universe flared forth fifteen billion years ago in a trillion-degree blaze of energy, constellated into a hundred billion galaxies, forged the elements deep in the cores of stars, refashioned its matter into living seas, sprouted into advanced organic beings, and spilled over into a conscious self-awareness that now ponders and shapes the evolutionary dynamics of Earth.

These are, as scientists like to say, the "facts." But what do we do with them? How does the fact of cosmogenesis—this great fact that is a culminating achievement of millions of humans laboring now for 100,000 years—how does the discovery of cosmogenesis affect human consciousness?

My own intuition is that those philosophers are correct who predict that over the next few centuries this knowledge will work its way deep into the strata of human consciousness, and will blossom into the fourth great mutation of *Homo sapiens*. But I could be wrong, of course. And many thoughtful people think I am. So the question I want to consider here is this: "What is it that happens that leads a person to regard cosmogenesis as not just a scientific theory, or a string of empirical facts, but as a new religious attitude enabling a creative, cosmological orientation within the world?"

I don't have the answer, but I do have a story that might shed some light.

This took place on Halloween. I was wandering with Denise and our two sons through the dark streets. Near the end of the night, worn-out, I decided to let the three of them go ahead and fleece the remaining houses on the cul-de-sac. To ease the pain in the small of my back, I crouched down close to the ground. There it happened. For just one moment, I left "California" and entered the "Universe."

I need to state at once that I am speaking here of the most ordinary thing. I was just crouched down in the middle of the street. It had been raining softly all evening. I was close to the ground and I noticed the thousand edges of black asphalt glittering with soft points of light from a street lamp overhead. For some reason all my roles seemed to vanish, or dropped out of sight. I was no longer "Dad," or "husband," or "college teacher," or "Californian." I was not primarily in a "city." I was not part of a "holiday" of the "United States." I was suddenly just there, just this being, breathing, in the mist, rained upon, thinking.

Such tremendous things had to happen before I could crouch there. Vast galactic storms. Explosions so violent they were beyond the reaches of the human imagination. Subtleties of cellular electricity in a quintillion prokaryotes. I could not recount them all consciously, but I could feel them in a sense; I rode upon them as if I were treading water at midnight in the middle of an ocean with a deep current flooding up from below me. I sat crouched, amazed at the story that we now know, and amazed at the story of greatness that we would never know because it would stay hidden forever in the chasms of the past, but a story that had even so unfurled over billions of years into this moment where this crouched and breathing being was now surrounded by those same opaque mysteries that, for unfathomable reasons, had taken on the form of asphalt.

Something moved. Crawling into my moment was a narrow black insect. She, too, was suddenly just there. I didn't know her name, but she was drenched. She was moving very slowly. To me she seemed hesitant, or confused. She changed directions uselessly.

Crouched down, I met her on a primordial level. I found myself thinking that she would never comprehend "California," or "humanity." I sat staring, thinking how she was unable to read up on the situation, unable to learn how to deal with roads, unable to learn how humanity had emerged and had flung up a thousand changes impossibly beyond her capacity for understanding. Here before me was a mentality of astonishing capabilities, one brought forth through a 400-million-year creative adventure, but a mentality unable to grok the meaning of finding herself in this sea of "asphalt."

I had learned years before that through some supremely mysterious process the molten lava of Earth had, over four billion years, transformed itself into organic life; but in that moment, crouched in the rain, I experienced this understanding directly. It had been decades since I had first learned that the same genetic language informed humans and insects, but now I could feel how I and this insect had been woven out of those same intelligent patterns. It had been so long since I first learned that all the elements of our solar system had been created in a star, and then scattered by a supernova blast five billions years ago, but here in the night I experienced directly how I shared a common flesh with my confused and struggling kin.

Of course, I realize now how vulnerable to ridicule all this is. What fun a *New York Times* type could have with this scientist going soft over an insect's plight! But in the moment such thoughts were the furthest thing from my mind. In the moment, I felt that I had suddenly understood, once again, the inner meaning of all our scientific studies.

The discovery of cosmogenesis is the discovery of a way of entering a more profound relationship with our companions of this great community of existence. On occasion, in an entirely haphazard manner, I have found my way into a brief taste of this—haphazard because such moments were not planned; haphazard because each such experience feels as if it is the first, so effectively do I erase any memory of the experiences in between.

It is possible that unless one experiences cosmogenesis directly, the significance of its discovery remains hidden. Perhaps the next era of Earth's adventure depends upon humans consciously creating educational forms and spiritual disciplines trained on evoking the embodiment of cosmogenesis.

52

BEVERLY RUBIK

Beverly Rubik, Ph.D., is director of the Center for Frontier Sciences at Temple University in Philadelphia, Pennsylvania, and editor of *The Interrelationship Between Mind and Matter* and *Frontier Perspectives* magazine.

Changing Science, Changing Ourselves

Modern science and technology have changed our lives and the face of the Earth. Powerful penetrating spacecraft have been launched to explore and conquer space. "Smart" remote missiles are capable of fighting push-button wars. We have an increasing number of nuclear reactors for greater energy production. There is a vast array of tools and appliances that consume that energy and ease our daily work. We have developed a plethora of new synthetic chemicals with the promise to fight insects, weeds, and disease, or improve upon natural products. The information revolution is underway and escalating toward more powerful computers and better global communications. With a modern scientized medicine, we have declared war on heart disease, cancer, AIDS, and other contemporary plagues. Based on recent discoveries in molecular biology, we are at the dawn of a new revolution in biotechnology where we can manipulate life itself.

These are considered as among our greatest accomplishments. But what's wrong with this picture? Virtually all were accomplished in the spirit of conquering, controlling, and capitalizing upon nature. Our conduct goes back to that of Francis Bacon, the father of modern science, who said that science was to tease and torture the secrets out of nature. Likewise, we have shown her little respect.

Whereas our knowledge is limited, our technologies have been potent and widespread with serious consequences. Life is now threatened globally by chemical, nuclear, and electromagnetic pollution. Rain forests and other ecohabitats are disappearing along with whole species dying by the minute. With our capability to tinker with the gene pool, we can now alter the course of natural evolution with unforeseen consequences. We have created holes in Earth's protective ozone membrane. Our modern medicine is invasive and often makes war against the body as it fights disease. Moreover, we are losing the "war on cancer" and the "war on AIDS." Clearly something is wrong with our approach. We are beginning to understand that when we confront nature, we only defeat ourselves in the long run.

Whereas nature is a seamless whole, we have created a world marked by fragmentation. The historical rift between science and spirituality still remains. Then again, we behave as if our minds are separate from our bodies. Furthermore, we see ourselves apart from nature and her deep wisdom.

Our deep fragmentation needs healing, both within the world and inside us. The present time is critical for us to change our ways. Can we overcome our apparent fear and loathing of nature that underlies our attempt to control, manipulate, and even wage war on her? Will the day ever come when we fall to our knees to embrace her, filled with awe, wonder, respect, and gratitude?

There is a vast domain within nature important to our survival that we have ignored—her softer, gentler, nurturing aspects. We know very little about the subtle interconnections that render the cosmos a living community that sustains itself. We know even less about the subtle powers within us, such as the role of consciousness in our health or in the physical world.

I am hopeful about the future, because new perspectives that might lead us to renewed relations with nature and ourselves are already emerging, although they are not yet widespread. There are an increasing number of courageous individuals who have risked stepping outside of the mainstream, frontier scientists and scholars, who are working to explore the subtle realms, heal our fragmentations, and build a new holistic science. They are asking new questions that go beyond the limits of the old science. Some have come to realize that science is not an objective enterprise, but context-dependent and filled with human projections. They are working to remove the isolation and bring meaning and values into science.

Interest is rapidly increasing in "soft" medicine, complementary to our present high-tech "hard" medicine. "Soft" medicine includes more natural, noninvasive medical modalities previously considered unconventional, such as therapeutic touch, acupressure, and herbal medicine. Those interested in consciousness are beginning to examine subjectivity as well as the objective realm. Many are concerned about bringing gender balance to science, not so much in terms of larger numbers of women scientists, but recognizing that every aspect of science has been colored by patriarchal traits, and that other approaches are needed in order to touch the gentler features of the universe.

Because our culture is strongly dependent upon science and its worldview, a new holistic science will undoubtedly have profound impact on our future. The new science, however, is still in the making by those few who have responded to a personal "wake-up call" and joined together in new alliances to work for the greater whole. It is not yet a mainstream activity or a collective institutional effort.

It appears to me that many of our institutional systems are dried up and staid, unable to respond fast enough in a changing environment to new ideas that have life value. Nonetheless, people are gradually waking up, experiencing a new integrity within themselves and in relation to nature. We are at the threshold of a new order of being. Before that, however, I anticipate at least a partial collapse of the old order. Although this would bring hardship, from a larger perspective the breakdown of our deteriorated structures is essential if we are to renew ourselves, our culture, and our planet.

53

LYALL WATSON

Lyall Watson, Ph.D., is a life scientist and anthropologist who lives aboard an ocean-going trawler, exploring the unusual and reporting his findings in a series of best-selling books such as *Supernature* and *Lifetide*.

We Are Midwives to Matter

We have a problem.

Humans have broken the mold. We have, just by taking thought, found ways of adding considerably more than one cubit to our stature.

It started simply, with tools and mechanical aids that freed us from various forms of drudgery, but it was not long before these new appendages gave rise also to a growing sense of alarm.

Such concern is not surprising. It is natural enough, the territorial response of a species whose niche is under potential threat from a rival. This archetypal unease was first given resonant form by Mary Shelley in *Frankenstein*, but more recently it has grown into a sort of technological theology, a new iconography in which robots have become more like mechanical gods, immortal and omnipotent, truly divine machines. And what makes this really scary is that such creations are no longer just part of some science fiction scenario. They exist.

There have been two recent developments, both evolutionary leaps, that make artificial life not just possible, but inevitable.

The first, of course, was the invention of the silicon chip. This little device is the mechanical equivalent of the "breath of life," turning myth into nascent reality, making it necessary for us to take the whole scenario seriously. If machines do not yet think, they very soon will. It is impossible to stop a process with the sort of momentum that brings it a thousandfold increase in complexity every twenty years. Robots with human intelligence could be amongst us in fifty years and commonplace inside a century.

The second vital development is less well-known, but just as seminal. If life is a special combination of matter and information, the addition of a set of basic biological instructions to certain powerful computers seems already to have irrevocably blurred the line between the living and the nonliving. In the last two years, computational biologists have succeeded in producing digital versions of the process of natural selection, creating artificial organisms that reproduce, grow, and evolve, increasing in complexity, displaying independent behavior in wholly inorganic but truly open-ended ecosystems. There is nothing, it seems, that limits life to carbon chemistry. It can just as easily be based on silicon.

The implications of this breakthrough are both exciting and terrifying. We have entered, almost by accident, into another Faustian bargain—exchanging the knowledge we need of nature for the responsibility of unleashing autonomous, self-perpetuating, semimetallic lifeforms on the universe.

The deal may have been inevitable, written into our contracts in the sense that it has always been our destiny to lift, nudge, and cajole inanimate matter into life. Perhaps this is our job—the bright person's burden, our part in bringing the universe to some kind of sentient completion. We are, if you like, midwives to matter and can derive some consolation from the thought that the labor pains have only just begun.

With a little luck and imagination, we may still have time to do more than just take part in the delivery. Perhaps we could influence the outcome, shaping the future in our own image, giving it the best of our many faces before we pass on the evolutionary baton. It would be nice to believe that our usual catastrophic hubris might yet be converted into a legacy worthy of our long gestation on this extraordinary little planet.

54

CHRISTINE HARDY

Christine Hardy, Ph.D., has conducted cross-cultural investigations of altered states of consciousness and techniques of mental self-control for several years, while traveling in the Middle East, the Far East, and Africa. She has published numerous works on progressive scientific research, including *La science et les états frontières* and *La connaissance de l'invisible*. She is currently president of Interface Psi.

The New Science and Culture

The transition to a new worldview can be long and arduous, but at this point, we definitely can distinguish the main values of the emerging paradigm. Its priorities will be to further systemic, holistic, synergistic outlooks. The ecological point of view, emphasizing harmony between humanity, society, and nature will come to predominate. The movement bringing together East and West, initiated in the 70s, will gather new force, renewing our focus upon human potentials and their fulfillment in terms of spirituality, relationships, mind, psyche, and body. It will renew our search for a left-brain/right-brain balance, both in individuals and in society.

Scientific research is going to be turning away from the study of isolated objects and closed systems and shifting to process, interactions between open systems, fluidity, and transformations.

In this context, I believe that some of the greatest scientific advances in the coming century will spring from the human sciences. In psychology, the self will once again be considered worthy of serious study, and internalized processes reclaimed. Cognitive psychology will undergo radical changes as a result of discoveries in artificial intelligence. The general concepts of mind, intelligence, consciousness, thought, logic, rationality, and knowledge will come to be totally redefined, acquiring new meanings and addressing higher levels of complexity. In particular, our understanding of mind and intelligence will evolve on the basis of four essential developments:

- the general recognition that intelligent information processing is achieved not just by the conscious mind but by the unconscious as well—with logical organization and linkage of concepts, purpose and goal-directedness, choice and decision. This will lead to the realization that there exist other ways of treating information and creating new knowledge—processes that are currently subsumed under the general rubric of "intuition." It will then stimulate the exploration of different forms of spontaneous logical linkages, and thus lead to the recognition of the possibility of multiple types of logic.
- the recognition of true intelligence in future generations of computers, when they come to show an ability to exchange in natural language, to learn, to make complex inferences, to weigh and decide, to generate novel information. The development in artificial intelligence will render computers most valuable tools, helping us to reflect, to process information in different ways, to consider and compare diverse interpretational grids.
- the discovery and investigation of different kinds of extraterrestrial intelligence and logic, and the associated understanding of the relativity of our categorization, classification, and organization schemes—even in the "hard sciences."
- the theoretical postulation and actual detection of an order of reality that, partaking both of the mental and the physical, acts as the interface where mind-matter interactions take place. Of crucial importance to our understanding of this interface will be sophisticated transdisciplinary investigations of psi phenomena.

Turning to society, the trend toward recognizing global interdependence will certainly grow. We will increasingly come to sense an urgency for creating international regulatory organizations that would oversee issues such as ecology, global economy, human rights, and health. This positive trend, however, could readily shift to a tendency to impose uniform solutions, across borders and diverse cultures. It thus contains the seed of a major threat: the subjugation of diversity and uniqueness to a single, overpowering civilization. In the long run, this would be disastrous to humankind's evolution, bringing forth a uniformization of our planet that would freeze human creativity and innovation. For, as far as innovation is concerned, diversity and a certain margin of disorder are crucial.

This, then, is one of the most important challenges we will face: finding the right balance between the need to institute global regulation and the need to protect cultural diversity and uniqueness of worldviews, values, customs, tastes, and lifestyles.

Perhaps the spread of computer networking will serve as a metaphor for the cohabitation between independence and shared ground. As occidental civilization increasingly moves to a society of overlapping networks, each organized around a particular theme and linked through telecommunications, we may come to appreciate the importance of both sharing common values and accepting differences, divergence, and decentralization.

The future is not simply "out there," a destiny awaiting our arrival. We are all creating our future, at every moment, through our day-to-day choices, but also through our anticipations, the projection of our thoughts into what we believe to be the future. A multiplicity of probability lines parade in front of us and are touched by the way we look at them, by our questions, our fears and hopes. We are all co-responsible for the future we face. In looking in its direction, we lay down the path we will follow.

55

PIERRE A. FORNALLAZ

Pierre A. Fornallaz is emeritus professor of mechanical engineering at the Swiss Federal Institute of Technology. He is the founder and first president of the Swiss Society of Solar Energy, a founder and former president of the Foundation of Appropriate Technology and Social Ecology, Langenbruck, and former president of the Swiss Association of Environmental Research.

To Have and *To Be*

In his profound work *To Have or to Be*, Erich Fromm examines the conflict in the human soul between two forms of existence: "Having" is based on material possession; "Being" expresses itself in inner growth and creative activity. Is there no way to reconcile these two aspects?

In the production process, goods are manufactured from raw materials, then used and discarded at the end of their life span. Raw materials can be utilized in many ways; in other words, they have a low level of entropy. Discarded products—or waste—are useless, are in many cases harmful to the environment where they are deposited, and have a high level of entropy. The production process thus transforms low-entropy materials into high-entropy goods, thereby contributing to chaos and disorder. It may create prosperity and comfort, but it does so to the detriment of life on Earth. In scientific terms, the conservative devolution of the structure-preserving system strives for balance and is opposed to the evolutionary process of life.

In contrast to the production process, life is the only organization of matter that is capable of countering entropy. This ability of life to diminish entropy is called *syntropy* and is found both in biological systems (for example, in photosynthesis) as well as in social and political institutions. A well-functioning, efficient society that gives its members a sense of purpose and well-being is a powerful anti-entropic system, which sustains, strengthens, and enhances life itself. The final goal of all organic systems is the battle against entropy and the advancement of life. This is evolution, scientifically speaking: the dissipative self-organization of open evolving systems that, rejecting balance, strive toward higher forms of organization.

In the interest of the further development of life, this scientific reflection thus advocates that production and consumption be contained as far as possible. On the other hand, we know, of course, that we have economic development to thank for our current prosperity. Is there a contradiction here? I maintain that both are true: In the sector of primarily material expansion, we must seek to curb the growth of entropy to the greatest extent possible; in the sector of principally nonmaterial growth, we need to encourage the growth of syntropy.

All growth begins in the "Having" sector in the satisfaction of largely material needs. Here, one should make sure that real needs are, in fact, met, rather than surrogate ones. The scientific and technical task at hand is to minimize the growth of entropy through the sustained utilization of unlimited resources and by promoting cyclical processes. Recycling and safe disposal are major aspects of production.

Further growth should come from the "Being" sector, through the advancement of largely nonmaterial needs. What is important here is the experience of life in all its dimensions—not the material aspect alone.

Society's task consists in liberating human beings from the pressure to earn money and consume and should aim to promote the development of their creative powers. This development is boundless, but it is contingent upon limiting the growth of the GNP. Without this restraint, the current trend willl prevail, accompanied by uncurbed GNP growth and a further deterioration in the quality of life. The results of this unfortunate trend are already to be seen in Switzerland, where most social indicators point to a decline in the quality of life.

In accordance with this view, the economy must set a new course for the future. In the cultural ecosystem, the economy represents the material foundation that makes possible the cycles of matter and energy to serve the advancement of humanity as a working species. Material production is merely a side effect, which must be critically viewed in terms of its real utility. Profit is never a goal in itself, but is only the prerequisite for sustaining this process.

A parallel can be found in nature's ecosystem. Nature is the material foundation that, through the transformation of energy and the recycling of matter, creates conditions for the development of life.

In both the cultural ecosystem and the ecosystem of nature, material growth is limited. It represents no more than a means to sustain, strengthen, and enhance life.

56

CAROL ORSBORN

Carol Orsborn is the author of *Inner Excellence: Spiritual Principles of Life-Drive Business* and *Enough Is Enough: Simple Solutions for Complex People.* She speaks nationally on the application of spiritual principles in the business environment.

The Next Revolution

Taking a leap of faith, our early farmers revolutionized agriculture by letting their fields lie fallow from time to time. Giants of the industrial revolution took another step forward with the introduction of machines for mass production.

Today, in the age of information, we sell our products and services on the basis of our peoples' talent, our problem-solving ability, our teamwork. But in a business environment that celebrates the workaholic who puts career before quality of life, we treat both our fields and our machines better than we treat ourselves, our employees, and each other. We may be doing our very best, but more often than not, this turns out to be only the best that exhausted, stressed people can produce.

As we approach the turn of the millennium, a growing number of individuals in business believe that the age of information deserves its own revolution: faith enough to revitalize contemporary business' greatest natural resource—the spirit of its people.

Over the past twenty years, as co-owner of a communications company providing marketing and communications consultation to six hundred companies, I have seen both the price of fear-driven management—and the rewards of transformation.

Using our company as a guinea pig, we have experimented with new ways of working, discovering that there need be no discrepancy between individual values, quality of life considerations—and success. What we have accomplished we propose to be a role model for the future of corporate cultures in America by the year 2000.

By working to foster an environment that encourages people to take more chances, not only in their assignments, but in the level of honesty and risk-taking they bring to their relationships with fellow workers and bosses, we have invited the return of vitality into our organization. Respecting the need for a healthy balance between personal and professional lives, we have discovered that the reduced number of hours at work is offset by the increase in efficiency and creativity. We have learned to work less and achieve more: Profits as well as morale are at an all-time high.

But this spirit of Inner Excellence is not only about making more money. In fact, I contend that in the dawn of a new era, success in traditional terms will be a by-product of the real purpose of doing business as a way to support humanity's highest aspirations—rather than our lowest. Taking our cue from mystics, saints, and heroes of times long past, we have begun the lifelong process of redefining success to encompass all of life—not only those times when we are manifesting externally on the material plane, but when we are reflective and loving and creative—regardless of what we have to "show" for ourselves. We detach more and more from society's standards and expectations and reclaim our own inner authority and experience.

When we are freed from externally generated purpose to find our own path through the world, we find ourselves benefiting from a point of view that allows us to function with the highest degree of strength, courage, and clarity: and that is to place our faith in a universe that, despite appearances at any one given time, has a master plan for us that always has our best interests at heart.

From our limited, human perspective, we cannot always understand why we are faced with the challenges that come our way in business and in life. But through the application of spirituality to our ambition and work lives, we can find ourselves on a path that allows us to function at the highest level possible for ourselves given the circumstances with which we are faced at any particular instance. Rather than bring our worst possible selves to work each day—reactive and fearful of what the day might bring—we bring our best with us.

We have learned to let our fields lie fallow from time to time; we have mastered mass production. And each revolution brings with it great changes on the most personal of levels. As we approach the next millennium, I foresee that by doing spiritual and growth work on the most personal of levels, we can contribute to the next great revolution for business—a philosophical shift that holds the promise of liberating not only our bottom lines, but our spirits.

57

FRANCES KINSMAN

Frances Kinsman, M.A., is a futurist, business consultant, writer, broad-
caster, and lecturer. He is the author of several books, including
Millennium, president and founder of The City Liaison Group, a
cofounder of The Business Network, and a qualified counselor for the
Centre for Transpersonal Psychology.

Something Else is Going On

Bad business has gotten us into this mess. Only good business
can get us out of it.

Forget governments, they are too big. Forget most individuals,
they are too small in the short term, and we haven't got too much term
left. It is only the newly ethical, newly concerned, constructive businesses in the middle that can rescue us and all that sail with us—
because they will go bust if they don't, and they would rather not do
that. The profit motive—the *optimum*, not the *maximum* profit motive—
will decide if they succeed or fail in this endeavor, a spur unavailable
to either the government agency or the voluntary organization. Fond
dream of a capitalist running dog? Absolutely not.

Take two captains of British industry in personal interviews
with the writer:

"The manager cannot be separated from human problems. He
cannot be brutally effective and rich anymore. Dr. Johnson said that
nothing so needs a philosophy as does business, and this is what it
boils down to. The whole essence of business in society must be
rethought through, and ringingly restated in human terms" (Sir Peter
Parker, lately chairman of British Rail).

"We must love our employees more" (Sir John Harvey-Jones, lately chairman of Imperial Chemical Industries).

Over the eight years since those and other encouraging interviews were conducted, there have been sporadic signs that the penny is beginning to drop more often—not only in Britain but throughout the developed world—with the recognition that there are acceptable profits to be made from decent, globally sensitive corporate behavior.

When Perrier withdrew the whole of its stock, its open attitude was favorably compared with that of Exxon's over the Valdez oil-spillage disaster. The case of Extra Strength Tylenol can be cited, too, where $50 million was lost when the cyanide-spiked product was withdrawn, but its position as U.S. market leader was regained three weeks after its safe reintroduction.

Even so, most managers are still too cautious or too greedy to risk the scrupulousness, openness, and imagination that will be vital to business success as we approach the new millennium. As yet, they fail to recognize the fact that Something Else Is Going On. This Something is the emergence of a whole new "postindustrial" philosophy, miles from the "industrial" and "agrarian" value systems that have preceded it. Opinion research reveals that some eighty-five percent of the population of the West belongs to one or the other of these three invisible clubs, and that the clubs themselves are of roughly equal strength and muscle. Social turbulence is in the offing.

First, and familiar to most of us, the "agrarian," or sustenance-driven group is concerned with maintaining the status quo. It is change-averse, risk-averse, tribal, stable, class-conscious, and nostalgic. Its mainspring is the dependency culture, both for those who depend and those who are depended upon.

In contrast, an "industrial" philosophy is what characterizes the outer-directed group. Their vision is focused outward, always looking to see the impact they are making. Theirs is the world of competition, aggression, materialism, thrust, discovery, glitz, cleverness, and independence. It is inhabited not only by the yuppies and the tycoons, but also by the assistant sales manager's wife, ogling the chairman at the company dance in order to secure her Wayne's promotion.

Finally there are the "postindustrial" inner-directeds, who are largely responsible for the "green" revolution we are now experiencing. Their demands are not only for conserving the environment, however, but also for conserving the people who inhabit it, for their self-fulfillment, self-development, and personal empowerment. Health and education, openness and autonomy, interdependence, and a human scale for all human activities are their concerns. They are growing fast, but are hard to pin down. Prince Charles is their unofficial spokesman in Britain. The others call them wimps.

This is, of course, a vastly oversimplified picture. All developed societies do exhibit these divisions, but their proportions differ widely by country, as do the national subdivisions into which the three main groups are split. However, regular opinion research in seventeen different countries since 1973 is backed by both established psychological theory and media evidence here. There is strong support for the basic premise of a society divided into three philosophical parts, rather than the conventional two of "Us" and "Them," with the third, inner-directed group now making the running.

Business must now understand the nature of the inner-directeds as consumers, as investors, as employees, and as representing the public at large. Some organizations are getting the message; for a role model you need look no further than The Body Shop, successful in everything it touches, and faithful to the principles of imaginatively decent conduct. Businesses that follow this path are not only going to "do well by doing good," they are going to provide the mainspring for the regeneration of the whole planet.

58
GARY COATES

Gary Coates, M.A., is professor of architecture at Kansas State University and editor and author of *Resettling America: Energy, Ecology and Community.* He is currently writing a book entitled *The Architecture of Erik Asmussen,* which focuses on the ecological community Asmussen has designed for a number of anthroposophical groups living in Jarna, Sweden.

Reflections on Resettling America

In 1981 I edited a book called *Resettling America: Energy, Ecology and Community,* which argued that industrial civilization is fundamentally flawed. It embodies an egoic way of life based on materialistic values, inaccurate descriptions of reality, and institutionalized forms of exploitation of the Earth and the majority of the peoples of the Earth. I documented the "ecology of scarcities" being generated by the routine operation of the current social order—the accelerating depletion of finite sources of energy and minerals; the progressive, and in some cases irreversible, degradation of the Earth's major biological systems; and escalating patterns of violence within and among nations. I concluded that urban-industrial civilization is inherently unsustainable and argued that only by changing our current values, institutions, and settlement patterns could we make the transition to a metaindustrial society in which human needs could be met without diminishing the prospects of future generations.

Since all of our problems come home to roost in the places where we live, I argued that the great task before us is to create ecologically sustainable buildings, towns, cities, and bioregions powered by renewable forms of energy. I called for the resettling of America based on the principles of equity, justice, cooperation, and the sacredness of all creation. Following economist Kenneth Boulding's dictum that "whatever exists is possible," nothing was proposed that was not also illustrated by practical examples. Detailed case studies by leading authors and activists from around the country demonstrated how we could destructure our cities into more self-reliant neighborhoods and create rural new towns and sustainable agricultural landscapes and bioregional economies. Taken as a whole, the book showed that it is both necessary and possible to integrate our architecture and human settlements gracefully within the energy flows, material cycles, and biological rhythms of the natural world.

At the time *Resettling America* was published, I sincerely believed that we were poised on the brink of such a radical transformation of nature, self, and society that the book could help inform and inspire a movement in that direction. I believed that the kinds of changes envisioned in the book not only offered a way to avoid the social, economic, and ecological catastrophes toward which we were so clearly headed but were also a means of realizing the perennial American dream of transforming this continent into a peaceful and plentiful land in which nature and human culture are joined within the harmony of a greater whole. However remote the possibility, I thought that we stood at the threshold of resacralizing and reinhabiting America. We had only to choose life, and, since the alternatives seemed so unthinkable, the choice seemed clear.

Of course, with the perfect vision of hindsight, it can now be seen that I underestimated completely our compulsive commitment to the addictive and self-destructive rituals of the consumer society. As we recoiled from the abyss that opened up with the energy and economic crises of the 1970s, Ronald Reagan came along to tell us the lies we wanted to hear. Using the hypnotic power of television, the "great communicator" offered us a vision of a past we never had, a present which did not exist, and a future which could never be. Rather than being a time of social and spiritual renewal, the 1980s turned out to be the decade of Reaganomics, an era in which egoic self-possession, unfettered greed, and the denial of ecological limits to human activity combined to create a kind of collective trance state. We seemed enchanted, held captive by a delusory reality that was rooted in fear and denial. The Reagan era was the Ghost Dance of American empire and industrial civilization.

As it turned out, however, we did resettle America but we did so according to the logic of Narcissus, the separate and separative self. Rather than creating pedestrian-scaled, locally self-reliant, and ecologically derived cooperative communities, as I had called for in *Resettling America*, we built what Joel Garreau has called "Edge City," a sprawling postindustrial landscape of corporate campuses, regional shopping malls, and lifestyle-specific, age-, race-, and income-segregated residential enclaves. Distances in these unnameable agglomerations of citylike functions are so great and the path and pod development pattern so daunting that walking as a means of transportation finally has become obsolete, although jogging trails and fitness clubs now abound. In this soulless and fragmented landscape, where the majority of Americans now live and work, the radical monopoly of automobile, airplane, television, and electronically mediated communication is nearly complete. During the 1980s we carried out the most revolutionary change in the last one hundred years in how we build and dwell, by constructing the most alienated, privatized, and unsustainable form of human settlement ever conceived.

While we were building the new American anticities for those wealthy enough to escape our increasingly unlivable cities, the health and viability of the living systems of the earth rapidly worsened, outstripping even the most pessimistic predictions I made in *Resettling America*. It has now become clear to most educated observers that human activity has already pushed many key natural systems beyond sustainable limits. We have entered an unprecedented era of ecological and social instability which threatens the continuation of life on this planet as we now know it.

Vaclav Havel proclaimed in a speech in February, 1990, to the U.S. Congress that "without a global revolution in the sphere of human consciousness, nothing will change for the better in the sphere of our being as humans, and the catastrophe toward which this world is headed—be it ecological, social, demographic, or a general breakdown of civilization—will be unavoidable."

While we still have it in our power to create a sustainable society that works humanly, ecologically, and socially for all the world's peoples, it is obvious that we have failed to demonstrate the will to do so. While miracles such as the disintegration of the Soviet empire and the resulting reduction in the likelihood of all-out nuclear war are always possible, I no longer believe that a revolution in human consciousness can or will occur as a way of avoiding the catastrophes that now appear inevitable. During the 1980s we lost precious time needed for building a bridge to a sustainable future, and every day that passes without fundamental change only hastens and deepens the crisis that looms ahead. As a society, we seem to be like addicts trapped in vicious cycles of our own making, unable to see through the veils of our illusions or to escape the inevitable consequences of our self-destructive behavior.

What then can I say about the human prospect as we approach the next millennium? It is hard to be both informed and optimistic. If the addiction metaphor is an accurate way of understanding our condition, then we can only assume that as this century winds down, we shall play out the dark logic of our egoic selves on the stage of world history. Things are likely to get a great deal worse before they even have a chance of becoming better. Like the alcoholic or drug addict, we shall probably have to hit bottom before we can begin to find the wisdom and motivation to change. And hitting bottom in itself is no guarantee of understanding nor is it a promise of a shift toward wholeness and health. There is only the certainty of greater suffering.

Having chosen not to prevent the catastrophes that face us when we had the chance, the only questions that still remain are related to what we shall do when things really do get bad. Will we transcend ourselves to realize our highest possibilities, or will we succumb to our worst tendencies? Or, as is presently the case, will we see some strange mix of both possibilities in a world turned suddenly upside down? How will we respond when rising sea levels created by global warming cause the flooding of many of the world's coastal cities and the creation of whole new populations of environmental refugees? When unprecedented changes in climate and weather patterns lead to massive ecosystem collapses, crop failures, and food shortages in wealthy as well as poor nations, will we develop more compassionate and effective forms of mutual aid? Will we find a way to work together to build self-reliant local communities when exponentially rising costs and declining supplies of fossil fuels combine to disrupt the continued functioning of the global economy? What will be our response when the wars over scarce resources that have already begun to occur become chronic threats and pervasive realities? In short, what will happen when the current order of egoic society finally collapses under the sheer weight of its life-denying tendencies? This is the question that everyone alive today shall have to answer.

If we ever do experience the kind of spiritual revolution spoken of by Havel, it will not occur as a way of avoiding catastrophe but as a way of grasping its meaning and transcending its motives and implications. Perhaps in the face of the terminal crisis of our technological society, we might finally begin to understand that there is no separate self, that the independent ego that we have hard-programmed in our architecture and pattern of human settlements is a fiction and form of suffering. Perhaps, through experiencing the almost unimaginable effects of the disruption of the whole planetary web of life, we shall come to understand that we are related to and dependent upon everything that exists and that whatever we do to each other and the earth we do to ourselves.

We might even come to see that the pursuit of happiness through the unlimited consumption of material goods and the addictive acquisition of all forms of experience is not only doomed to fail but that it is this search itself that threatens our continued existence as a species on this planet. And, perhaps, by grace, we might one day learn how to release our fearful attachment to the bondage of self so that we can simply stand free, capable of expressing love in all relations. Only then will a truly human life become possible and only then can we begin to create the kind of world I envisioned in *Resettling America.*

══ 59 ══
JAMES A. SWAN

James A. Swan, Ph.D., is one of the founders of the modern field of environmental psychology and one of the developers of the modern concept of environmental education. He is president of The Institute for the Study of Natural Systems in Mill Valley, California, and author of *Sacred Places*, *The Power of Place*, and *Nature As Teacher and Healer*.

Recovering Our Roots in Nature

The times we live in hold great promise and peril. We hold in our hands the capacity both to make unprecedented advances in human civilization and to destroy ourselves through the misuse of technology and through overpopulation. Our species is called *Homo sapiens*, implying we are thoughtful animals. Looking toward the future, it seems that applying our minds to the question of how best to live on Earth—personally and collectively—must be the central concern for all of us, especially when we face the fact that environmental problems ultimately arise from human actions.

In his book *Megatrends*, John Naisbitt speaks eloquently of our future success as a function of blending unprecedented levels of technology with heightened human awareness. One example of "hi-tech" that is important to our survival is James Lovelock's invention of the gas chromatograph, which has allowed us to be aware of minute levels of toxic substances in the world around us, and which enabled Rachel Carson to bring the perils of toxic pollution to our awareness in *Silent Spring*. Considering the fact that the chemical journals of the world report an average of some six thousand new chemicals synthesized each month, it behooves us to build upon Lovelock's invention and create, as soon as possible, a host of highly sensitive technologies of awareness to monitor the world around us. Many of the worst pollutants of our times are present in quantities that are far below the levels of detection by any human sensory process, and the effects of exposure to them may take years to detect. The sad fact that the guidebooks of laws for fishing in many states now carry the advisory statement that because of heavy metal and toxic substances contamination, pregnant women and children under eighteen should not eat fish from natural lakes in many regions is a chilling warning of how we befoul our nest. Science can no longer be allowed to avoid responsibility for the consequences of its actions.

To balance increasingly sophisticated technologies of awareness, we desperately need to cultivate new ways of thinking and behaving as a species that are more grounded in the reality of who and what we are. The traditional cultures of the Earth, long regarded as primitive and archaic, hold many important clues as to how we can recover our senses and learn to make living in harmony with nature a sensory experience; this knowledge is not something that we can acquire through reading or listening to television. It is all too often not understood how, consciously and unconsciously, our personal agendas and needs influence our social behavior. And, because of the sensationalist nature of the media and the information overload of our times, often the people who get heard are those who make the most noise or have the best catch phrases rather than those who have the most to say. Many people today suffer from "well-informed futility." Clearly the education system is a prime cause, for seldom do we teach *how* to think, which is more difficult than *what* to think. A tendency in many people is automatically to reject modern culture altogether, and perhaps embrace fully another culture or an earlier age that has certain qualities not found in modern times. Evolution is a process of species finding increasingly better fits to their niche, which reminds us that our challenge today is to build upon the past to create a new integration of its wisdom with the present. Successful evolution of the human mind calls for integration of the human potential on ever-increasing levels.

Carl Jung said, "He who is rooted in the soil endures," and that is very good advice. An old Sufi saying is that the right path for action—the sort of thing that the *I Ching* also seeks to instruct us on— is to align yourself with nature, develop your mind, and then act accordingly to be at the right place at the right time. My own research on the development of an ecological conscience clearly shows that true love for nature begins with strong, positive psychological bonds to the natural world that seem to arise from early childhood experiences; from later-life transcendental experiences in nature, often associated with visits to sacred places; and from discovering how nature can be a force for healing. Considering this work, it seems worrisome that social researchers find that average Americans spends more than eighty percent of their life indoors, and to an increasing extent, use various technological devices to ascertain what is going on in the world around them, rather than using their own senses and mental processes. This research also suggests that we need natural areas and exposure to them to keep ourselves rooted in nature at a very basic level.

An education for right livelihood with nature ought to begin with getting our hands dirty. Many people today have no contact with growing or harvesting the food that they eat, and because of the lack of a visceral, sensory comprehension of our dependency upon nature for survival—food does not come from the supermarket!—they do not have firsthand awareness and understanding of our primal place in the food chain. Among those people who do understand how, as Joseph Campbell put it, "Flesh eats flesh," the relationship between people and other living things almost always becomes ultimately a matter of spirituality and deep reverence, whether you eat meat or not.

And throughout life, we need now, more than ever, to spend time alone in nature to reflect on our basic oneness with all creatures. Inside of each of us is an "inner zoo" that is our basic identity. The natural images of our dreams and reveries that resonate with nature are our core personality, for symbols seem to penetrate deeper into the waters of truth than words, in many cases. Personal health, in my experience, comes not from denying our primal link with nature, but from discovering and prizing it, which leads us to a heartful reverence for life itself. Research shows that for most people, spending half a day alone in a pleasant natural setting causes us to ponder our most basic qualities and values. Somehow nature must have planned for this, as I now feel that contemplating nature must be one of the most basic of all homeostatic processes for humanity.

Fritz Perls urged us to "Lose our minds and come to our senses." With an awareness of personal identity rooted in nature, our own and the natural world itself, it seems to me that people will set aside the mechanical thinking of the Newtonian-Cartesian school and become "tinkerers"—people who seek to comprehend how we each exist as the result of the interplay of a wondrous and intricate spiderweb of interrelationships, and how when one element of life changes, all else is affected. Tinkerers do not automatically look for quick fixes to agricultural pest problems by "discovering" new poisons. They look for bugs to eat bugs; new, hardier species of plants; or natural pest repellents.

Learning to love nature involves a sense of surrendering personal ego. Looking at successful human relationships and organizations, it seems that all too often the thing that keeps us from achieving our greatest potential is the need to control and protect our own egos, rather than seeking out a deeper truth that will get the best results. Once nature has worked its magic in our lives, it is up to us to apply these energies and insights in a fashion that creates community. Martin Buber said that true "relationship is reciprocity." If we could apply this to all things and seek out our right relationships with all things from a position of *sapientia* or wisdom, I think our chances for long-term survival on Spaceship Earth are greatly advanced. For it seems that because we as a species have such an ability to create technology, we must now learn to apply it to making life on Earth prosper for all species.

60

WILLIAM ANDERSON

William Anderson is a poet and author. Among his books are four volumes of poetry, the latest being *What I Am is Stillness*, and several prose works, including the award-winning *Dante the Maker* and *Green Man*. He is also an honorary senior research fellow of King's College, London, and acts as a consultant on educational and environmental matters for an international chemical company.

The Green Man: Image of Transition

"Now God be thanked who has matched us with this hour!" We can say that line of Rupert Brooke's, not in the spirit he wrote it at the outbreak of the First World War, but because, after a century of mass wars, mass industrialization, and mass applications of science and technology, we are faced with challenges on a scale never known before in the recorded history of humanity. We should be proud to be given such challenges, proud to live in an age when we are given a vision of earth and of the interdependence of living things upon that earth that was impossible for our forebears to conceive, and proud of the potential creativity of our own humanity.

As a poet I am interested in the archetypal images that arise from the depths of the human psyche at particular periods of history. One such image is that of the Green Man, the man whose face is formed of leaves or disgorges leaves from his mouth. I find it extraordinary and encouraging that this image, long forgotten, should return at a time of environmental crisis. In the myths connected with him, he is the challenger, the tester of our courage and our intelligence, and I think he is recurring now to challenge us to stand up to the test of creating a new civilization that will be based on a harmonious relationship between humanity and nature. To the Gothic masters he was the chief symbol of the creative power on which they drew to create their masterpieces. In his Indian form he is known as "The Face of Glory," and he signifies the creative energy of God. He is our protection in the jungle of life.

As a student of creativity and of the origins of civilization, I see our current crises, not as the accumulated instances of pollution and thoughtless destruction, but as the birth pangs of the new civilization. I see the great themes on which we have to concentrate in order to bring about the full flowering of that civilization as consciousness, creativity, and the environment. If I said above that we should be proud, before these themes we should be humble—simply because we still know so little about them.

I see consciousness, creativity, and the environment as interlinked for the following reasons. Consciousness and the capacity for the experience of unity in consciousness are what distinguishes the human races from other species in the animal kingdom; all our other distinguishing characteristics, language, social behavior, and physical natures, are incidental to that. I find it encouraging that more and more scientists and thinkers are turning their attention to the nature of consciousness, and also that through the revival and spread of the practice of meditation and other forms of contemplation, so many people are enabled to experience the stillness and the unity that are in the depths of our true selves. If these movements continue to prosper, then we can look forward to a new science that can interpret findings in the light of inner guidance, new and older forms of art that appeal to what is most true and most universal in their audiences, religions that are based on experience instead of authority, and philosophies that are truly the love of wisdom.

The creative experience is one of great simplification. It is when we *know* what we have to do and make. In such moments of clear direction, we are given a taste of the unity of consciousness. The separated sides of our natures, our waking and our dreaming selves, are drawn together into a fresh and powerful coordination, when all kinds of solutions and unrealized possibilities are laid open to us. It is upon such experiences that all civilizations depend for their origins and their renewal, and it is upon such experiences that we will depend for the solutions of the problems that face humanity.

If many of the problems of the environment arise from the

misguided applications of human ingenuity and discovery, then they can only be solved by human creativity and intelligence, in the light of wisdom and experience. As we learn more about the nature of consciousness, so we will learn more about our inner environment, the sphere of mind of which we are all part and which determines so much of what happens in the sphere of life that surrounds the earth. Then perhaps we will develop a new art, the art of living together in harmony and of seeing in one another—with the attention we give now to whatever we love most, whether it be music, sport, fishing, or watching television—''the true self which is in the hearts of all.'' Then each word we speak will be a leaf from the mouth of the Green Man, and whatever we look at will shine with the energy of the Face of Glory.

61

ANDREW ROWAN

Andrew Rowan, Ph.D., is director of the Tufts Center for Animals and Public Policy and associate professor, Department of Environmental Studies, Tufts School of Veterinary Medicine. He is the author of numerous articles and the book *Of Mice, Models and Men*, the editor of *People and Animals Sharing the World*, and the founding editor of *Anthrozoös*.

A New Vision of Nature

As a young boy who had the great good fortune to grow up without fear of hunger or deprivation in some wild (Tristan da Cunha) and beautiful (Cape Town, South Africa) places, I used to think about what the year 2000 would bring. However, it was then very difficult to imagine what I would be like at the age of fifty-four, let alone what the world would be like. Now it is easier, and I much prefer my preteen ignorance.

I mourn the gradual encroachment of humans on, and the degradation of, all those magic spots I knew as a boy where the wind whipped sand across the dunes and the plovers still had places to nest undisturbed (except by us, of course), where mountain streams trickled below the dappled sunlight of oak and chestnut trees, and where the only sound in the desert air was the cracking of the cylinder block as the engine cooled behind one. I see the blight caused by human consumption and yet am as much to blame as my neighbors. I hear the predicted population growth and wonder how we are to fit all those people on the planet without destroying the wilderness and hence changing ourselves as well forever. My scholar's mind concludes that one can only be a pessimist and view the next century through the gloomiest of glasses. But my optimist heart refuses to concede defeat.

There are signs of hope for the next millennia. Societal forces are beginning to move toward a redefinition of human interaction with nature. In pre-Reformation times, Nature was viewed as a nurturing mother before the philosophies of Bacon, Descartes, and Newton turned Nature into a wanton harlot that had to be controlled and dominated by humankind. We are beginning to turn away from the wanton harlot vision of the past four centuries and see Nature as a fragile entity that needs our nurture as much as we need hers. Whether the change is too slow and too late cannot be answered here, but at least there are many signs of a change in direction. I cling to these signs and try to influence them in my own small and insignificant way. I owe it to my children, to my neighbor's children, and to the children of all the world to do what I can to ensure that both they and Nature will survive both the most creative and destructive power on earth today—human ingenuity and imagination.

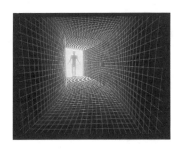

MINDING THE BODY,
EMBODYING THE MIND

62

ANDREW WEIL

Andrew Weil, M.D., is associate director of the Division of Social Perspectives in Medicine of the College of Medicine, University of Arizona, and has a private practice in Tucson, Arizona. He is an internationally recognized expert on drugs, drug abuse, altered states of consciousness, and alternative medicine, and is the author of many scientific and popular articles and five books, including *The Natural Mind*, *The Marriage of the Sun and Moon*, and *Natural Health, Natural Medicine*.

A Change in Consciousness

We are in the habit of imposing lines and divisions on the continuums of nature. Calendar divisions, like the upcoming start of a new millennium, are artificial, not part of the natural world. In reality they have no significance.

Nonetheless, the fact of so much consciousness focused on the turn of the century makes this point in human history special and provides an opportunity to reflect on where we have come from and where we are going. And the possibility that the human race may not have much future must be uppermost in the minds of all who can see what is happening.

The root problem is overpopulation along with overconcentration of population in cities. All of our troubles derive from these facts of the twentieth century. Within thirty years the number of human beings on planet Earth will reach such critical levels that present ways of life will certainly be impossible. Just what sorts of disasters will occur in that time are hard to predict, but it will surely not be business as usual. Even if all human effort were to be redirected toward reversing population growth and environmental destruction, it would probably be too late to save the situation, and that change is not about to happen.

I think we will be able to glimpse the future of cities by watching Mexico City and the future of nations by watching India. These are the likeliest places to see first the effects of runaway population growth, and the prospects are ominous.

I am sure that human civilization as we know it will be forever changed in the next century. It is even possible that human life will end. That does not mean the end of life, nor the end of consciousness, which has, I believe, always existed and will always exist. Consciousness strives to know itself better and experiments constantly with new life forms. It may be that the human experiment is fatally flawed: that our ability to manipulate the environment so far outruns our ability to control our own emotions that we are bound to do ourselves in. If so, other experiments may succeed after we are gone.

Only a change in consciousness can save us. I don't dismiss the possibility that such a change can occur in time to avert disaster, but the hour is late, and the clock ticks on. Our time on Earth has been a fraction of a second in the history of our planet, and if we were to disappear, we would scarcely be missed. Of course, I will continue to work for the necessary change of consciousness, and of course I will continue to celebrate the mystery and miracle of our present existence.

These are some of my thoughts at this moment in history.

63

WILLIS HARMAN

Willis Harman, Ph.D., is president of the Noetic Institute of Sciences, Sausalito, California. Prior to that he was a senior social scientist at Stanford Research Institute International and is emeritus professor of engineering-economic systems at Stanford University. Among his many books are *An Incomplete Guide to the Future, Global Mind Change, Higher Creativity,* and *Creative Work.*

Changing the Self to Change the World

My hope is that people will reexamine their most deeply held beliefs and change the ones that need changing. My fear is that they may not do it in time. Let me explain.

When an individual life is in real trouble, it typically takes the form of multiple problems—problems at work, a failing marriage, health problems, financial problems, relationship problems, addictions, and so on. Such a problem-laden life almost always stems from deeply held beliefs, primarily picked up in early childhood. These beliefs are so deeply and firmly emplaced that the person is often not consciously aware of them. Belief in unworthiness rather than self-esteem, for example. Belief that the world is a hostile place and you have to hustle to compete and get your share. Belief that fulfillment comes from externals—wealth and possessions, record of accomplishments, relationships with important people, reputation for altruistic acts, and so on.

Thus an individual life is shaped by basic assumptions, formed in childhood, about "who I am, how I am related to the not-I, and what kind of universe I inhabit." Society is like that, too.

Society is shaped by assumptions that were picked up through the course of its evolution. What kind of universe is this? How do we relate to one another and to the universe? When modern society is beset with a host of global problems for which there seem to be no solutions —for any one problem, let alone when they are taken all together—we may suspect that bad assumptions could be the source.

A Native American elder summarized the native view in two short statements: *"Everything* in the universe is alive" and "We're *all relatives."* How different from the modern white man's "scientific" view of an essentially dead universe, operating according to fixed scientific laws, with the rest of the universe available for exploitation by humans in pursuit of economic ends. If God created the universe, there is in this view no evidence of divine meddling in everyday human affairs.

Modern science is explicitly based on a set of fundamental assumptions that include the implicit separateness of humans from nature, mind from matter, and observer from observed; the non-reality or unimportance of what cannot be observed or measured physically; and the ultimate explanation of everything in terms of fundamental entities such as particles and fields. Most persons, including most scientists, relate to those assumptions as though they were scientific findings. But they are not; they are metaphysical assumptions.

From those assumptions derive other assumptions that underlie the industrial-economic system: the goal of material progress; humanity's exploitative relationship to the Earth and its creatures; the primacy of economic motivation and the superiority of economic rationality; the necessity therefore for continued economic growth; the high positive value thus placed on consumption of economic product.

Now, in the latter part of this century, we are faced with a host of critical issues and tasks that stem directly from the successes of the industrial-economic system—controlling global climate change, protecting the ozone layer, conserving biological diversity, combating deforestation, preventing soil erosion and desertification, protecting fragile coastal areas, managing fisheries, regulating manufacture and disposal of toxic chemicals, conserving fresh water, and on and on. Programs are put forth, politicians' promises are made to deal with these. But they are all attempts to "patch up" the system that caused the problems.

It is difficult to admit that these measures are bound to fail.

They can at best ameliorate the problems and buy time. There is no solution without changing the underlying assumptions.

We typically underestimate the pervasive power of these basic beliefs. The native population of Mindanao have seen much environmental destruction in recent generations. Their perceptive explanation for this is that "when the foreigners came to the Philippines, they put God too high in the sky."

But to change deeply held assumptions is to change the self. When a person has an addiction to alcohol or other substance or behavior, there is no real sobriety short of fundamental change in the individual's core beliefs about self and relationship to the universal process of which he/she is a part. If we are members of a society that is addicted to control, exploitation, economic growth, and consumption, then there is no cure for our global symptoms short of widespread change in the underlying assumptions.

Persons brought up in this society are steeped from birth in a deep belief in the assumptions of the industrial-economic system and the scientific worldview. Any one of us will encounter deep fear and resistance to discovering that the present form of the world economic system is essentially unworkable, and that the modern scientific worldview is fundamentally misleading.

The effectiveness of the well-known twelve-step programs for dealing with addiction lies precisely here. The twelve steps are not aimed at curing symptoms, but at fundamental personal change. The first two steps are usually the hardest: admitting that one's life has become unmanageable, and recognizing the presence of inner resources previously ignored or denied. There is a direct analogy: The only ultimate solution to the global dilemmas is through admitting the unmanageability of the planet in the ways we have been attempting it, and recognizing the inner knowing and inner resources that have been denied us by our "modern" beliefs about reality.

Hence my most fervent hope is that people will reexamine their most deeply held beliefs, and change the ones that need changing. And my fear is that they may not do it in time. If not, the planet, *Gaia*, will take care of herself but there will be much human suffering.

64
RINA SIRCAR

Rina Sircar, Ph.D., has been a teacher for thirty years and is the co-founder and resident meditation teacher of Taungpulu Kaya-Aye Monastery and its San Francisco center. She conducts retreats worldwide on mindfulness, insight, and healing in the Theravada forest tradition. In 1981, she received the honorary title of Vidasanachariya from Calcutta and, in 1982, Dhammaratna from Bangladesh.

Toward Open-Mindedness

We should be pleased that we are living in an age when there seems to be nothing that cannot be conquered. Maybe there are still some diseases that challenge humanity. Maybe there are still places in the universe where we would like to be but have not yet developed the technology to get there. But it appears as if everything is within our reach. Therefore, we must be optimistic about our capability.

If we are to reach the great summits ahead, we must slowly train ourselves so that we can first progress spiritually. We must get rid of speculative thought, ideologies that are full of wishful thinking or rosy promises but lack a practical implementation. Now there is a call for a way of living given to factual thought, one that is without superstition, that has a rational outlook that will lead to a scientific approach to life. It is high time to search inside and not outside for that practical mentality, for all power is within us.

Modern civilization is a mixed blessing. Science and technology echo the tremendously rich and powerful promise of turning this world into a paradise, and today there is ceaseless work going on in every direction to improve the world. Though all these improvements have their advantages and rewards, no one can yet invent or discover anything that is not subject to change. Above all, the mind is subject to change, and it seems the more we try to control it, the more it changes.

Actually, we should train the mind to behave like the hen sitting on her eggs. Though she looks lazy, she is very active. Whereas the squirrel who runs incessantly in the revolving cage looks so busy, yet cannot show any fruit for all his spinning.

Mind, though an invisible force, can create heaven and hell. Of all forces, the force of the mind is the most potent. This is the lesson taught by the Buddha. He introduced us to a new phase a step beyond the old, a new evolutionary path of human consciousness. His teaching is pure science and in-depth psychology. Newton discovered the law of gravitation; Einstein discovered the law of relativity, but higher than these two laws is the Buddha's discovery of the law of karma. Karma is not a belief, but rather an understanding that can be seen and experienced in everyday life. It is the unique marriage between theory and practice that can be a beacon light of practicability and the religion of heart.

It is also important to cultivate the practice of open-mindedness. In today's world, can we ever forget that we are living a life of competition economically, politically, and culturally? In whatever form, this competition has brought tension and stress that has done much damage by way of ailments to the body: heart disease, cancer, insomnia, and even nervous breakdown. Most of our illnesses are caused by anxiety attacks, the nervous tension of modern life, economic distress, and emotional unrest as well as competition. Therefore, what we need now is a trained mind, a well-developed mind that can be controlled at will. That is, a mind that does not go in all directions; a mind that is alert to discover itself; a mind that looks within to face the problems, find the secrets, and all in all seeks out the reality of life. This open-mindedness is one priceless treasure that we can possess if and only if we can give up wishful thinking, the weakest force possible for trying to build a world.

Obviously, the situation is such that we are expected to lift ourselves beyond the dangers of procrastination. For when we put off action, even for a day, we are like the man waiting at the ocean's shore to take a bath, but only when the ocean is calm. Even if someone were to come and offer to take us to Nibbana at this very moment, in our procrastination we would say, "Can I wait until I win the lottery?" or "Can I wait until I finish my Ph.D.?" or "Can I wait until I get married?"

Be prompt in your endeavor, and share your knowledge, your thinking, and your experience. This is the Open Path; it is what we need now.

65

SHIRLEY J. NICHOLSON

Shirley J. Nicholson is former senior editor for the Theosophical Publishing House and Quest Books. She is the author of *Ancient Wisdom—
Modern Insight* and compiler or co-compiler of several anthologies,
including *The Goddess Reawakening, Shamanism,* and *Gaia's Hidden
Life.* She is presently acting director of the Krotona School of Theosophy
in Ojai, California.

A New Mind of Unity

The divisive nature of the human mind is dramatically displayed everywhere today. I need not enumerate the frictions, factional
strife, and ethnic conflicts all over the world. As Krishnamurti and
others have pointed out, these clashes are generated by the human
mind, by the tendency to think of oneself as separate and apart from
everything else. It is extraordinary that, without even thinking about
it, we divide the universe into two categories—myself and everything
else. We think of the self in us as something separate and independent that interacts with others. There is not space to give the mounting evidence from science, psychology, and spiritual traditions that
this is not so, that we are part of one whole, part of a seamless unity
that cannot be broken.

H. P. Blavatsky and others who have understood the ancient
wisdom—that esoteric philosophy that has been with humanity
throughout the ages—have painted a vast picture of human evolution.
According to this view, humanity as a whole goes through great stages
of development, each of which emphasizes a unique aspect of con-

sciousness. We are now in the midst of a development of the mind, the thinking principle, *manas*, as it is called in Sanskrit. With this comes the spectacular technical achievements of the Western world. The characteristics of the rational part of the mind that led to modern science are categorizing, analyzing, dividing things into units. But this separative aspect of mind is also the seat of egoism and enhances the tendency to separate ourselves from everything else. It is behind the grasping quality that drives consumerism, competition, the urge for power.

The next stage of development, according to esoteric philosophy, is that aspect of mind called *buddhi*, which has inadequately been translated as *intuition*. It involves empathy, the state in which the knower is one with that which is known, a fusion of consciousness with that with which we interact. In this state we do not stand separate and apart but merge with the environment and with each other. The erroneous sense of egoism—that one is more important than anything else, which fires grasping for oneself—falls away, and the wholeness of nature and humanity becomes the guiding vision of life. The Buddha called such a revolution in perspective "turning about in the deepest seat of consciousness," from the outward, apparently divided world known through the senses to an inward view that includes all.

According to the ancient wisdom, evolution of humanity from the mundane mind of separation to the new mind of unity is a long, slow process that will take centuries. But it has already begun. Witness the numberless meditators and meditation centers, the wealth of literature based on the concept of interconnectedness, holism, and the oneness of everything, even in science. As this new sense of unity quickens, the other part of the mind that separates and clings to separate ego identity reacts in backlash. Hence the two powerful trends in the world today—factionalism, ethnicity, tribal identity on the one hand and global consciousness, consideration for the interconnection of all people with one another and with the planet, on the other.

I see these two poles of the mind in opposition for some time to come, seesawing back and forth in society and even in individuals in whom the sense of oneness is dawning. But eventually the forces of evolution will awaken a deep-seated sense of unity in more and more people until unity becomes dominant and inspires a new attitude on a wide scale.

We can do our part to quicken the process by training ourselves even now to think of the good of the whole, and especially through meditation, inspiration, and altruism to awaken awareness of that deeper consciousness in us that perceives we are always one with the whole of things.

66

ALAN VAUGHAN

Alan Vaughan is the author of *The Power of Positive Prophecy, The Edge of Tomorrow, Incredible Coincidence,* and *Patterns of Prophecy.* He has taught intuitive techniques to over 10,000 people and recently finished a major research project in training intuition with Psychic Reward software.

Using Intuition in the Future

The mind's hidden powers of intuition are on the threshold of entering into the mainstream. My recent report in *Subtle Energies* on software for training intuition shows that twenty-four percent of people possess latent capabilities for attaining statistically significant skills in intuitive decision-making. Moreover, a significant majority (seventy-one percent) of people improved their ability to make successful decisions about the future. The impact of reliable technology for training intuition could affect major areas of human endeavor.

Government. By relying on intuitive decision-making, government leaders and their advisors will be better able to foresee the consequences of their decisions. They could bring the world community into a time of high prosperity and avoid decisions that lead to economic collapse. They would avoid such crucial mistakes as giving billions of dollars to a foreign dictator who will use the money for weapons to invade other countries.

Business. Highly successful business executives have demonstrated in research at New Jersey Institute of Technology that they have superior intuitive skills (commonly called "gut feelings" or "good instincts"). As more CEOs rely on intuitive decision-making, their companies will prosper by making goods and providing services that the public will want to buy. Any important business decision involves the future, and it is the ability to foresee that future that leads to success.

Finance. Financial markets, such as stocks and commodities, have been shown to behave randomly. From 1929 to 1992, studies of stock-prediction strategies have all shown the same result: no better than flipping a coin. Only intuition can penetrate the veil of the future. The use of intuitive prediction techniques will enable more people to make successful financial decisions.

Science. As the most skeptical group, scientists will be the slowest to advance the use of intuition in solving scientific problems. However, such champions of intuition in the past as Albert Einstein or Jonas Salk will find future counterparts who will defy conventional wisdom and hit upon brilliant solutions to difficult problems.

Law Enforcement. Police will be trained in the use of intuitive techniques to aid criminal investigations. Police will become far more efficient in locating criminals and evidence that can convict them. Young would-be criminals, in turn, may be deterred from a life of crime if they see how efficient the police are in catching them.

Medicine. Doctors will be trained in using intuitive techniques in diagnosis to narrow the number of tests needed to identify medical conditions. Bioenergetic healing techniques will become an accepted medical adjunct. Medicine will become less costly and more effective.

Education. As techniques for intuitive problem-solving are introduced into schools to serve as a balance to rote learning, more emphasis will be given to training people to achieve creative solutions to life's practical problems. As more people discover their intuitive capabilities for making successful decisions, they will be able to enhance their lives and productivity. They will show that educating the individual to his or her full potential (especially the presently repressed intuitive potential) will lead the way to achieving full potential of communities, cities, states, nations, and the planet.

67

JOEL AND MICHELLE LEVEY

Dr. Joel Levey and Michelle Levey are cofounders of InnerWork Technologies, Inc., in Seattle, Washington. Their pioneering work with hundreds of organizations around the world focuses on building synergy between individual and organizational transformation. They are co-authors of *Quality of Mind: Tools for Self Mastery and Enhanced Performance* and *The Fine Arts of Relaxation, Concentration & Meditation: Ancient Skills for Modern Minds*.

Aspirations for Tomorrow

We circle around, circle around, in the circle of life.
All things are connected . . . connected . . . connected . . .

When we contemplate the immensity of the accelerating global dilemma in every area of human experience, it is easy to feel quite despondent. It all seems too big, too pervasive and multidimensional, and perhaps even too late, to begin to turn things around in a sustainably healthy way at the root level. Never before has humanity had the range and degree of destructive capability to demolish so much so rapidly. Yet the source of all the major global crises is in the human mind, and this is ultimately where the work must be done. Our expanded technological capacity enables us to externalize the internal conflicts, toxicities, and psychological wastelands rooted in ravaged self-esteem, spiritual impoverishment, and love-deficient abusive families, in ways of expression that go directly mind to mind, through mass media information dissemination, as well as through physical violence, war, and ecological decimation on an unprecedented scale.

In the face of all this we ask ourselves: What can I, one not-yet-fully-enlightened being, do to contribute in the greatest possible way toward reversing this self-destructive course that humanity seems to be hurtling itself and its fellow earthlings along?

What we come back to inevitably, and evermore unshakably, is the firm conviction that social transformation is only possible through the concerted commitment, compassion, and creativity of consciously evolving individuals working on themselves and working together. We have, on this planet today, unprecedented opportunities for tapping into the wisdom teachings of every tradition of inner science that exists, coupled with the networking and communication technologies made available to this generation through conventional science, to link up, share, and disseminate our insights and inspirations as well. We can, and indeed must, transcend inherited tendencies toward narrow identification with rigid and divisive sectarian boundaries, and learn to honor and celebrate the richness and uniqueness of our cultural diversities. It is an imperative of this time that we also consciously and actively seek out, celebrate, and build on the universal patterns and truths that we share in the web of life.

What it will take to accomplish this turnaround is nothing less than enough of us recognizing our true nature of interdependence, our "interbeing." Living in accordance with that we will naturally refuse to continue the dysfunctional egocentric, ethnocentric, and anthropocentric patterns of the past. Where this process begins is nowhere else than within each of us, in our own individual body, speech, and mind. To think, feel, speak, and act with the recognition that each other being is in essence "another myself" (this is the translation of the ancient Mayan word for *you*), will require a totally new quality of attention, faith, and trust in our larger wholeness, combined with a commitment to take that leap of faith into birthing a totally different tomorrow. Today.

Standing here on the threshold of tomorrow, we remember that tomorrow is actually arriving here and now moment to moment. Each of us lives with different kinds of aspirations throughout the course of our life, and these aspirations are in essence our prayers. These aspirations, our conscious or unconscious yearnings and prayers, organize our attention as we move through the world. If we walk down the street and we are hungry, we will notice restaurants and fruit trees. If we are lonely, we zoom in on the people with and without companions. So, if our hearts' yearning and prayer is for personal change or transformation, our minds will be more open to recognizing and taking advantage of the learning opportunities that our life brings. And if we are really serious about contributing to global change and social transformation, we have to generate big-time prayers and hold big-time aspirations, and be ready to catch the waves of opportunity that contribute to fulfilling this yearning.

As our understanding of this process deepens, we discover that we live in a responsive universe. If you drop a little stone in a pool it sends out and draws back a little wave. If you drop a big stone in the pool, it sends out and draws back a big wave. The moment there is a yearning in our hearts or a question in our minds—consciously or unconsciously—there are echoes of information available to us. The answer or clues might be revealed in the patterns of a cloud, in a bird's song, or by what the person three seats away is saying. As we learn to listen more deeply, we discover that the answers are often here, though generally speaking our circuits are too jammed to hear them.

The key to calling forth the kind of inspiration we need for creating meaningful change in our lives and in our world is learning to live our prayers in a passionately receptive way. We must learn how to tap the power of the quiet mind and to be present for the revelation of the answers to our questions and prayers. To access the quiet mind, we must know how to quiet the turbulence within us. This does not mean that the noise has to go away, it simply means that we discover the quiet within the noise, the fearlessness within the fear, the peacefulness within the agitation.

The closer we come to discovering what is true, the more we live with the resolution of paradox. Understanding this, we learn to smile through our tears, and with a quiet, open mind, embrace and take to heart the sufferings of our world in one hand and the beauty in our world with the other. As our hearts get broken open again and again, the suffering serves to awaken compassion in our lives while the beauty we encounter teaches us to rejoice and be more grateful. Moment to moment the mystery reveals itself to us, and through the experiences of our lives we discover the answers to our deepest yearnings and prayers. Standing here on the threshold moment to moment, taking the world into our hearts, how deeply can we yearn and how deeply will we learn to listen?

68

DENISE BRETON & CHRISTOPHER LARGENT

Denise Breton and Christopher Largent are coauthors of *The Soul of Economies: Spiritual Evolution Goes to the Marketplace*, team-teach philosophy and religion at the University of Delaware, and codirect Idea House/The Center for Applied Philosophy and Practical Spirituality in Wilmington, Delaware.

Fun on the Threshold

The old Chinese curse, "May you be born in interesting times," applies to no time better than our own. Between dire prophecies and daily tragedies, most of us wish the times were a bit less interesting.

But this is only half the story. Out of the chaos—ancient and modern prophets tell us—will come a new humanity and a new world. A time of great danger is also a time of great opportunity. The faster we respond not with fear but with a transforming vision, the less traumatic the transition will be.

Physical pain occurs, researchers say, when dying cells do not get out of the way fast enough for new cells to replace them. This is the physical analogue to what is happening on the planet metaphysically. As we let conflict-based worldviews die off naturally—as we refuse to be intimidated by fear-for-survival models, especially when it is clear they create the worlds they claim only to describe—new models can be born with less pain.

In short, the more we go forward with inward changes, the less outward suffering we will experience, since outward upheavals occur to help us notice that inwardly—philosophically—we are on the wrong track. The good news is that inward changes seem to be speeding up everywhere.

An oppressive educational system based on competition and mystery-learning is being replaced across the country with quality-based mastery-education. These "schools without failures" invite students at all levels to take charge of their learning process and to enjoy it.

Businesses are looking at more than next quarter's profits. They are taking holistic management, team learning, and community and environmental awareness seriously. For example, they are discovering that authoritarian management models squander a company's greatest resource, its employees, while profit-only thinking undermines the communities on which businesses depend. Business people are too practical not to notice that if they destroy the human and natural communities, they will not have a world in which to do business.

But educational and economic systems are not alone in experiencing deep changes. Frustrated with the political system, the Socratic sleeping horse of the American electorate woke up and participated at record levels in the election of 1992. New faces appeared in both parties, while independents drew millions of new supporters. For the first time since Lincoln's election, voters reclaimed the self-government truth that elected officials are servants not rulers of the people.

Perhaps most encouragingly, people are embracing their own spirituality and its power to transform humanity. In many cases, this spiritual awareness is emerging from the pain of addiction. Strong and growing, the recovery movement is not limiting itself to personal recovery. People are reclaiming their lives from abusive rules and addictive systems not just at home but also at school, at work, in church, in government, and in the media.

Nothing could be better news. Beyond the sensationalism of some newly uncovered abuse lies a reawakening of a long-denied inner selfhood. As author and ex-psychotherapist Anne Wilson Schaef puts it, recovery liberates us to "see what we see and know what we know"—to trust our inner knowing enough to name an addictive worldview for what it is: not as "conventional wisdom" nor as "realism" but as a "progressive, fatal disease."

The effect of all this may be a millennium like none humanity has seen. We ourselves are likely to evolve into new beings, exercising powers of consciousness that we are only beginning to explore—another ancient and modern prediction. So far, we have been using only a fraction of our brainpower and genetic potential. What is the rest there for, and how can we tap it? How might we be different as we do? The frontier of outer space yields to that of inner space—a frontier we all can explore.

With an awakening humanity, societies must follow. Communities built on cooperation, economic justice, political freedom, and ecological wisdom are not utopian dreams. They are the only practical models for the future.

How do we get there without killing ourselves? To start, we could relearn how to have fun together. As consciousness researchers Sheila Ostrander and Lynn Schroeder documented in *Superlearning* and *Supermemory*, learning, creativity, and performance go off the charts when we are relaxed and enjoying ourselves. Yet we have structured our lives together in ways that maximize stress, insecurity, and drudgery. No wonder we are all feeling stymied as we face humanity's greatest challenges.

Abusive philosophies perpetuate themselves through heaviness and fear. Philosophies that encourage bigness of vision, lightness, and joy are the logical antidotes, because they give us the inward space and enthusiasm to evolve beyond dead-weight, status-quo thinking.

When we come together, for example, we can explore ways to join forces that pattern symbiotic play rather than one-up, one-down gaming. That way, we learn from the roles we have each assumed in this cosmic drama, rather than putting one up by pulling another down.

In this spirit of cooperation, physicist David Bohm suggested converting arguments into dialogues by looking behind each other's positions—exchanging assumptions and goals instead of crossfire. Pooling our inward resources to tap deeper dimensions of knowing, Bohm suggested we ask ourselves such questions as: How did we each arrive at our positions? Beyond our immediate interests, what are our real concerns? By looking behind our official fronts, we begin to understand each other from the inside out.

To expand the arena of fun, we can also abandon roles that do not fit and that only narrow our interactions with each other. Stereotypes about males and females, majority and minority groups, or socioeconomic classes are dinosaurs in the face of solid research on the human potential. Within our present social categories, the differences among us seem insurmountable. But compared to the potential we all have and can develop, the differences become trivial. As dysfunctional mind-sets fade and economic pressures subside, we will have the time of our lives getting to know "them," whatever nationality, race, sex, or type "they" may be.

Transforming learning into play, making business a game of

co-creation, reclaiming politics from closed-system power elites while rebirthing real self-government, and discovering the freedom of connecting with our soul-self and that of others, we bring the spirit of celebration to the threshold of tomorrow. At the same time, we open doors on what we can become.

After all, heaviness and drudgery never achieve what they would have us believe. Laboring under them, we take ourselves too seriously and give ourselves heart trouble. By contrast, real learning, producing, administering, governing, and interacting go on as we relax and enjoy the process together.

As we face the trial of transformation, then, we might consider that the new millennium and our getting there could be—if we let it—more fun than a barrel of monkeys. Why not?

69

RICHARD HEINBERG

Richard Heinberg is a violinist and publisher and editor of the monthly newsletter *Museletter*. He is the author of *Memories and Visions of Paradise* and *Celebrate the Solstice: Honoring the Earth's Seasonal Rhythms with Festival and Ceremony*

New Myth, New Culture

As many of us have learned from the works of Carl Jung and Joseph Campbell, myths are not merely pathetic tales invented by unscientific peoples to explain natural phenomena; they are stories that serve to constellate the meanings of a culture. Thus, we in the modern West have every bit as deep a need for vital myths as ancient or tribal peoples, the systematic study of whom is the rather arrogant purpose of anthropology.

Science itself, though it is formulated in a way quite different from traditional myths, serves in part a mythic function: It tells us how the universe began, where the first people came from, and how the world came to be the way it is. And, a hundred years hence, our current scientific views on these matters may appear in retrospect to have been about as fantastic as anything our ethnographers have coaxed from the tongues of reluctant natives.

Now, of course, our world is caught in an extraordinary dilemma. If we stand by and do nothing, within a few decades civilization will probably succumb to overpopulation and environmental collapse. Meanwhile, all our cultural institutions, all our forms of community—from the family to the church, city, corporation, and nation—are showing the strain. We need a fundamental change of direction. But where will this bolt of inspiration come from, and how can it present itself in a way that is potent enough to get everyone's attention?

As early as the 1920s, Carl Jung suggested that part of our culture's problem is that its myths are dying and that we need a new myth to revive our sense of meaning. As the greatest politicians, artists, spiritual leaders, and even scientists know in their gut, only a new myth can inspire creative cultural change.

Of course, it is always possible to engineer a new myth—to study the requirements and simply tailor one for the occasion. Quite a few of our culture's current myths came into being this way, but perhaps that is precisely why they are so anemic. Truly great myths are not manufactured; they are dreamt and sung and danced and lived.

One of the core manufactured myths of civilization is that of *conquest*. God has given us, His people (note the pronoun), dominion over the land, plants, and animals, and it is our destiny to subdue not only these, but also any other tribes of human beings we may come across. It was a powerful myth, but it has run its course: We have subdued just about everything that moves. Where do we go from here?

I will skip here the explanations and justifications and say simply: I believe that the new myth is staring us in the face. In fact, we have to shut our eyes tight in order to ignore it (and many of us are doing a pretty good job of that). We could call it the myth of *humility*. It exists in many versions; here is my current favorite:

About ten thousand years ago, everyone lived by hunting and gathering. Wild game had been plentiful—so much so that the human population burgeoned. But now many of the big game animals were being hunted to extinction. In addition, climates everywhere were changing and sea levels were rising, drowning the most populated areas. All of this amounted to a catastrophe. How to respond?

There were two ways to go. Some people decided to learn more about their environment so that they could adapt themselves better to it. They dreamed myths that encoded meanings having to do with protecting populations of wild animals, with keeping the size of the human population in bounds, and with honoring the diversity and interconnectivity of the web of life.

Other people decided to adapt the environment to themselves. They domesticated plants and animals; they cleared and plowed the land. They chose the best places and built permanent settlements. The population of these groups continued to grow unchecked. As settlements increased in size, social arrangements became more stratified. A few individuals became wealthy and powerful; the rest tried to make themselves useful. As their territory expanded, they came into conflict with other settled groups, with whom they fought or formed alliances, or with the hunter-gatherers, whom they killed or enslaved.

Wherever they settled they exhausted the land. After a few generations famine would strike and they would move on. Eventually, however, their populations and territories grew so large that there was nowhere to go. Meanwhile, virtually all of the peoples who had taken the first option were now absorbed within the lands of the planters and herders.

As the whole Earth began to cry out in fatigue, and as hunger gripped the poorer classes of the planting-and-herding groups, the youth of the latter began to seek out the few remaining peoples who had learned to adapt themselves to the land. The planters, who had been so arrogant, began to humble themselves before their cousins, from whom they had departed so long ago and whom they had ruthlessly butchered and enslaved at every opportunity. They began to humble themselves before the wild things and the wild places of the Earth. They vowed to heal and renew the land and to forge sacred ties of mutual respect and aid between species and cultures. And they vowed to remember, so that they would not make the same mistakes again.

70

MORRIS BERMAN

Morris Berman, Ph.D., has taught at several universities in Europe and North America and has lectured widely on the themes of personal and cultural change. His published works include *Social Change and Scientific Organization*, *The Reenchantment of the World*, and *Coming to Our Senses*.

Living in Limbic: A Few Thoughts for the Third Millennium

When I reflect on the things I have written over the past twenty years, and especially over the past twelve, I realize that there has been one unstated, if very commonplace question that has animated a good deal of my research. The question is: Is the human race a flawed species? I still do not have an answer, but I am convinced that it is as decisive a question for us as Einstein's famous "Is the universe friendly?" For this is about our *internal* universe, and if we really are our own worst enemy, what hope is there?

I am not playing devil's advocate here; I am genuinely worried. I subscribe to the *Manchester Guardian Weekly*, and not an issue goes by that I do not read about a famine and/or massacre occurring somewhere in the world. Reading Jane Goodall's remarkable book *The Chimpanzees of Gombe*, I learned that our closest primate cousins attack, murder, and eat each other in the wild. They also organize themselves into hierarchies, pecking orders of dominance and submission. This is the human story, of course, and we tend to want to blame it on civilization: the Neolithic Revolution, the Scientific Revolution, the Industrial Revolution, and so on. And this is understandable, because if our troubles can so be blamed, then some sort of "paradigm shift," allegedly set to occur in the next century, is going to bail us out; or so we would like to think. Thus a friend recently wrote me that she is "recovering from Western civilization." "Wonderful," I wrote back, "but how do you intend to recover from your limbic system?"

The limbic system, of course, is that part of the brain that governs things such as sexuality, the emotions, and aggression. Chimps have it (as the paleomammalian brain), and so do we. As we evolved, and the cortex exploded in size, so did the limbic system. In her recent book *Braindance,* Dean Falk reviews the biological evidence and comes to the gloomy conclusion that our only hope is cortical control of the emotional part of the brain; keeping the lid on, as it were. It is not a hopeful prospect; if we are going to have to violate our own biology in order to survive, it is going to be an uphill battle, at best— as Freud pointed out long ago.

How is all this going to translate into the twenty-first century? No one knows for sure, of course, but with only a few years left of the twentieth, the broad horizon lines can already be seen in science fiction (*Blade Runner* by Ridley Scott, or *Neuromancer* by William Gibson) as well as political economy, e.g., Jacques Attali's convincing essay "Millennium." The vision of the new world order that seems likely to emerge is a global corporate economy based on the microchip, in which the United States, Japan, and the European Community vie for hegemonic control of the globe. The gulf between haves and have-nots, between rich center and impoverished periphery, will become wider and deeper; dominance, hierarchy, and a life based on power and control will be the order of the day. Large, poor nomadic populations will arise that may eventually threaten the power blocks that feed off the energy and resources of these peoples. "The losers will outnumber the winners by an unimaginable factor," writes Attali, and adds: "The horrors of the twentieth century will fade by comparison."

Attali is drawing no moral conclusions here; he is merely stating what he feels is likely to occur. Myself, I cannot help asking: Have we learned nothing at all? Here things get a bit tricky; for one thing, it depends on what one means by "learning." "Limbic reality" may be a kind of bottom line, but it is not the only one, because there is biology and there is biology. At least part of our biological heritage (cortical or otherwise) must involve cooperation, because without it, we would have been naturally selected out of existence a long time ago. In addition, we do possess a few spiritual traditions that attempt to cultivate both the undoing of the ego and the avoidance of fixed formulas; and although these traditions are the products of culture,

I cannot believe that they are entirely without biological roots. The brain (and the body) may contain more than just a warring ego and id, each intent on having its way. It may also contain a "third path," so to speak, that leaves the two ancient enemies fighting it out while it goes off in entirely new, and unpredictable, directions.

What directions? Here we have to distinguish between micro-history and macrohistory. The global corporate world depicted in "Millennium" is, of course, macrohistory, and it is not likely that individual efforts, or a new brain path, can do much to change its basic outlines; at least not in the foreseeable future. But on the individual and private level, there is a lot going on that falls into the "third path" category, things that could conceivably make a difference by the *end* of the third millennium, if not at the beginning: a renewed interest in the sacred— not necessarily the dramatic kind of sacred experience that has generated great religious movements, but the kind that endows ordinary, daily events with an aura of "suchness," of presence or immediacy. The attempt to modify our conditioning, to live out of what might be called essence rather than personality. Experiments with nonhierarchical relationships, and with what might be called nonheroic behavior. The shaping of life in such a way that, to the extent that it is possible, it becomes an act of service and beauty, a kind of gift (both to oneself and the culture at large), rather than being an exhausting chase for personal influence or self-expression.

All of this is a tall order, and not without its own set of dangers, for "third path" perception can easily degenerate into sloppy thinking, confusing desire with analysis, and ideology with understanding— an obvious feature of today's "alternative" landscape. It can also, virtually overnight, get pressed into the service of ego and influence— historical examples of this are legion—and much-touted "paradigm shifts" quickly get converted into fixed formulas, to be coopted and used by the very global corporate economy they were designed to reject or outflank (indeed, it is happening even as I write). Be that as it may, "third path" experiments are necessary if we are going to create ways of being and thinking that are truly different, and which exist outside of the dictates of the limbic reality system. It is within such "loops" in the fabric of (macro)history, if sectarian "certainty" can be avoided, that real breathing space might occur, and a freer life be experimented with.

And this raises, finally, the question of the relationship between micro- and macrohistory, for the question of how the former actually does get translated into the latter is an enigma that no historian, poet, or social scientist has managed to solve. Indeed, in this area, unpredictability is at an all-time high. Rosa Parks will not go to the back of the bus, and thirty-odd years later, our understanding of race is very different; much deeper and better, I would say, the Rodney King incident notwithstanding. Someone starts recycling waste products in Northern California, but if (as Attali notes) such eco-habits were to be extended to the Third World, they would occur at the expense of the latter's economic development, effectively safeguarding the wealth and comforts of the privileged First World. Years of private, individual dissent, of *samizdat* poetry circulated on the q.t., finally open out onto *glasnost*, the end of Communist dogma and Soviet repression . . . which in turn opens out onto a reawakened racism and "ethnic cleansing."

This is the way of the world, that the private, the courageous, the decent, and the innovative must be undertaken in order to live any sort of authentic life, and that the outcome of such an effort is anybody's guess, because it is simply out of anybody's control. All we can do is work on these things and hope that we are forging a new link between nature and nurture, one that enables the human race to navigate the next millennium in a less violent, less formulistic way. Even chimps are not preoccupied with pecking orders *all* the time!

71

DON HANLON JOHNSON

Don Hanlon Johnson, Ph.D., is a professor and director of the Somatics graduate degree program at the California Institute of Integral Studies and is director of Esalen Institute's Somatics Research and Education Program. He is also executive director and founder of The Healing Center for Survivors of Political Torture in San Francisco, a contributing editor of *Somatics*, and the author of *Body, Spirit, and Democracy*.

Toward Recovery of a Sensible Intelligence

How can we work together?
to heal a world that makes little sense,
that makes little of the senses,
that is fast eroding the senses, replacing them with prosthetic video display terminals and virtual realities?
How can we together become more impelled by a respect for commonly felt human needs for food, shelter, decent work, and health care over greed, nationalism, and religious sectarianism?
How can we make a consensus?

Consensus originally meant ''sensing together.'' It recalls older ways of interaction where people passed time with each other eating, drumming, chanting, sharing tobacco, often in silence, teasing their raucous spirits out of the ethereal and divisive realms of untethered opinions into their shared feelings of the fire's heat and the smell of soup. Cut off from those older ways, beset by the turbulence of city life, we have to find our own peculiar ways back from ghostly private and sectarian ideas to a communal sensibility. Refugees from cultures decimated by centuries of war and economic rapacity in the recent or distant past, we all now live in the same neighborhoods.

We have to clean up our streets together, walk our children to the same schools. No matter what our beliefs about ultimate reality, we have to deal with the degradation of the atmosphere, topsoil, rain forests, and water. Our spirituality has to reflect our everyday experiences of struggling to get along with people from many cultures and religions in an endangered ecosystem. We also have to come to grips with the demons of cancer, heart disease, AIDS, chronic fatigue syndrome, addiction, and schizophrenia that affect so many in our communities, independent of ethnic background, sexual preference, and religion.

The sources of an archaic sensible intelligence lie in many regions. Some are in memories preserved in the older cultures: Cree, Iroquois, Inuit, Dinka. Others in the radical mystical traditions of Christianity, Judaism, Islam, Buddhism, Taoism, Hinduism. Poets and artists often crack through the illusions of modernity to the bedrock of the immediate. So do ordinary people who have forged their wisdom out of lives of caring for their families, suffering, recovering from addictions, and sharing their newly won capacities for healing. Still other sources are carried forward in the cellular memories of our bodies, memories that surface in quiet breathing, conscious sitting and walking, careful and reverent touch.

I have often wondered what it would be like if Christians, Jews, secular biologists, Muslims, psychoanalysts, Mormons, and other sectarians would take their various cosmic systems as we take the distillates of a given region: champagne, pilsner, slivovica, grapa, Irish mash. Instead of seeing them as the Truth to be clung to at the expense of all else, they would be honored as unique essences, wrung from centuries of a given people's struggles for identity, shaped by their unique tastes and imaginations. To be savored, if one likes, rather than argued about. For we are torn asunder by religious and secular ideologies; we are united in our breathing, digestion, patterns of movement, and neurological functioning. We are also united in our resistance to greed, addiction, heartlessness, and violence. A return to our roots in those sensual and emotional experiences might ground saner designs for our community life.

72
DEANE JUHAN

Deane Juhan is the author of *Job's Body: A Handbook for Bodywork* and was a member of the Esalen Massage Crew from 1973 to 1989. He is currently a Trager instructor and teaches anatomy and physiology to bodyworkers of all kinds throughout the United States, Canada, and Europe.

Touching the Future

The developments that have absorbed most of my attention for the past twenty years have been those in the field of therapeutic massage and movement education.

The collective successes in the twentieth century of industrialism, capitalism, science, technology, and modern medicine have been truly spectacular. But the ways in which we have pursued them have at the same time produced a population that is painfully and dangerously "out of touch"—with ourselves, our children, the institutions that regulate our lives, and with competing global concerns. In the midst of transforming our environment and our society, we have lost contact with ourselves in important ways, and this sense of physical, psychological, and social isolation haunts us, mocks our material progress, frustrates our attempts to translate greater prosperity into greater human happiness.

The overwhelming evidence from many avenues of research is now unquestionable: Touching and physical interaction between individuals is absolutely necessary for normal healthy growth and behavior. Varying degrees of touch deprivation reliably result in emotional problems, learning disabilities, severe neuroses, physical deformities, derangement, even death. There is a crucial stream of sensory information—and a functional integration of that information—that simply does not occur without adequate amounts of pleasurable physical contact, and which cannot be replaced by any other means. In short, we learn much of what we need to know about ourselves, one another, and the world *only* by a large amount and a wide variety of touch and movement experiences.

I believe that in the next century we will see a steadily increasing interest in effective bodywork and basic movement education of many kinds. The National Institute of Health is currently initiating a funding program for research in various modalities of bodywork. More and more health professionals will become interested in these methods. More and more consumers will experience them, benefit from them, and demand coverage for them from their insurance carriers. These trends will enormously enrich our healthcare system, not only by greatly improving prevention and rehabilitation, but also by revivifying the interpersonal warmth, caring, and contact between health professionals and their patients, by improving quality of life when we cannot offer a cure, and by developing together—professionals and patient—effective means of coping with many conditions that neither surgery nor drugs can fix. After all, the major killers in our culture are much more directly related to stress than to germs or genes. Moreover —and this is not a minor issue in our current healthcare crisis—bodywork will prove to be extremely cost-effective. Perhaps it is not too much to hope that it could be the penicillin of its era.

Educational touch and movement will also become a major new element in our primary and secondary school systems. Presently we teach our children far more about handling an equation or a computer than we do about living with their own bodies. This new focus will not just be upon children's *understanding* of how their bodies work, but also upon the active *creation* of their own strength and health and vitality. Far more than simply adding another subject to the curriculum, basic bodywork skills and movement education will enhance children's physical and intellectual capacities in general, bringing fresh insight, enthusiasm, and creativity to every enterprise they engage in. They will discover that it was no accident that the Greeks were not sitting in isolated desks in orderly rows dutifully marking multiple choices when they were formulating the major scientific, philosophical, and aesthetic themes of Western civilization. These pleasures and discoveries will make future children's educational experience so refreshing that they will want to sustain it for a lifetime.

Innovations in healthcare and education will only be the beginning of the ramifications of more and better touch in our culture. Expanded sensory awareness will bring with it fuller and more accurate perception, and improved perception will increase our abilities to recognize and solve a wide array of problems in ways that now seem remote to even our wisest. Once we can actually *feel* and *acknowledge* the sources and results of our own personal pollutions, our collective responsibilities toward our common environment will cease to be either a mystery or an undue burden. Once we actively engage in the lifelong *process* of growth and improvement in our own organisms, it will not be so difficult to sustain a long-term view of the gradual improvement of our government, our economy, our society. If we can literally connect with, and consciously grow with other individuals in an immediate, tactile fashion, the concept of global connectedness will already be immeasurably closer.

It is difficult for me to imagine that something so simple, so available—and so pleasurable in the bargain—will not increasingly find its place and purpose in our efforts to better human life.

73

EDWIN M. McMAHON

Reverend Edwin M. McMahon, Ph.D., is cofounder and research coordinator of the Institute for Bio-Spiritual Research in Coulterville, California. His experience as a therapist, researcher in the psychology of religion, priest, author, and teacher has been passed on through workshops, training programs, retreats, and in some twenty-five booklets and books over several decades, his most recent book being *Beyond the Myth of Dominance: An Alternative to a Violent Society.*

Focusing:
The Awareness of Our Bodies is Holy Ground

''**F**or the first time since World War II, no nuclear weapons are being produced in the United States.'' I sat stunned by these words, not from some government report, which may or may not be true, but from an article by a respected science journalist and mother of two preschool children. As I thoughtfully set the pages down, my gut said: ''After being lied to for so many years, just maybe I can believe this woman because she has so much at stake with those two tiny kids.''

The article went on to describe a growing cooperation between Russian and American scientists. The ''spin-off'' applications of weapons technology were now being turned toward cleaning up our environment as well as discovering new energy sources from deep within the earth. It was exciting to reflect on the implications. But what suddenly connected in my mind with this breathtaking and hope-filled occurrence was a recent phone call concerning one of the very scientists involved in this challenging work, a scientist whose personal life at the same time was literally in shambles. The stark contrast between this man's highly disciplined and brilliant mind and his primitive knowledge of human relatedness (beginning with his own body and its feelings) struck me as a universal and tragic symbol of our time.

Ironically, other areas of human development and scientific advancement can move forward without there being one iota of corresponding maturity in this area of potential growth. Experimental research on how to process our feelings has been extensive. But it has received little recognition and been accorded even less priority within our religious and educational systems.

To cite but one example, the brilliant contribution of Eugene T. Gendlin, which could have enormous social benefits in any culture if introduced into educational, healthcare, or other social systems, remains unknown to the average person—including those working in the fields of human relations. In religion, if spirituality could be grounded in what Gendlin calls "Focusing," it would make the difference between religious practices that are superficial and often pathological and a healthy spirituality solidly rooted in the process of human wholeness. This is something that people of all ages who are looking for deeper meaning in their lives could really become excited about!

We deplore the killing, suffering, and endless violence that erupts not only in the Balkans but from within our own schools, families, and neighborhoods. Yet, there is still little realization that the most basic cause of such destruction lies not in the external environment but arises directly out of the way we carry hurt, scared, angry, blocked, and stuck feelings inside our bodies. When churches, schools, and parental upbringing provide children with literally no knowledge whatsoever and no social support for processing these painful feelings, they simply fester inside. Sooner or later they destructively explode into all our relationships. External circumstances may be the immediate catalyst of a violent response. But we know, today, that this is simply the tip of the iceberg.

With the end of the Cold War, as we turn our priorities toward creating a more healthy global human existence, the time has never been more opportune than it is now to invest in providing our children (and ourselves) with an alternative to the inevitable violence that erupts from unprocessed feelings. Such suffering need not continue nor become the future for our children. Today, there is another choice.

This is the service and mission of the Institute for Bio-Spiritual Research. What we call "levels programs" are our way of beginning this change and offering an alternative in living rooms, classrooms, church basements, retreat centers—wherever a small group of people can gather who are willing to learn the peace process from inside.

The awareness of our bodies is holy ground. It is a place of new beginnings. Most of all, it is a sacred inner space where all human beings can listen to the unique "Word of God" that they are as this revelation of their own story speaks from within. "Focusing" is the body-awareness process we use in this reverent listening.

Learning how to create the inner and outer climate for this truth (our own spirit) to be born and grow is what a "levels program" is about. Step by step these stages teach us how to open our whole being to the body-feel of gift. Then, living in the truth of our spirit "in the Spirit," we can better connect with all living things in a way that nurtures peace and unity. This is a bio- or body-spirituality.

The levels programs are designed to give people enough support and regular sessions at each stage in this development so that they are able to: 1) acquire a body-feel for the process of Focusing; 2) learn the same practical knowledge for guiding others; and 3) nurture a deep enough experience of the sacred and community-building potential of Bio-Spirituality through Focusing that they will be capable (if they wish) of becoming part of a Focusing Companions relationship.

This is a special quality of nondominative, nondirective shared Focusing together in which mutual vulnerability creates a community presence that empowers and frees each person. It is a relationship radically different from the teacher/student, guru/disciple, doctor/patient, parent/child model upon which we have based our social organization for centuries.

As I look toward the twenty-first century, I am hope-filled. I see my life's work gradually spreading as more and more people become trained Focusing guides and then pass this on to others. New communities and relationships of nonviolence will mature—rooted not in theoretical visions of the mind, but in the experience of the transformation of the human body.

For adults, all this takes time, commitment, practice, and the assistance of an experienced focuser, because it is so countercultural. For children, not yet programmed into disconnecting from their body-consciousness, it comes naturally and joyfully, like breathing and playing. Nevertheless, adults can learn how their bodies provide answers and direction that cannot be arrived at by thinking. Bio-Spirituality returns us to our bodies as the bridge into that inner wisdom of "the Body" that speaks through our individual bodies, if we can learn to carry whatever is real inside us with openness and availability. Then, what Gendlin calls a "symbol" comes unbidden (as a gift) and connects with the body-awareness carried in this invitational posture, bringing with it a physiological shift. The body-feel changes, and it now sits in us in a different way—less blocked, unknown, tight, scary, hurting, or whatever else needed to loosen and unfold. A step toward more wholeness has taken place.

Although the Institute has only several thousand members now, I see this nuclear group building a solid foundation for a global spirituality in the next century. One of the main reasons for this is that Bio-Spirituality through Focusing does not jettison whatever is psychologically healthy within any religious tradition or secular system that prizes the development of a caring, life-giving presence to each other and our environment. We do not waste time and get into the unproductive and divisive confrontations about whose interpretation of life's sacred experience is right or wrong. Instead, we help each other come home to the common bond we all share—a sacred human body. It is through this body that we are capable of experiencing ourselves and all other living things as integral cells of some Larger Living Body, waiting to gift us with enriched life and meaning if only we will live in our own bodies as invitation.

74

JOHN BRIGGS

John Briggs, Ph.D., is associate professor of English at Western Connecticut State University. A widely published science writer, he is the author of *Fractals: The Patterns of Chaos* and *Fire in the Crucible: The Self Creation of Creativity and Genius* and coauthor of *Metaphor, Turbulent Mirror,* and *Looking Glass Universe.*

The Balm of Irony

Desperately our species flails for a means to save itself from a crushing oblivion in the twenty-first century—oblivion beneath the weight of its own greed. The problem is clear. One doubts that any idealism will save us because there are too many cynics and too many idealists eager to impose their conflicting ideals. One doubts that evolution can save us because the time scales for evolving a new faculty of harmony are too long—and our greed is too quick. To save ourselves, one suspects, we will need to expand on a faculty we already possess. My proposal is irony.

In "The Second Coming" Yeats says, "Things fall apart; the centre cannot hold;/Mere anarchy is loosed upon the world." His apocalypse is ironic. What does the phrase *"mere* anarchy" portend? That something awful and monumental is about to transpire, or something fatuous and small? Polonius advises his son, "and it must follow as the night the day,/Thou canst not then be false to any man," failing to appreciate the irony that Polonius himself is false to everyone. In irony such disparate perspectives as "mere" and "anarchy," or "falseness" and "truthfulness," are brought together in a potent mixture that flushes out the holes in our worldviews, widens the cracks in our knowledge, and lets mystery pour through. What do we really know? For example, do I really know that I am less hypocritical than Polonius?

In music, painting, poetry, and nature, irony is the conjunction of forms that are both harmonious and dissonant. Making and perceiving such forms can free us from bondage. That bondage is our thought, our attempts to escape thought, and our thoughtlessness. These tie us down and gobble up everything. The drive of mind to digitalize the flux of life into packets of what we know is so great that we have transformed the world into something contrived and hidden like the pixels on a television screen. Illuminating the dots with the scanning machinery of our imagination, we have made a picture that seems real. In the digitalized dark spaces on this screen even what we *don't* know (or don't think about) seems to lie. But *is* it real? Or is it merely one-dimensional and sad.

An Ode to Pac-man
ENDLESSLY DECEPTIVE SONG:

Thought and nothought,
like a feasting dot,
engulfs
the eyes' nerves,
spiraling snowflakes,
lips,
galaxies—
and all the vast complexities
of starts and stops.

Nothing escapes our
swollen famished dot—
but
a certain deep place
of gauzy green sunlight.

I've never been there.
No one has.
. . . Yet the dot of
thought-nothought
engulfs it.

Against this trend are humankind's old, sacred texts and stories— riddled with irony. There, tricksters abound, and parables turn in on themselves and tangle into mystery. These texts and stories remind us of how big things are and how small our knowledge. From irony: humility.

The perception of ironies gives us pause, plunges deep into being. Through the cultivation and practice of irony, we may find our common ground. Virginia Woolf said, "If we don't jump to conclusions, if you think, and I think, perhaps one day, thinking differently, we shall think the same." Hearing Woolf one is reminded, in our own era, of the dramatist turned leader of Czechoslovakia, Vaclav Havel. Havel said: "It must seem a paradox: I write mercilessly skeptical, even cruel plays—and yet in other matters I behave almost like a Don Quixote and an eternal dreamer, foolishly struggling for some idea or another." As a politician, Havel continued to cultivate the ironic attitude, which apparently bred in him a respect for diversity, a generous humanity, a humility, and a hardheaded realism that is visionary. It also has helped him cope with disappointment. Irony is curative, a balm. Yeats called it a "gaiety transfiguring all that dread."

But how do we cultivate irony? We might begin simply, with a modest skepticism about our certainties; raise an eyebrow at our platitudes (a platitudinous belief in irony included). As Joseph Conrad advised John Galsworthy: "The fact is you want more skepticism at the very foundation of your work. Skepticism, the tonic of minds, the tonic of life, the agent of truth,—the way of art and salvation." In other words, irony is the fine art of wedding certainties with doubt. Da Vinci wrote that "he who has no doubts will accomplish little." In doubt lurks much; in a doubt-wracked certainty lurks more. Irony is an attitude of uncovering, honoring, and momentarily suspending ourselves in the swarming contraries of existence (or our description of it)—a process that through the ages has shown us Truth (or, anyway, Something).

The faculty of irony is already in us. Nothing new is needed. In facts, we are ironic creatures. It is the key to our creativity. Perhaps through exercising and developing our ironic faculty we may discover that our role as a species is to be life's artists. Who knows? Infusing our minds with the cold heat of irony, might we melt down our weapons and violence so as to forge them into sculptures? Of course I have no great hope that this will happen. Am I too ironic? Or idealistic? It hardly matters. Or it matters a great deal. Mere irony is loosed upon the world:

REFLECTIONS ON THE DEATH OF LI PO AND
OUR ASTRONAUTS LANDING ON THE MOON

That night the poet, in a small boat, drifted
on the empty lake, accompanied by
friends. Across the desolate hills their lyric
drunken laughter. Was it more than wine
intoxicated thoughtful Li? Night was clear
and windless. Moon shone sheer as
thought upon the silent water. One feels he
said, "My venerable friends, I'll fish this
frail conceptual pearl for you."
Cold still image
of the moon held purely,
until shattered
where
he fell . . .
We stroll by a summer lake. Moon that
men have landed on (into its dry and
desolate seas) floats palely in the vast dark
night. . . . A pearl. I conjure Li, who dreamed
and reached, and fell—and disappeared.
Moon lies still in the watery universe, is
sheer; is clear . . .
Quick, cold moon floats near . . .
as if it were an image
of what lies
beyond us . . .

75

JACOB LIBERMAN

Jacob Liberman, O.D., Ph.D., is a pioneer in the therapeutic use of light and color and the art of mind/body integration. His groundbreaking book *Light: Medicine of the Future* has received international acclaim. In addition to an extensive lecture and seminar schedule, he is in private practice in Aspen, Colorado, and is president of Universal Light Technology, Ltd.

We Are All Healers

I have experienced many miracles and changes in my own life. For twelve years I wore glasses, and found that through opening to healing myself at a deep level, I "graduated" to clear vision. I have also found myself transitioning from optometrist to therapist to author to teacher, and what I have discovered is that we are all meant to be teachers—to inspire learning within each other.

This is an exciting time. We are seeing paradigm shifts in all aspects of healing and relationships. The current medical paradigm is crumbling; in its wake, a new perspective and awareness of how we heal is emerging. It is only a matter of time before even the most skeptical scientists confirm that we, as human beings, are the most powerful medicine in the world. We have the power to heal ourselves and our planet, and this is part of our inevitable evolution.

What will the FDA do when we are all healers? How will it regulate us when we talk to each other on the phone and healing occurs? Or when we touch each other and healing occurs? These things are already happening for many people. I experience them all the time.

229

But do not simply believe my experience; create your own healing shifts. Open yourself to receive deep healing. Take risks. Planet Earth is a bold adventure that we are on, and I believe that within our potential for destruction lie the seeds of our healing.

There was a time when humans were deeply attuned to their surroundings and their inner selves. They were able to read the language of Nature. It told them what healing remedy to use in any situation. The first healers were highly sensitive, intuitive people who could sense what was happening within another person. You can still see this today in some of the so-called primitive cultures. However, in our modern world, we have all but forgotten that ability and have instead learned to label it as "witchcraft" or "imagination." Scientists are beginning to prove that we actually can interact in these subtle, nonmaterial ways, and that we are fundamentally connected to everything in the universe, just as the ancients knew. I am seeing this continually in my own work, and in the discoveries of many of my colleagues.

At a recent workshop, someone said, "So you use light . . . that's your main technology, right?" And I said to them, "You only need to *use* the light until you *see* the light." The meaning here is that our techniques are just a means of bringing our awareness to a forgotten area; and once our awareness is expanded, the whole world becomes our tool for healing and expanding our vision. And we become the tool for the healing of our people and our earth. Although the world is changing rapidly around us, the most important changes are what are happening inside me, inside you, and how we come together in our healing. This is where the healing of the Earth and its peoples ultimately rests.

76

YOGI AMRIT DESAI

Yogi Amrit Desai is the founder and spiritual leader of Kripalu Center for Yoga and Health in Lenox, Massachusetts. He is the developer of Kripalu Yoga and an internationally recognized authority on the yogic principles of self-transformation and holistic health. He is the author of several books, including *Happiness is Now, Working Miracles of Love,* and *Food for the Soul.*

We Heal the Planet as We Heal Ourselves

When we look at the world today, it seems to be in a state of accelerating crisis. That is not necessarily a bad thing, however, because crisis is actually an opportunity for transformation. It is an opening, rather than something to fear.

If we fear crisis, we reinforce it. The attitude we take determines whether crisis becomes for us the opportunity it is or an experience of fear and resistance. Crisis always calls us to reexamine our paradigms and value systems and reassign our priorities. If we are willing to change our personal priorities, the entire world will change.

Now more than ever, the world is experiencing shifts in social, cultural, and spiritual values. Technological advances in transportation and information systems have turned the globe into a village. What happens anyplace immediately shows its impact everywhere.

The first effect of that phenomenon is the spread of materialism from the technologically advanced and rich countries to the poorer ones. Materialism travels fast, faster than spirituality. People embrace materialism as a quick and easy solution to their problems, one that will not require internal change on their parts. So the desire for prosperity and the feeling of freedom that often follows it are spreading worldwide, but such freedom and prosperity are superficial.

Superficial freedom is the freedom to prioritize and pursue one's desires, fantasies, and false hopes for fulfillment. However, indulgence in desires and greed result not in fulfillment but abuse—abuse of personal and universal resources. First, people take steps to convert universal resources into personal ones. Once they feel they own those resources, they feel free to abuse and waste them, all in the name of pursuing prosperity and freedom. The result is not freedom, but license and abuse—both of the planet and of people, including the abuser himself, whose personal health and well-being usually suffer as a consequence.

The alternative is to prioritize *true* freedom, which is freedom from the compulsions that drive our self-destructive behavior. It is our unwillingness to face and master the compelling forces of greed and unconsciousness that leads us to settle for a false freedom grounded in escape and denial.

It is time for each of us to look at our personal drives toward the abusive and indulgent behavior that leads ultimately to self-destruction and global destruction. To get to the core of society's problems, we must go to the core of our selves. Real change will occur only when we are willing to change our personal values, for personal and planetary consciousness are intimately interdependent.

Personal, individual responsibility must be the central part of all our attempts to heal ailing humanity. I do not mean responsibility as an intellectual or psychological concept, but as the daily practice of actions that focus our scattered mental, emotional, and physical energies, energies that now cause conflict within us as well as a feeling of separation from each other.

Such internal conflict—which gets mirrored as external conflict—results from our alienation from the source of oneness that is within each of us. It can be resolved through a perceptual shift that embraces that oneness.

But to change my perception, I must change my internal chemistry, which is determined by the mental, emotional, and physical conditions I create with my values and actions. Through my values and actions, I choose whether or not to live according to the universal spiritual laws that protect my health and promote my capacity to embrace oneness with humanity and all of existence.

The primary spiritual law is "Thou Art That." All that we consider to be outside us is really just the extension of us, and we are the extension of God, who manifests through creation. When we recognize that who we are is God, and recognize every living being and every resource in that way, we heal the inner split that causes alienation. Our love, like God's, becomes a nonexclusive, unconditional, universal love that knows no separation.

The individual body is not separate from the body of the universe; the individual soul is not separate from the universal soul. Once our behavior and priorities begin to manifest in context with the whole rather than in the greed and unconsciousness that causes alienation from the whole, we will begin to bring into experiential reality our inborn divinity. It is through opening ourselves to the universal source within us that we bring forth the unifying principles of love and compassion toward all beings and all existence. And that is the greatest contribution we can make to integrative planetary consciousness and transformation.

77

VICKI NOBLE

Vicki Noble is a feminist shaman healer, working primarily with hands-on healing in a group ritual context. She is cocreator of *Motherpeace Tarot* and the author of *Motherpeace, Shakti Woman,* and *Uncoiling the Snake.* Her next book, entitled *Down is Up for Aaron Eagle,* is about her seven-year-old Down's Syndrome son.

The End of the Millennium:
An Opportunity for Healing

As we approach the end of this epoch, prophecies made by native people and medieval monks seem to be coming terribly true: the overtaking of Nature by metal and concrete, disturbing the natural balance in such a way as to court disaster and bring about the "end of the world." The Mayan calendar ends with the year 2013, leading us to seriously contemplate what it might mean for one age to finish and the next to commence. Will humans (and more specifically, whites) survive these changes? Are we the 144,000 "chosen ones" meant to live through the transformation of our planet into a new century and a new millennium? Are we an embodiment of evolving consciousness (the "brain of the planet") or just a decadent society on its way to (necessary) extinction?

Most of what has been suggested by modern New Age spokespeople looks delusionary to me at best and dangerous at worst. To look around at what the Western world has wreaked on the rest of the planet and theorize, even for a moment, that we represent some pinnacle of achievement or evolutionary (awakening) consciousness seems just plain dumb to me, a clear-cut state of denial. It takes no genius to see we are messing things up everywhere on the globe. Our consumer-oriented, objectifying consciousness has taken over even the most beautiful places, such as Bali, and introduced the foulest kind of constructs into those formerly innocent cultures. Our incredible greed for limitless profit is creating genocide in the whole Third World, making a multinational totalitarian government to replace all the democracies on the planet, and bringing about untold and utterly unimaginable destruction to the body of the Mother herself.

But then intelligent people have been describing this problem for fifty years, at least since Rachael Carson's *Silent Spring*. The really interesting thing about the end of this millennium is the level of recalcitrant unconsciousness on the part of those in charge, and the high degree of mental rationalization and brainwashing being used as weapons in the epochal battle against life on Earth. For it was a mere five thousand years ago that this war on Nature began with the first clear-cutting of the sacred groves. From China to Mexico, from the British Isles to the southern tip of Chile, the same pattern emerged: destroy and conquer the ancient female-centered cultures. Cut down their trees, dismember their Goddess and colonize those who serve her, create a pseudo-reality to replace the natural one, put military men in charge of it in the "divine" image of a newly invented, monolithic God-the-Father, and call it "civilization." Spend the next five thousand years carrying through on the task of destroying ancient, earth-based cultures everywhere on the planet, and when the last tree is felled, the last shaman murdered, have a new futuristic civilization in place, fully equipped with space travel, virtual reality, and Star Wars to protect it.

The situation looks apocalyptic all right, like a battle between good and evil, dark and light forces. But such dualisms are not usually valid on the deepest levels, and good and evil must ultimately be reconciled within each of us. When I awakened fifteen years ago, I had visions of the end of the age—images of chaos and breakdown, confusion, sickness, famine, earth changes, and death. But I was given at the same time a deep abiding faith in transformational healing, a body-based belief in the potential of any body to spontaneously heal itself of the most outrageous illness and dis-ease. Like other healers and spiritual teachers of this period, I have been groomed to respond to something I cannot quite imagine—the potential extinction of my own species, along with the other life on the planet.

As a shamanic healer of cancer patients and other terminally ill people, I have come to respect the body's deep intelligence and its natural ability to rid itself of invading illnesses, realigning the cells to work properly (for no apparent reason). I have witnessed brain tumors shrinking to nothing after simply being exposed to sacred drumming, chanting, and hands-on healing. In our groups we never attack the cancer cells or try to kill the illness itself; rather, we attempt to awaken and catalyze the healthy cells to hum together in harmony. It is this group humming that seems to heal the organism by overpowering the disease with love and vibration.

If I have any hope for us as a species on this planet, it is for this spontaneous awakening and humming together. As cells in the body of the Mother, we have the potential to respond to her call, to allow her healing vibrations to flow through us and transform us, and to both witness and midwife the expulsion of this five-thousand-year-old virus from our collective body. If we do not do this, the body may die. But then, the enduring mystery of the twenty-five-thousand-year-old Goddess religion is that of death and rebirth, cyclic regeneration, and the unalterable fact that nothing dies without returning as something else.

The so-called 'population problem' looks more like a curtain call to me—kind of a command performance at the end of the millennium. I think all the souls are in, all of us having been called back into bodies, so that we might be present and accountable at this time of reckoning. In chaos theory, when a system breaks down (the way ours is clearly doing at the end of this age), there are opportunities for something that has been peripheral (such as earth-based consciousness, for example) to become a new "nucleus" of a new system. Like Riane Eisler suggested in *The Chalice and the Blade*, I am praying that those of us who love the Earth are magnetic enough to bond together and form the new nucleus of a system being birthed right now in these times of death and destruction. If that is true, then all the work we have done to make a personal shift to healthy, earth-based ways of living on the planet will have prepared us for this healing time. And if our species instead becomes extinct, then we will experience the ripening of our understanding that all things change from one form to another, and still the circle of life cannot be broken.

78

DEENA METZGER

Deena Metzger is a writer and healer living in Topanga, California. Her latest books include *Writing For Your Life: A Guide and Companion to the Inner Worlds*, *A Sabbath Among the Ruins*, *What Dinah Thought*, *The Woman Who Slept With Men to Take the War Out of Them*, and *Tree*.

Rebuilding Our Lives with Sanity

If I were to speak in the language of discourse, I would speak about the way our lives are governed by the demon of increase and how our lives and therefore our souls are devoured by the demand and the need to be known, to be seen, to respond to everything, to have more, to be more, to use more.

Working with people who are ill, I have learned that we cannot heal the body or the mind without healing the life first, that health exists in a context and the context is what is ailing. Therefore, when trying to heal, it is essential to find single gestures that are healing or sustaining for us as individuals and also simultaneously for the body politic and the planet as well. When we speak about illness, we must see how that illness we are carrying is also expressed in the community and on the earth—the cancer in us, for example, which devours our body and which is manifested as imperialism in the body politic and as commercial exploitation of the forests or minerals, let's say, can be approached with single actions that undermine *all* aspects of pernicious and maniacal growth. The way viruses alter our DNA and make us ill is not dissimilar from the way fascism alters our minds or science has determined to alter the genetic codes. The viruses are, therefore, the mirrors of our behavior, messengers rather than enemies. These states are reflections of each other, they are the causes and the conditions of the suffering we have created. Restoring health requires nothing less than fully dismantling our lives and rebuilding them with sanity, awe, and passion for the life force.

79

DEBORAH GOLEMAN WOLF

Deborah Goleman Wolf, Ph.D., was trained as a folklorist/anthro-
pologist and integrative therapist. She is in private practice in New York
City, trains and supervises peer counselors at the Manhattan Center for
Living, and is on the board of the New York Open Center.

Psychotherapy as Sacred Art

As we approach the millennium from this beautiful, tender, fragile, magnificent place that is our home, we see various themes of our time emerging. These are an awareness of the interconnectedness of individual people, of communities, of species, and a growing sense of responsibility for life.

Recently there has been an explosion of knowledge from esoteric traditions that has never before been available so widely to the uninitiated. Age-old prophecies have decreed that the time to reveal these teachings is now. It is no accident, I believe. Anyone who is drawn to them has access, for example, to Native American ritual, esoteric mystical traditions of the East and West, sacred practices that lead to the contacting of a higher wisdom. It seems to be part of the evolution of the species at a time of need, when the Earth is in danger of terminal pollution and deep fragmentation among her inhabitants.

I see the last half of the twentieth century as a time when Spirit and spiritual practices are coming out of the closet as reverence and responsibility are coming back into our lives. With the growing awareness of a mind-body-spirit interconnectedness, it is clear that a healthy body and an enriched mind are not enough. There is an imperative to connect deeply with a higher Power, with new kinds of family of choice, with one's self in a deeply spiritual way.

This interconnectedness recasts ancient traditions in new contexts. In healing, for instance, we use shamanistic drumming to work with the dying; therapeutic touch, a modern form of laying on of hands, to help premature babies gain weight. Meditation and support groups, a modern form of community, have been shown to help heart and cancer patients. For many of us the epidemic of AIDS and other life-challenging illnesses has meant that we look to ancient forms of healing coupled with the latest medical discoveries to uncover the most effective treatment for our clients.

As many practitioners and clients have their own spiritual practice, we are finding that the nature of psychotherapy is changing radically. The office can become a sacred space with a mixture of client-centered therapy, ritual, the use of myth and archetype, visualization, and imagery to connect the client to a deeper personal truth, and the use of the nonverbal to anchor insight deeply in the psyche, the awareness of spirit and soul—all have become part of the vocabulary and tools of the therapeutic process.

And there has been a shift in the American *Zeitgeist*, as well. From a self-directed frenzy of consumerism and reckless devouring of natural resources and throwaway relationships, we see a new imperative to connect, to find a deeper purpose in life.

As we move into the new millennium, the still small voice is becoming a mighty roar. We have more dedication, better tools, a deeper sense of how little time may be left and how to use it fully as we lurch toward yet another level in evolution—where we will achieve a true awareness of interconnectedness, responsibility, and reverence. Where we can each make a commitment to become more spacious, more compassionate, to "know," as the poet Joy Harjo writes in "Eagle Poem," "that we must take the utmost care and kindness in all things."

80

ANNE WILSON SCHAEF

Anne Wilson Schaef, Ph.D., a former psychotherapist, is the originator of the healing work of Living in Process. She is also a lecturer, organizational consultant, and workshop leader and is the author of *Women's Reality, Co-Dependence, When Society Becomes An Addict, The Addictive Organization,* and *Beyond Therapy / Beyond Science.*

We Must Be the Whole

What a challenge to put down my "personal hopes and fears about the future!"

I have long since said that the society in which we live (Western culture, to be specific) is an addictive society and functions exactly like an active addict. One of my fears stems from knowing that an addict, in order to recover, often has to "hit bottom," and I shudder as to what this means for an entire planet. Yet, I see that happening.

Several years ago, people in workshops that I do around the world began to remember early incest memories. Initially, I was shocked and astounded by the number of people who had been sexually abused as infants and children. Still, their body memories were impressive, and I believed them and knew that whatever memories they were recovering were important. I was also astounded that this was not just happening in the United States. It was happening all over the planet.

Now, I see the same phenomenon occurring with respect to ritual cult abuse. People, planet-wide, are recovering memories of hideous torture and programming, most of which have taken place in our most revered institutions. Can we, indeed, be hitting bottom?

We have developed a science that has become a religion and a religion that is enmeshed in a mechanistic science, neither of which search for truth or healing. Our sacred and secular institutions have become more interested in self-preservation than in meeting the needs of the planet. We pollute our air, destroy our environment, hoard our resources, and live out of a drunken self-centeredness.

As I travel around the world meeting with tribal and aboriginal elders, and as I meet with persons on the cutting edge of a new scientific paradigm, I see much hope. Although Western science and culture are systematically trying to destroy native people and native wisdom, a new force is rising.

Mechanistic science has reached the end of its path as a worldview, and we are beginning to see the wisdom and sophistication in tribal knowledge. We are beginning to listen to our elders. Our science has come full circle and is now evolving from and recognizing the whole and that we all must relate to and participate in the whole. We must *be* the whole. We must become ourselves in community. None of this evolution is possible without our recognition of and participation in our spirituality. We *are* spiritual beings. We are not necessarily religious beings.

I shudder at how far an addict has to push her/himself, at times, before seeking recovery. I hope this human experiment does not have to hit a bottom that leaves us no options.

It is time for truth speakers. "You shall know the truth and the truth shall make you free." We need to see what we see, know what we know, and be willing to speak out for what is important to us.

81

JAMES CLARKSON

Jim Clarkson is an addiction counselor and Focusing facilitator with
the Institute for Bio-Spiritual Research. He is currently completing
graduate studies at The Institute of Culture and Creation Spirituality
at Holy Names College in Oakland, California.

Threads of Compassion, Circles of Healing

I write in gratitude for the doors opening as we approach the
twenty-first century. There is a saying, ''There's nothing more practical than a good theory.'' There are many of us, young and old alike,
who are riding the crest of a vast wave—a paradigm shift that is making valuable old ideals and theories useful, concrete realities. This wave
is a wave of trust and compassion. We are beginning to trust that the
universe, and within it the human organism, is unfolding into an ele-
gant tapestry of wholeness and goodness, and it is the magic of radical
compassion that appears to be the nutritious soil in which this unfolding takes place. Cosmologist Brian Swimme suggests what mystics
have known throughout the centuries, that perhaps compassion has
been woven into the very fabric of the universe from the very beginning. Although this cannot be proven, data tells us that if the original
''flaring forth'' of the universe had happened a millisecond faster than
it actually did, or a fraction slower, Earth, nor any of its splendid
millions of species, would not have existed at all. It was as if the universe conspired to create each one of us. Yet, in this technocratic era
of control, dominance, and addiction, many often find themselves

divorced from an awareness of compassion, and, being out of control on the inside, seek greater control and dominance of others and the planet.

In working with young people, I see firsthand the consequences of an addictive controlling society. Levels of sexual abuse, trauma, and addiction are stunningly high. Like many in the counseling field, I have had to struggle with finding a practical method to reintroduce these young people to a compassionate experience of themselves and others who are safe. Monarchal, second-hand theology and morality would not work. Intrusive, dominating psychology served only to drive their trauma deeper behind more elaborate masks. I discovered in the work of Fathers Ed McMahon and Peter Campbell a way that seemed to allow young people to tap into the wisdom of their own bodies. It was a radical shift, trusting that there was indeed compassion woven into the very fabric of their bodies and that following the signals from their body would begin the process of moving toward wholeness.

So much of what passes as education these days is what Alice Miller refers to as "poisonous pedagogy"—any experience that teaches mistrust or devalues one's own inner feelings and perceptions. The process that Ed McMahon and Peter Campbell teach is a version of the Focusing process pioneered by Eugene Gendlin. It is the antithesis of "poisonous pedagogy" and a "vaccine" against addiction. It is by no means a "loving away" of the young person's pain or trauma. It instead teaches the young person to sit with whatever is real in their bodies in a compassionate way. It does, concretely, tap into the compassion woven into the fabric of the universe. When these painful places begin to feel compassion, they begin to unfold—to tell their story. What greater gift can we give our young than a way of being present to what is real in their bodies, to the wisdom woven in every cell, in a caring way!

There is great hope for adults and children alike who can gather in communities and share what is most real, in their bodies, with each other. When groups can do that there seems to unfold a powerful, numinous quality. This, I believe, is a body-feel of being an open instrument of a higher Power, a voice of the Cosmos, if you will.

Recently a Native American teacher was giving a workshop I attended. One of the comments she made, jokingly, as she tried in vain to have the mostly white audience circle up their chairs, was "I can always tell when I'm with the Anglos. They just can't get into a real circle. They always make an egg." I thought about the literally thousands of circles I have sat in over the past eight years. Circles of healing. Circle of trust. Circles of honesty. Each day and night across the globe, perhaps a million people or more gather quietly in the churches, libraries, and back rooms of halls. They come together seeking healing, knowing that healing will come if they can speak their own truth. They come knowing that only a Power greater than themselves can lead them to wholeness and that this power will manifest at the moment they can share their own truth. These meetings, pioneered by Alcoholics Anonymous, are truly leaderless. The leadership is shared—they say their leaders are but trusted servants. It is possible for societies to grow in an organic, nondominative way. Right here, at the end of the second millennium, it is happening! It seems the Native Americans, much more aware of the connectedness and innate goodness of all creation, were comfortable in circles where all life was seen as an expression of the Divine. Perhaps now, as we become aware of the truth and wisdom contained in our bodies, we too will become more comfortable in circles, rather than hierarchies.

It is no surprise that out of the soil of compassion comes creation. Otto Rank, who was sexually molested as a child once remarked, "I must create every day or commit suicide." Focusing and Twelve-Step groups are but two "laboratories" in which the new cosmology of compassion and trust can be experienced. It is my deepest hope that with the turn of the century each person can become his or her own artist—riding; high the freeing wind of compassion and unleashing the wonderful creative energy of the universe!

82
ANN MARIE BUYS WYRSCH

Ann Marie Buys Wyrsch is a certified clinical specialist in mental health nursing who has facilitated co-dependence recovery since 1986. She is the coauthor of a chapter entitled "Spiritual and Religious Dimensions of Psychiatric Mental Health Nursing" in the fourth edition of *Psychiatric Nursing in the Hospital and the Community,* edited by Ann Wolbert Burgess.

Discovering and Recovering

My vision of the future is of a world where each of us lives congruently with our inner and outer reality. It is a world where individuals surrender to the source of enlightenment and empowerment within, which I call God, or our Source of Life. It is a world where persons continue to live consciously and freely, growing in a truthful relationship with self, others, the world around one, and God.

In this world, we can live in mutual vulnerability, sharing our journey at a deep and personal level, and truly caring about and for ourselves and each other on this planet. We will actively use our spiritual power to make choices and accept the responsibility for these choices. We will own our human limitations and no longer need to deny them in a way that leads us to attempt to control and dominate ourselves or others.

Living congruently with our inner and outer reality presupposes what I have come to call "original birthrights." These birthrights include our physical, emotional, mental, spiritual, and social dimensions. They are:

I have a right to be, to recognize my body's needs and
    to be able to meet them.
I have a right to be fully human, to feel bodily all my
    feelings and to respect and listen to them, and to
    learn to recover from emotional trauma.
I have a right to choose my beliefs and to change them.
I have a right to connect with my source of life within
    and accept my personal power to co-create my life
    with that source.
I have a right to boundaries that enable me to achieve
    healthy interdependence, and to learn skills to
    relate to others in a way that is healthy for me
    and for them.

Evidence of the consequences of not experiencing these rights are manifest in the addictive process that is so prevalent in our culture. The addictive process cuts us off from our inner and outer reality. We learn to look only to the outside for the meaning of our experience, rather than how to allow that meaning to unfold from within. We very early learn to deny our anxiety, how to ignore body signals and emotions, and how to use a behavior that brings relief without awareness. We thus live on automatic pilot, repeating familiar patterns over and over, yet expecting different emotions. We become masters of denial and control.

Fear is what keeps us in denial and in need of controlling. For the past ten years, I have had cause for hope that the paradox of surrendering to a power greater than ourselves, while owning our personal power and responsibility, is realistic and achievable.

One reason for this hope is witnessing persons moving beyond pervasive denial to become aware of their birthrights and discovering life can be lived more fully within our human limitations. Because of the fear that locks in the pervasive denial, this awareness is initially achieved best in a gentle way. Individuals sharing their story of growth awaken possibilities that were hitherto unknown. Rather than more controlling, a vulnerable sharing of how life was, what happened to change it, and how it has become has planted seeds of awareness.

An even more compelling reason for hope is persons acting on that awareness and acquiring remedial skills to move toward experiencing those rights. A key to recovering is to develop congruence. A process called Focusing facilitates this congruence. Focusing is about learning to notice, owning the body-feel of what is real, and holding it in a caring nonfixing way so that Grace can move it forward. Gradually it is possible to more and more surrender to and follow an inner source of enlightenment and empowerment.

I believe all those who aspire to do so can claim or reclaim "original birthrights." These birthrights are basic to experiencing "life to the full." Focusing, in conjunction with other experiential learning, fosters growth in connectedness with our humanity, and paradoxically at the same time, with our true spirituality. We learn to take "safe risks" to experiment with new ways of being. What follows is a healing spiral of ongoing discovery and recovery. The best is yet to come!

THE NEW MORALITY

83

PETER SINGER

Peter Singer, Ph.D., is best known as the author of *Animal Liberation*, sometimes described as "the bible of the animal liberation movement." He has written several other books, including *Practical Ethics* and *The Expanding Circle*. He teaches at the Centre for Human Bioethics at Monash University in Melbourne, Australia.

Beyond Traditional Religion

When we mark the end of the second millennium, we use a system of dating that takes the alleged date of the birth of Jesus of Nazareth as the beginning of the modern era. There is, therefore, a certain irony in the hope that I now express: that the coming "third millennium" will be the millennium in which we remove the hold that religion has had, for most of the first two millennia, over our thoughts and ideas. I voice this hope because I believe that religion, and particularly the now-dominant religion of the West, has reinforced our tendency to think of the planet as "man's dominion," and of all things as existing to serve our interests. Without it, we can all hope for a better future.

Some fear the decline of religion and of traditional ways of thinking. They worry about human arrogance, about our control over nature, and our coming ability even to shape our own nature by intervening in our genetic inheritance. We are an arrogant and dangerous species, and we have, up to now, always put our own interests ahead of those of other species, or even of future generations of our own species. Yet I see no hope of salvation, whether on Earth or anywhere else, in a return to the closed-mindedness of traditional religions.

We need to develop a wider ethic that goes beyond the bounds of our own species. This is a large step forward, one that can only be compared in its scope with the step that was taken, over the last two hundred years, to abolish slavery and include all human beings within the bounds of equality. Yet it is possible. Free and secular thinking about ethics is still relatively new. I hope that the next millennium will begin by extending equal consideration of interests to all sentient beings.

84
DAVID LOYE

David Loye, Ph.D., is a social psychologist, futurist, systems theorist, and the developer of a new theory of moral sensitivity. A former member of the psychology faculty of Princeton University and former professor at the UCLA School of Medicine, he is a founder-member of the General Evolution Research Group and is codirector with Riane Eisler of the Center for Partnership Studies in Pacific Grove, California. He is the author of several books, including *The Healing of a Nation, The Leadership Passion, The Knowable Future,* and *The Sphinx and the Rainbow.*

Moral Sense and the Partnership Vision

For a decade, driven by increasing evidence of the moral senselessness of our time and the disastrous co-option of the stance and language of morality by rightist fundamentalists, I have been completely reevaluating the nature, origins, present condition, and future prospects for what historically has been called the moral sense, or the drive for goodness in humans.

Most people concerned with this drive for goodness who are acquainted with social science are aware of the work of Lawrence Kohlberg and Carol Gilligan in psychology, Robert Bellah in sociology, or Robert Coles in psychiatry. What is not generally realized is that within science as a whole, work of this type is still seen as little more than an insignificant blip along the far edge of the screen.

In other words, here we live in a time when thousands of scientists as well as possibly millions of the rest of us fear that we may be headed toward extinction of our species. Yet the exploration of the nature of morality—that is, into the nature of what, against all the odds, drives our species to care for others and to care for our environment—is very, very low on the list of either our scientific or our social priorities. But at the same time there is this paradox: Within the range of science as a whole, almost wholly unknown even to the scientists themselves, lies a vast storehouse of precisely the kind of information about this drive toward goodness that we badly need to understand and put to use at a time of critical evolutionary challenge.

It is this much larger body of work that I have drawn on in my research—in addition to the fields of psychology, sociology, and psychotherapy, I have drawn on anthropology, archeology, history, systems science, brain research, and moral, feminist, racial, gender, spirituality, and evolutionary studies.

Moral sense, long shattered, lies scattered in fragments in all of these fields. A primary purpose of what is becoming a series of books I am writing on my findings is to gather in these fragments and see where and how they fit together. In this way we can build the new science of moral sensitivity—as well as develop moral *sensitizing* as a new therapy and course of learning—which is needed if we are to understand not only what moral sense is and where it comes from but also where it seems to be trying to take us and of how we may get there.

It is a central finding for this work that morally we have reached what is known—in terms of new evolutionary theories—as a bifurcation point. We have reached what is, in effect, an evolutionary door in time. Prior to this point we have been mired in the state of moral senselessness exemplified by all the personal, political, economic, and spiritual imbalances, disorganizations, dysfunctions, and ultimately insanities of our history and our present time. In effect a blocked-up backwater in evolution, this state is what I term the pre-door or "old" consciousness. But now, if we will make use of a three-hundred-year investment in the massively neglected and often suppressed aspect of science my research has uncovered, it is within our power to use moral sense to attain a new state of greater personal, social, and spiritual balance, organization, and sanity.

Among many forces driving us through trans-door or a transitional consciousness toward the post-door or "new" consciousness are the four I primarily focus on—which also seem to foreshadow the nature of the "new" consciousness lying beyond this evolutionary door in time.

First is the evolutionary drive of an innate tendency toward goodness in human beings. Long disputed by innate evilists in regressive Christianity and by moral neutralists in science, I have uncovered in evolutionary studies, brain research, and psychology what seems to me strong proof of goodness as an embedded drive.

Second is the global transformation in gender relations whereby, in Riane Eisler's terms, we are moving from an "androcratic" or "dominator" mode to a "gylanic" or "partnership" mode and ethos, such as prevailed in an earlier time in our cultural evolution. In line with this new evolutionary theory, I develop the case for "three worlds" of morality. There are the "two worlds" detected by Jean Piaget—as well as by Immanuel Kant, Marx, Engels, Freud, and a surprising number of other founders of modern social science: one a dominator moral insensitivity and morality, the other a partnership moral sensitivity and morality. The third "world" of morality, which becomes evident once one grasps the nature of the basic two, is the misleading, hypocritical, and indeed literally crazy-making hybrid of the basic two that has been passed off on us for centuries as the one and only morality—which underlies and has been used to perpetuate the moral senselessness of our time.

Third among the forces driving us toward a "partnership future" is the thrust of the drive toward freedom and equality. Given many different names at levels of science ranging from the molecular to the social, this I find to be the elemental thrust to moral sensitivity itself.

Last is the awareness—globally spreading since the explosion of the first atomic bombs in Hiroshima and Nagasaki—that unless we change our attitudes toward one another and toward the environment we face species' extinction.

Based on the findings of this research, and the writing of these books, here is where I would venture we are headed.

Basically, the "new" consciousness that can shape the world of the future looks like much the kind of consciousness that existed in the earlier goddess-worshiping culture. Emerging from the works of Eisler and archeologist Marija Gimbutas, James Mellaart, and Nicholas Platon is a picture of an unusual state of gender equality, peace, high creativity, and a general sharing of the wealth with the many rather than a hoarding of the wealth by the few. The chief difference between this deep past for humanity (circa 10,000-1500 B.C.) and our likely future will be the vast upgrading of our lives through the new power for liberation of the mind and heart and soul that nondestructive technology can provide. Even more important will be a mind filled with this incredibly hard-won new knowledge of how precious is this new life we are attaining—and how critical it is to prevent any chance of its loss again.

The specifics, I believe, will mainly derive from an updating of the moral characteristics that differentiate the earlier time from this hard time we have known and at last now have the capacity to put behind us:

- a world, once again, peaceful beyond our present capacity for belief;
- a new feeling for art as an expansion and liberation of life rather than as commercial fraud;
- the celebration of diversity that more and more I realize is the underlying key to it all;
- the reverence for life we have lost but through the impact of the environmental movement are now swiftly regaining;
- the feeling of responsibility for ourselves and for the welfare of others that we have lost but can regain;
- an abundant wealth widely shared;
- the Earth imaged as our home;
- sex as mutual pleasure, rather than as socialized sado-masochism;
- men and women, while obviously different in sexual characteristics, seen as remarkably similar in other qualities;
- empathic freedom as a realizable goal;
- equality as the recognition of the vital bond of our linking of one to another and a realizable goal.

It will be a time, in short, when people who want all this for themselves, and their children—and for all the other people of this Earth—no longer have to feel like lost and hunted creatures dropped off by mistake on an alien planet.

85

ROBERT BRIGGS

Robert Briggs attended Auburn and Columbia Universities and served in the Korean War. Before launching Robert Briggs Associates in 1972, he was a bookseller in New York and San Francisco and cofounder of the San Francisco Book Company. He is the author of *The American Emergency: A Search for Spiritual Renewal in an Age of Materialism.*

A New Basis for Moral Life

Turning toward the twenty-first century, we find ourselves faced with a unique, American emergency symbolized in many ways by what might be labeled the successful failure of the New Age promise. At the same time that we have benefited from the evolution of new psychotherapies, holistic medicine, East-West spiritual exchange, and a broader understanding of the philosophical implications of "new" science (ironically, introduced in 1905), we discover we were fleeced by a host of movie-starred gurus, a string of questionable crystal and lotion merchants, and a glut of counterfeit notions.

Now we are all faced with the mandate to "make a difference," not only in our own lives and communities but on the planet as well. In the midst of grave economic and ecological crises, we realize that we must turn away from the isolation of individualistic separation toward a more humane integration with people and places previously beyond our perspective.

We will be unable to assess the degree to which the future has been clouded by cultural hubris until we begin to deal with the uncertainty in both our lives and science. In order to cope with the confusion such a climate creates, we must further public understanding of the principles of awareness and consciousness. Above all, we must reaffirm the psychological and spiritual advantages of the *idea* of reincarnation.

> Twentieth-century problems
> are more understandable,
> but unimaginable.

Dismayed by an inequitable distribution of wealth, we have begun to suffer from the stress of shrinking income, debt, overwork, inequitable tax burdens, cancerous costs of living, and a monstrous federal deficit.

Indeed, it sometimes feels as if the sky *is* falling! There are mornings when stress seems to seep into meditation, afternoons when we can almost feel ozone warnings or smell the ravage of acid rain, and evenings when the shadows of the homeless and hungry are melancholy reminders that in a true democracy, the destitution of anyone denigrates the well-being of everyone.

Throughout the world, communities are freaked by racial and religious prejudice and rising crime, and neither neighborhood nor national governments can begin to provide adequate law enforcement. There are not enough prisons in which to incarcerate the intolerable.

Contributing to the social meltdown is the fact that two of the most important social stabilizers, education and healthcare, are in alarming disarray. Costs have risen to dizzying heights, with little relief in sight. Across America education and healthcare are being rationed —to those who can pay for it.

> Obviously,
> such absurdity
> cannot be tolerated.

Though no one denies that the guarantee of a technological future is fatally flawed, some are beginning to suspect that "crisis" itself is often nothing more than planned political impotence designed to disguise the cost of yet another political failure.

> Others fear
> that trust
> is a ruptured ideal.

We must acknowledge the fact that, despite all that was useful in New

Age influence, the need for change is still momentous. In order to rupture the stasis of the twentieth century and face the uncertainty of the twenty-first, individuals must forge a greater commitment to global consciousness.

Far more people need to be made aware of ways that greater consciousness can be achieved through the unification of daily exercise, lifetime diet and meditation, continual revision of lifestyle, and consideration of the implications of reincarnation.

Until we do, it will be impossible to see that the limitations of traditional ethics can be revised through a new understanding of the human condition: that wellness, not medicine, is the best antidote to disease; that deeper appreciation of the spiritual mystery can be enriched by a sympathetic view of other religions; and that our endangered planet can be saved only through respect for the importance of forms of life previously sacrificed to progress, or profit.

Reincarnation provides that shock of recognition that magnifies perspective and shrinks the urgency of the life we are living. The realization of reincarnation allows us to see the mystery of birth and death differently. It makes more plausible the belief shared by two-thirds of the world's population that birth and death are but recurring episodes in the journey of the soul.

The freedom to grow and change and the independence to explore our minds, bodies, and the environment we inhabit are part of this primeval inheritance. But rather than augmenting our awareness of these "life rights," the socialization process dulls our consciousness and replaces natural intuition with "conventional wisdom."

An acknowledgment of reincarnation can lead us back to a reality bathed in instinct—that "child's garden of consciousness" where the first moments and months of life are filled with awe, and only love, warmth, food, sight, and sound mattered. Then, it was natural to believe that the world was a place in which

> the beauty of a weed equaled
> the majesty of sky
> and cats and elephants were
> brothers and sisters.

If, in our informative years, these instincts had been nurtured, the rights of life would have been obvious, and it would have been simple to see that time and space were artificial constraints.

We might have been spared old confusions and freed from that peculiar feeling that decades later caused us to pause on a street corner, or in any empty room, where we suddenly realize that something was missing from all we had experienced.

Life rights affirm one's faith to weather the tyranny of time and intransigence. They inspire recognition of the life-and-death cycle and create a locus at which personal transformation begins.

As we approach the twenty-first century, we must deny the domination of scientific determinism. Only then will we truly understand that

> Gaia or Ourantos
> were not created
> by the Big Bang.

Only then will we see that we are born to grow, age, and connect the death we die with other lives we are to lead.

Only then can the power of aging be realized, the "denial of death" be denied, and the second half of life be incorporated into the rhythm of existence.

Only then can we know why D. H. Lawrence said the young were always "half-hearted," and why he felt "one has to be seventy before one is full of courage."

86

RICHARD RYDER

Richard Ryder worked for many years as a clinical psychologist in Oxford where he was part of the pioneering "Oxford Group," which began the modern revival of intellectual interest in animal rights. In 1970 he coined the term "speciesism," which has earned a niche in the great philosophical debate of recent years. He is the author of *Victims of Science* and *Animal Revolution* and the editor of *Animal Rights—A Symposium* and *Animal Welfare and the Environment*.

Painism: A New Morality

My consciousness is my universe, and my universe is my consciousness. Consciousness, in this sense, is everything. Yet consciousness is so fragile: a blow on the head, a deep sleep, death—and it is gone. Consciousness is the great mystery that still defies explanation. Somehow it emerges from our brains. Perhaps it is no more extraordinary than the images that emerge from a television set. It is merely one of the many *emergent* phenomena we encounter—so different in quality from its constituents. Like electricity. Who could have explained five hundred years ago how something so potent, dangerous, and unseen could emerge from copper wires rotated within a magnetized lump of iron? Electricity is so entirely *different* in quality from its material basis. So also with consciousness.

Consciousness plays a central role in quantum theory. In the dream world of quantum reality, it is said that observation (or measurement) itself affects events. Does observation have to be conscious to have such effects? Will the consciousness of a cat serve as well as that of a human? Can an ant serve as an observer? Can a machine? Before consciousness evolved in complex organisms, how did quantum events occur? If consciousness is such an integral part of physics, then are we not in some sort of huge loop? A loop driven into a spiral by time—spirals within spirals?

The idea, common among quantum physicists, that one event A can cause another event B *instantaneously* in a distant part of the universe, or even *before* A occurs, becomes less weird if you think of our universe as all one system, as small to some outside observer as an atomic nucleus appears to us. We think it is odd, but not *so* odd, that events within a nucleus can occur synchronistically. We say it is one system.

So why not regard the universe as one system within which events can occur synchronistically without involving mechanical cause and effect? What appears to us to be one complex small-scale event may seem to a microbe to be separate events mysteriously acting on each other at a great distance. So much seems to depend upon sheer scale.

Perhaps quantum mechanics will help us explain consciousness. Free will—or the impression of free will—seems to be one of the primary ingredients of our consciousness. Yet subatomic particles can appear to have free will, too. So also can "self-organizing systems." Are they also conscious? Is everything, to a greater or lesser degree, conscious? Yet, unlike some quantum events, consciousness is firmly anchored in time and space. I cannot transfer my consciousness to you or to anything else; it is rooted in *my* brain. It is also rooted in "the present"; consciousness is the slave of time. Again we are faced with the marked limitations of consciousness—it seems to have feet of clay.

Another common feature of consciousness is that every experience is either painful or pleasant. It is never neutral. Like positive and negative in electromagnetism, and like approach and avoidance, conscious events are either nice or nasty. Consciousness reflects the great dichotomy in life between good and bad.

This is where morality comes in, too. Morality is a program we need psychologically. It tells us how to act and which decisions to make, but only insofar as our actions *affect others*. (The motivation of our behavior, as far as it affects only ourselves, is easy: We simply seek pleasure and avoid pain.) But when we realize that our behavior also causes pain or pleasure to *others*, then we have to engage morality.

I do not believe that the pains and pleasures of one individual are justified by the pains and pleasures of others. This is the problem with utilitarianism. The sadists' or rapists' pleasures may be said to justify the sufferings of their victim. This must be wrong. For me, the individual is paramount because consciousness, in particular the consciousness of pain and distress, is not transferable from one individual to others.

Morality should be based upon *painance*—the capacity of individuals to suffer pain. (By *pain* I mean *all* negative experiences—thoughts, sensations, moods, emotions, or perceptions.) All painients should be embraced equally by our morality; that is to say, *x* amount of pain in a rat is just as important morally as is *x* amount of pain in an elephant or *x* amount of pain in a human.

We must chuck out racism, sexism, ageism, and speciesism: The size, color, sex, or furriness of others is morally irrelevant. When purple aliens land on Earth and take us away to experiment on us they may say, "We don't hate you—indeed some of us keep humans as pets. We have discovered that you taste quite nice, however, and we are going to develop you commercially as a food source for our people. This will require some scientific experiments. We will not make these any more painful than necessary. Immoral? No, of course not. The advancement of scientific knowledge is a noble idea and we all have our careers to think of. Besides, none of you are purple."

Pain is pain regardless of who or what experiences it. The circle of our compassion, and of our painist morality, must include all painient beings—human and nonhuman, natural and artificial, terrestrial and alien.

87

CATHERINE ROBERTS

Catherine Roberts, Ph.D., is the author of *The Scientific Conscience* and *Science, Animals, and Evolution,* as well as numerous essays, articles, and reviews concerning the ethics of bioscientific advance from a spiritual and evolutionary perspective. With her death in April 1993, the animal rights movement has lost one of its most spiritually oriented and passionate spokespersons.

Human Freedom and the New Era

The imminence of the third millennium is causing Christians and non-Christians alike to speculate on what entry into this new era will mean for humankind and on what has defined and sustained us until now and whether it will be humanly adequate in the time to come.

Our current focus on secular freedom is a recent phenomenon. Before the rise of Western science, people were predominantly religious beings whose diverse faiths in the dominion of higher sacred powers sustained their daily lives, stimulated their intellectual and creative accomplishments, and helped curb their baser instincts. Although a common goal of world religions is to facilitate humankind's moral enlightenment, religious insight and exhortation have never made civilized humanity wholly ethical. Individual theocentric belief can be associated with great nobility of character and heartfelt compassion but also with profound injustice and appalling acts of cruelty, cowardice, and deceit. Civilized societies which profess religious faiths have, in fact, often been responsible for massive suffering, death, and devastation. Their limited success in improving ethical conduct was not, however, the prime reason for the weakening of religious authority. Their decline was largely due to the global advance of Western science and the growing perception that scientific knowledge is somehow more interesting and valid than spiritual wisdom. On the eve of the third millennium, the world seems to be on the threshold of a new spiritual awakening, yet still functions through a predominantly secular/scientific focus and its highly prized freedom and religious restraint.

Secularism, having dismissed as spurious religion's claim that objective, absolute standards of morality exist, has fostered a permissive civilization where the individual conscience is seen as the free and final arbiter in ethical matters. Yet the cumulative wrongdoing of the twentieth century reveals that so far as ethical conduct goes, people have not profited from their secular deflection from the sacred. With or without religion, we seem unable to become morally better human beings. So we often define our nature as a permanent mix of good and evil that will sustain us forever because, in this respect, we can never be substantially different from what we have been and now are. And we tend to emphasize the development of mind more than morals in a secular vision of open-ended evolution of men and women becoming increasingly free to direct their own future through ever-greater intellectual and creative achievements.

Any evolutionary vision reflects the mystery of the unknown, and no one can foresee the splendor of the human potential as it unfolds. Are we to become superintellectual creators and achievers free to avoid moral responsibility to secure our ends? Or are we to learn that conscience is not free at all but is rather a reverberation of a divine ethic to which we are forever bound? If the latter, then the unlocking of our higher potentials in science, art, and the humanities may depend on restraining our insatiable desire for evermore sweeping forward drives of human intellect largely dissociated from moral issues. The white-hot advance of the free inquiring mind that is responsible, for example, for rapid bioscientific breakthroughs may now appear both impossible and undesirable to curb. This is largely so because the advance of bioscience is still kept separate from spiritual truths as world religions accommodate themselves to unrestrained scientific advance even when it violates their basic concepts of right and wrong.

When a spiritual awakening emerges, as now, out of the omnipresent darkness of moral imperfection, religions may need to portray the human divine relation in terms of the evolution of universal moral enlightenment. In paradise the tree of knowledge was solely concerned with good and evil, and to taste of it was to become more godlike. We in the twentieth century certainly bear no resemblance to gods who can do no wrong, but spiritual wisdom perhaps more ancient than Biblical story is said to reveal that we are indeed to become more godlike because the whole of humankind is on an evolutionary pilgrimage back toward the spiritual Source of all things. When we perceive this Source as the transcendent Good, we will know that our further evolution depends upon fuller participation in earthly goodness. If every human being is destined to return to the Source, everyone has at his or her disposal a long succession of earthly lives whose trials and tribulations, successes, errors, and omissions all serve as necessary learning experiences in the understanding of virtue. Retaining its cumulative spiritual insight after the death of the body, the immortal part of each individual thus possesses at each incarnation increasing knowledge of the interaction of divine Good and earthly good—and all human endeavor gradually becomes limited and sustained by righteousness.

In this view it is an illusion to expect that the further realization of the human potential will mean increasing freedom from all restraint. Only in the short term do we have the freedom to be morally apathetic or ignorant and to conduct our lives accordingly, but as higher beings, such freedom will be denied us. In awareness thereof we have no choice but to try to conform in our successive lives to an evermore perfect alignment with the divine ethic. Spiritual determinism, interacting with absolute moral law, restricts our evolutionary freedom most mightily.

In this new era let us, then, rid ourselves of secular misconceptions about the increasingly free unfolding of the human potential, accept the spiritual inevitability of our moral self-transcendence, and redefine the human race as evolving beings slowly but surely becoming more godlike because of our sacred Source and the latent divinity within us.

88

ANDREW LINZEY

Reverend Andrew Linzey, Ph.D., is an International Fund for Animal Welfare senior research fellow of Mansfield College, Oxford, and also special professor of theology at the University of Nottingham. He has written or edited thirteen books on Christian ethics, including pioneering works on the moral status of animals. The latter include *Animal Rights: A Christian Assessment, Christianity and the Rights of Animals,* and *Animals and Christianity.*

Spiritual Openness Beyond Moralism

I remember when I was a student in London traveling every day into Westminster passing by the new huge buildings in Elephant and Castle. These buildings were vast, shiny, impressive edifices illustrative of a culture characterized by technological mastery. As I gazed up and down the latest new building, my eye caught sight of a homeless person who had squatted on the bright new steps leading to the entrance.

At that time I was struck by the utter contrast between technological accomplishment on the one hand and human squalor on the other. The scene has long remained in my mind as a foundational glimpse into the spiritual emptiness of technological society.

One response to this impoverishment is to moralize: to act, campaign, and protest against injustice—for the rights of the homeless, the rights of children, the rights of sexual minorities, and, not least of all, the rights of animals, who, like the rest, know only too well what it is like to be oppressed. In my lifetime I have done no little moralizing and my fair share of social activism.

But, looking back, I now see ever-more clearly that moralism is not enough. Of course we should do all in our power to influence, persuade, act—sometimes even heroically—for better world conditions. There is—at best—a camaraderie among those who protest that links them to wider goals and to a refreshed consciousness. But I do not think that social activism, however well-intentioned or expertly pursued, can by itself meet what is the most strikingly urgent need of our times, namely spiritual rebirth.

By "spiritual rebirth" I do not mean ecclesiastical allegiance, even less "born again" evangelicalism. The tragic truth is that Christian churches have become defective witnesses to the Spirit. Fundamentalism—especially in its idolatrous worship of the Bible—is arguably the most antispiritual force in the world today.

I mean by spiritual rebirth that openness to the Spirit that induces in us moments of sheer wonder, awe, joy, and celebration of the life of creation around us. These moments—and many others—enable us not just to become better human beings but to become human. True "in-spiration" of this sort leads to all kinds of creativity—in art, literature, poetry, drama—to an expansion of ourselves beyond hitherto determined limits—and, most of all, to the discovery of goodness and moral sensitivity. The Spirit is always available to us but never of our invention.

I do not think there are any shortcuts to spiritual renewal: no programs, no timetables, no chronology. Human history is certainly not a linear movement toward moral progress. In many ways, for example, we might hope for the moral heroism of long-lost Greek civilization. This makes being hopeful for tomorrow problematic. Despite all the energy invested in expectation of a better world, only our openness to the transcendent Spirit can fundamentally transform us. Whether humanity can become anything like human is the perennial question that lies before us—especially as we approach the end of the second millennium.

89
FRANK H. MEYER

Frank H. Meyer is a research physicist and emeritus professor of physics, University of Wisconsin System, Superior. He is a board member of the International Society of Unified Science (ISUS, Inc.) and editor of its journal, *Reciprocity*.

Ultimate Human Worth

For many generations humankind, with numerous other living creatures, has inhabited Earth, third planet of our Sun.

Generations from now, humankind, a most unusual whole, as I see us, will outlast Earth. The great longevity of our planet apparently is finite. Who knows when, if ever, humankind must or will end? Who knows when, where, how this most ornery living species now on Earth began? The human species will not be put off the Earth, as the dinosaurs are reputed to have been. Rather we shall stay and advance by becoming ethically better united among ourselves, toward the living world and with the physical world.

In the summer of 1992 I became seventy-seven years young. For over half a century I have been a theorizing and practicing physicist in industry, medicine, and education. When beginning my education, I was taught and postulated that humankind as a whole is a small, incidental, even accidental and unessential component of the physical universe. I took the finite physical world to be the whole of Nature and/or natural existence. This now is questionable science.

Now approaching the end of my life, I infer from abundantly accumulating evidence that the opposite is more likely to be true: that the finite physical world, the universe of motion or space-time, enormous in size and dimensions though it be, is just a small but essential component of the human universe, a whole of ultimate *infinite* human worth.

What makes the human universe an infinite whole is a *non-physical* sector of natural existence, believably inhabited by humankind exclusive of most, if not all, other living organisms of Earth. This nonphysical sector is not simply or readily visible, audible, or tangible. It includes numbers and the meanings of words, but not numerals or words themselves. Humankind as a whole can and does learn about the being of our nonphysical sector of existence by virtue of our native ability to create and reproduce adequate *physical* entities to represent nonphysical entities essential to our well-being: numbers by numerals, meanings by words.

Humankind as a whole and as its proper parts, the private woman and the private man, can and do participate in the infinitude of ultimate human worth *only* by way of our inhabiting the nonphysical sector or realm of the human universe. This is the realm of meanings, including discourse, number, arithmetic, human values, truth, beauty, humor, science, art, philosophy, and ethics of the human spirit.

The total quantity of money around our planet is finite (like all the grains of sand on all the beaches of Earth) and countable (if you have nothing better to do). Money is a commodity whose use value is to estimate and measure *only* finite exchange values. Once a famous American capitalist was asked, "How much money income is enough?" He replied, "A little *more*."

Ultimate human worth is *not* finite. Hence ultimate human worth cannot be counted with money and finite arithmetic. Finite arithmetic is governed by the postulate that any and every part of a finite whole is *less* than the whole. Finite arithmetic, adequate for counting the exchange values of commodities of the global market, is quite unsuitable for counting the ultimate worth of the whole of humankind. Ultimate human worth is not *finite*. Ultimate human worth is an *infinite whole*.

Not many years ago none of the professed mathematicians among humankind appeared to know how to estimate and count infinite wholes. Today infinite wholes can be and are counted with a method much like, while different from, the more familiar method of counting finite wholes.

Mathematicians refer to the method for counting both finite and infinite or transfinite wholes as "one-to-one correspondence." The difference is that when counting an infinite whole, *not any part will do*. In order to identify and count any infinite whole, *a proper part* of it must first be found. The fundamental postulate of infinite wholes differs from that of finite wholes: "The proper part of an infinite whole is *equal to the whole.*" A simple example: The set of counting numbers is an infinite whole (since there is no greatest counting number). In this infinite whole, the even counting number total can be demonstrated to equal the total of even and odd counting numbers.

The proper parts of the infinite whole of humankind are ourselves, all women and all men. *Persons are the most precious of all human wealth on earth.* The proper parts of the whole of humankind are not any of the physical parts of the human organism, not human hands, not legs, not hearts, not brains, neither human bodies, nor even the biological control units that are designed to govern survival of human bodies: human minds. The proper parts of the infinite whole of humankind are our spaceless and timeless nonphysical selves, our human spirits, if you like.

By virtue of the nonphysical self, provided only that in each particular case it continues integrating and growing instead of disintegrating to nonexistence, each individual self is equal to the whole of humankind in ultimate human worth. Since entities equal to the same entity are equal to each other, all women and men are by nature infinite, independent, and equal in respect to worth or human value. In no other presently known respect, particularly including human longevity and human biological or physical performance, are persons infinite or equal.

American civilization was first introduced to the human equality proposition, so far as I can tell, through Jesus Josephson. Jesus never said He is the *only* Son of God, but He taught rather that all Women are the Daughters of Nature's God and all Men are the Sons of S(he). The proposition was reaffirmed eighteen centuries later by Thomas Paine, author of the original draft of "A Declaration by the representatives of the United States of America in general Congress assembled."

From our equal creation we derive rights, nowadays called human rights, inherent and unalienable, among which are the preservation of life, liberty, and democracy.

The future of human rights on Earth relates to how humankind practices the human rights we profess. A primary attitudinal change among all humankind on Earth now is required for the future of human rights on Earth to be brighter. The change has to be composed of a rational rejection of the hoary bromide that all men are by nature finite and unequal in *all respects* while women are *less* equal together with the voluntary informed acknowledgment and positive affirmation that the human equality proposition is, after all, accurately true.

90

KENNETH SHAPIRO

Kenneth Shapiro, Ph.D., is the founding editor of *Society and Animals*, a journal of social-scientific studies of the human side of human-nonhuman relations, and the cofounder and executive director of Psychologists for the Ethical Treatment of Animals.

Transcending Self-Centered Utilitarianism

Jaded by the thinly veiled admonition (from strangers no less) to "have a good day," I welcome this opportunity to reflect on the possibility of having a nice millennium.

From many perspectives, the prospects do not look so good, and my effort here to adopt a light tone is strained if not fatuous. While many lately have dusted off God talk, to me the First Coming gets mixed reviews at best. So I think the worst we could do is become millenarians and sit on our hands waiting for the delivery of a second promised golden age.

Not that I do not believe in miracles. When taken outside of a theological frame, the term simply means "wonderful things." And whatever our present difficulties, it is and always will be wonderful and awesome that there is something rather than nothing, that there is life, that we can experience it, that we can love . . . (I resisted the Woody Allen finish, " . . . and that we can send out for dinner").

But there are also, well, these problems we've been having (really, *making*). You know: war, famine, overpopulation, various forms of discrimination, ethnic and religious strife, epidemic nationalism, and, one of more recent vintage, environmental global crises.

So what can and should we do and what can we hope for? For the last decade I have put stock in a particular shift in thinking about our relation to the world. In some ways it just builds on traditional values—individual rights, compassion for others, community. It simply extends that circle of rights-bearers, of community members, to nonhuman animals and, for some thinkers, to all other living things. But won't extending the circle just bring more of the same problems—as those values now being spread thinner will lose what ethical effectiveness they possessed?

In another way, this shift inaugurates a radically different attitude to the world, for the extension across the species border takes the exclusive focus off our own kind, off our sense of our own special entitlement. But we have lived through a series of such "shifts," and we still find ourselves with these problems. The revolutions of Copernicus, Darwin, Marx, and Freud each in its own way purportedly pulled us out of our special standing, relieved us of some aspect of our alleged unique autonomy and separateness, ourselves as the center of the universe or as made in God's image, or as unaffected by larger external forces (economics, language, history) or by internal forces (unconscious motivations). So why should this revolution be any different?

To be honest, I am not sure it will be—which is not all bad, for, despite our present plight, each of these earlier shifts arguably brought some gains. But the present shift is different. It flatly refuses and denies that foundational cleavage (at least in Western thought) between human and nonhuman. This shift toward giving moral consideration to the well-being of nonhuman animals and the integrity of the natural environment is powerful, for it reveals a ground common to several social and political movements—environmentalism, animal rights, the Greens.

In addition to these, other progressive social movements are sympathetic and potential allies. The Rainbow Coalition is becoming aware that environmental degradation is disproportionately fouling the homes and workplaces of ethnic minorities. In feminist thought, the androcentrism undergirding gender discrimination is also the prejudice lurking beneath the anthropocentrism that is the traditional apology for the exploitation of animals and nature.

If we can master the disappointment of not being number one, as individuals and as a species, we can let go of that narrow and short-sighted utilitarianism in which only our own kind count and in which everything else is an instrument to our own ends, a resource for us to harvest. In its place, we can relate to the world in its integrity and in its parts as a being and as individual beings with inherent value. I believe that this attitude gears into our present dilemma in a way that no other available point of view does. Its intellectual development and political expression provide a hope that the next millennium will be a better one, and, in any case, will not be our last. Have a nice one.

91
MONTAGUE ULLMAN

Montague Ullman, M.D., is a psychiatrist and psychoanalyst who founded the Dream Laboratory at the Maimonides Medical Center, Brooklyn, New York, and is emeritus clinical professor of psychiatry at the Albert Einstein College of Medicine. He is the author or coauthor of several books, including *Dream Telepathy* and *Working with Dreams*, and coeditor of the *Handbook of States of Consciousness*.

Dreams and a New Politics of Connectedness

Perhaps the most important challenge we face is how to connect our individual lives to the now obvious reality that the survival of humankind is at risk. Contributing to the mounting nature of the risk is our own failure to significantly impede the degradation of the environment and the equally significant failure to forgo violence as a means of settling disputes. There is a common factor underlying both these trends. Even more than gradual pollution of the natural world has been a more insidious and infinitely more dangerous form of pollution—the pollution of the human soul. The population at large has been conditioned to be taken in by lies, big and small, and not to see what is clearly there to be seen. While Nazi Germany is often singled out as an instance of a level of social blindness that left an entire nation impervious to the Big Lie, the possibility for tragedy on this scale or on an even larger scale is still with us. The underlying dynamics have never been completely rooted out. This is the formidable task that still confronts us. Are we capable of creating a citizenry that is able to see through the tissue of lies that obstructs its vision?

We will each have to find our own way to political truth (seeing through the lies our leaders tell us) and personal truth (the lies we tell ourselves), neither of which is easy. In regard to political truth, Anthony Lewis put it very well when, in an article in the *New York Times* in December, 1991, dealing with the vicissitudes of free speech in America, he noted: "Speaking truth to power is never going to be easy, not even after 200 years." There is a connection between the scale of deception, sustained by lies, big and small, and the way power is deployed in the management of human affairs. Only the cultivation of both social and personal honesty will enable us to discern the difference between the operation of power in a way that victimizes others (referred to by Abraham Maslow as asynergic power) and power that benefits all involved (synergic power). The former dehumanizes both the wielder of power and the victim. The latter nurtures the capacity of both parties to be fully human. In this it is somewhat akin to love.

As a psychiatrist, my concern is with personal truth. One road I have taken in pursuit of this has been to attempt to demystify dreams in a way that would make the personal honesty embedded in the metaphorical images of our dreams available to all. Dreaming is a universal phenomenon. In my opinion there should be universal access to the benefits that can accrue from them. For too long the public has been taken in by the prevailing mystique that serious dream work had best be limited to the clinical domain. Our dreaming psyche arises out of an incorruptible core of our being that, in contrast to our waking ego, has never lost sight of the fact that we are members of a single species. Our ability to endure as a species may depend on taking that fact more seriously than we have in the past. Dreams reveal the state of connectedness of the individual to his or her past, to others, and to the supports and constraints of the social order. Is it too much to hope that, as we move into a postindustrial society, the intrinsic honesty of dreams can be harnessed to this effort?

The political climate is not apt to change unless a transformation from below occurs that is great enough in its intensity to create leaders with the long-range vision needed to change the course our present leaders seem so blindly and so helplessly destined to pursue. We are in need of a politics of connectedness, one that will work toward matching our biological unity as a species with a cultural reality of communion and brotherhood.

92

JON WYNNE-TYSON

Jon Wynne-Tyson is the author of *The Civilised Alternative* and *Food for a Future* and the editor of *The Extended Circle*, an anthology of humane thought. He has written novels and plays and has been a publisher since 1954. His Kingship Library, a paperback series of classic and new works on animal rights, was launched in 1992.

Believe in Miracles, or They Will Never Happen

*M*y hope for the remaining years of this decade is that they will lay the basis for a millennium in which humankind shows it has learned its greatest lesson—that if we are to survive, and realize our potential, we must extend the circle of our compassion to all living creatures, regardless of color, creed, race, or species. We are all kin, sharing the same needs, joys, and right to liberty and life. If we persist in believing that we can outsmart Nature and forever exploit the environment for our own selfish ends, "She" will have the last laugh, and the Earth will be at peace—without us.

In the 1980s, waking one morning with the thought that there was not much more than a decade to go before A.D. 2000 hit us for better or for worse, I launched ARC (Animal Rights Cooperative) with the logo "PHASE OUT 2000." It was a modest solo attempt to represent a network of societies, groups, and individuals concerned to see animals liberated from human tyranny. ARC was not yet another organization, but a device, a declaration, to help speed the process of humane education so vital to building a more compassionate society.

It confirmed a shared aim to phase out by 2000 A.D. some of our cruelty toward animals.

Needless to say, with no immediate end product but the distribution of a simple printed statement of these aims, suggesting the use of the logo on letterheads, stickers, posters, leaflets, and so on, inviting the recipient to ask for further details, the "launch" got a handful of sympathetic reactions over a few months, then melted into the ground. Unstaffed, overloaded by work, I left it at that.

Voices on the Threshold of Tomorrow will, I hope, achieve more, especially if the voices are unified by the recognition that however many answers may be valid, they will be powerless without a common basis, a common link, a link that even today so many idealists fail to acknowledge.

Think back to the early 1980s. Do you remember the agenda of the First Assembly of the Fourth World? Wonderful intentions, a splendid passion, but were we being realistic to expect the warring, self-seeking, distraught, and rootless First, Second, and Third Worlds to recognize a collaborative basis in the twenty-five proposed forums, covering as they did just about every conceivable rightable situation, from twinning Western neighborhoods with Third-World villages, to little matters like settling the Irish problem? Wasn't there something missing?

Now, as then, surely, if the Fourth World has a hope on Earth of being anything more than the breathless bottom layer of a seething heap of conflicting human ambitions, it has got to do what none of the other three worlds can see the sense in doing, and that is to give proper weight and priority to the critical need for a true *philosophy* of environmental concern. All agitation about ethnic minorities, feminism, African politics, the nuclear threat, and the whole eco-politico-agro-you-name-it boiling amounts to so much hot air until each one of us focuses upon and absorbs the demands and power of a mature, compassionate, and ethically aware environmental philosophy.

The four worlds are blending into a single amorphous entity whose whole can be no better than its parts. The Fourth World's agenda displayed little that was not the microcosm of the larger worlds' concerns. The brief was, and largely remains, to tinker and adjust and correct the balances, and hope that somehow, by social engineering, legislation, power politics, talking it through, creating organizations and committees, lobbying and activating, pressuring and proving, grouping and regrading, the brave new world will struggle out on top and be a shining example to the lost majority. *It won't.* Not without the essential foundation. It is not that most of the targets were or are anything but right and proper. Their problem is the lack of a unifying "perennial" philosophy, a common and consistent ethic.

Nothing can be solved collectively that has not already come right individually. The pie is as good as its plums. Society can be no better than its members. History is the sad tale of imperfect people wanting good ends via bad means. Better people are not just people with political and social awareness and the right slogans on their banners and bosoms. It is not enough to cover the landscape with responsible wind generators; to bake our own bread; to recycle; to compost; to preserve whales and seals until there are enough to "cull" for human greed; to get the girls to sort out the boys; to ensure that sentient animals are butchered by gentlemen in their own backyards; to discourage human procreation; to preach humanism in the name of religion, and religion in the name of humanism.

The problem has to be tackled at the source. The source is *We*. *We* are produced by homes and schools. *We* are in need of major overhaul. *We* need to see the basis of all lasting reform as a fundamental, felt resolve to discipline and change our natures. Dare it be said in these days of scientific domination, but what I am banging on about might be called the Spiritual Factor. If once we dismiss the existence of a spiritual link between humans, and between humans and non-humans, as abstract rubbish simply because no white-coated savior has corked the clinical evidence in a test tube, we shall have boarded the last train for Genocide. We can acknowledge that link without having to postulate old men in clouds or explanations of that great red herring "Creation." I am not rooting for Christian revival or even for an eclectic religion offering the best of ancient and modern beliefs. Show me an organization and I will show you the dry rot in the cellar.

Individual commitment is the only name of the game; individual recognition of the link, the foundation; individual determination to rear our kids to know that while alternative technology, human rights, and the rest are hugely important, the vital ingredient is a deeply learned, deeply felt sense of the unity of all being. Love, if you like. Not *quid pro quo* love, but the kind that tears down the barriers of habit and seeks for all life, human and animal, those rights and joys that do not knowingly harm or distress others and which are consistent with a view of the human capacity for evolution toward a race of truly humane beings.

If I am wrong about this, then the wind vane in the meadow and the oven-baked loaf will have to take the full brunt of the future. I suspect it is beyond them.

93

JOAN BORYSENKO

Joan Borysenko, Ph.D., is a medical scientist, psychologist, and teacher of meditation whose vision is to unite medicine, psychology, and the spiritual traditions of the world in service of an expanded view of healing. She is the best-selling author of *Minding the Body, Mending the Mind; Guilt is the Teacher, Love is the Lesson;* and *Fire in the Soul: A New Psychology of Spiritual Optimism.*

The Birth of the Divine Child

The day before I sat down to write this piece, a young woman was murdered. She was a biology professor at Clark University, our son Justin's recent alma mater. Her life ended brutally and unexpectedly when she walked into her home and surprised two burglars. Although we did not know one another, her death touched a place deep inside me. I grieved for her, for her family, for the students. But today, as the sun rose on a brilliant fall day, I sat across the breakfast table looking at my stepdaughter Natalia. Her face was soft and her whole being radiant with the mystery of new life. In early summer she will be a mother.

My heart ached with the beauty of life to come and the grief of life snuffed out. And in the aching it became a little softer, a little more open. And this opening of the heart, I believe, is what will carry us across the threshold of tomorrow into a new era in the evolution of humankind. Never before has our delicate earth seemed so small. Not just because of the press of overcrowding, but also because of the magic of communication. We hear instantly of the death of a college professor in the next town and of the starvation of children in far-off Somalia. We can practically smell the burning of the rain forest. And as our hearts begin to open to the suffering, so do they also open to gratitude and to the realization that all things are interconnected. We are the murdered professor, the starving children, the burning rain forest. We are also Natalia's child awaiting its birth.

But wait, you say. The realization of interconnectedness has not struck most of us. It is still too easy to close off the suffering and turn our backs on the waste and lovelessness that have so decimated our planet. But life in the cocoon of denial is going to be short-lived as we move into the next millennium. The crumbling economy, the severe disturbances of weather, and the global AIDS epidemic are symptomatic of the end of an old era and the birth of a new one.

Nobel Laureate Ilya Prigogine demonstrated that chaos always precedes the "escape to a higher order" of any system, from the molecular to the cosmic. We are now, I believe, escaping to a higher order in which the realization of the essential Oneness of all life will arise in our hearts and change the very molecular structure of our bodies. A significant subset of people who have had near-death experiences, for example, have experienced physiological changes ranging from instantaneous healings to the development of electrical sensitivities. Such people literally stop clocks and put computers on the fritz because their physical energy structure has been fundamentally altered. Consciousness is often altered in tandem, the person suddenly becoming more intuitive, more compassionate, and present to a level of reality where the seemingly senseless facts of life become sensible in light of a greatly expanded perspective. These individuals are examples of the evolution that our entire species is currently undergoing.

We are the Divine Child, dreaming the extremes of heaven and hell in the spasms of our birth. The most important thing we can all do during the tumultuous process, to quote the Ram Dass of the sixties, is to "love, serve, and remember." We need to love ourselves, our families, our neighbors, and the world through word, thought, prayer, and social action. We need to speak whatever our truth may be and steadfastly refuse to capitulate to fear that has always been, and will evermore remain, the great separator. And we need to remember who we really are—part of a Consciousness so subtle, so sweet, so powerful that it has created a web of life that is infinite yet whose splendor can be savored by opening our hearts to a sunrise or to the forest birdsong. If we take a little time out of our busy lives to be still, then everything we need to birth ourselves into the future will reveal itself for,

In the secret recesses of the heart
beyond the teachings of this world
calls a still, small voice
singing a song unchanged
from the foundation of the world.
Speak to me in sunsets and in starlight
Speak to me in the eyes of a child
You Who call from a smile
My cosmic beloved
Tell me who I am
And who I always will be.
The soul of the world
And the song of songs.

All life is a wonder and a blessing.
We need only remember.

94
BROOKE MEDICINE EAGLE

Brooke Medicine Eagle is an American native Earthkeeper, teacher, healer, songwriter, ceremonial leader, and author of *Buffalo Woman Comes Singing*, who is dedicated to bringing forward the ancient truths concerning how to live in a fully human life. Based in the Montana wilderness, Brooke is the creator of EagleSong and the founder of FlowerSong Land and Life Foundation.

Giving Back the Gifts of Earth

The primary vision I see for our unfolding future is that we will come into a full awareness and experience of the great power that lives within us—the power endowed us by Creator. We as two-leggeds have been playing a game of "how much everything else in the world influences and determines who we are." We have, in essence, been victims in a material world that we must work hard *outside* ourselves to change. As the new paradigm becomes real for us, we will understand ourselves as spirit, space, and thought co-creating a world in which we are masters of our destiny. We will understand our ability to change with relative ease, not only the outer material world around us, but the inner world of body and feeling. Healing ourselves will become standard practice, and anyone who relies on some "outside expert" to tell them what to do with their own body will be quite laughable.

The great universal bonding and unifying principle of Love will live fully and consciously in our hearts, replacing the separating and frightening specter of fear. As we find ourselves in unity with all things, understanding that we are one with the circle of life, we will live a life of respect and communion with all our relations. The magic of cooperation with all beings and energies around us will become evident, and White Buffalo Calf Woman's teachings of oneness and respect will begin to make exquisite sense to us, not only as spiritual teachings, but as practical ways of living in our daily world.

So you can see that it is not a matter of outer technology, but of inner awareness and consciousness, that is the "dividing line" between an old and a new paradigm. Even today, at *any* moment in which we are living in cooperation, unity, oneness, wholeness, respect for all life, communion, and joy, then we *are* in the new world; yet when we are in the mode of separation, fear, alienation, conflict, hostility, resentment, and anger, we are living an old paradigm that is passing. That world will crumble, yet my elders remind me that if *we* are not participating in the world, not a speck of its dust or fallout will touch us. Our challenge is to live fully in harmony and respect with all things in the circle of life, now.

This is not a theoretical notion. It means creating homes that do not suck energy and resources (electricity, water, heat, food) from the circle of life, and then give back only garbage and toilet waste. It means standing firm on the ground where we live—taking our own power and communing with all the conscious and intelligent life around us to create what we need. In cooperation with the nature intelligences and our own deep Self, we can easily produce what we need to eat, use our wastes as fertilizer, catch most of the water we need from our roofs, grow and gather the medicines we need, create joy and beauty from our hands and our lives—taking very little and giving back the gifts we came to Earth to give in abundance and joy. Each of us will find that we ourselves are a wellspring of abundance, creation, and harmonious action. Our days will be radiant and sweet as a spring morning after a warm rain, and all will be good and growing.

95

STEPHEN GASKIN

Stephen Gaskin, M.A., is founder of The Farm Community in Summertown, Tennessee, one of the most significant hippie communities in the world. He is also founder and first chairman of the board of directors of Plenty International, an overseas relief and development company, and founder of many other projects on four continents. He is the author of several books, including *The Caravan, Mind at Play,* and *Rendered Infamous.*

The Key to the Future is Service

There is a great mass of mythology connected with the turn of the millennium, the year 2000, but fortunately it is only in the Christian calendar. The whole question becomes much easier to handle if you look at it as the Year of the Dragon as in the Chinese calendar, or 5753 in the Hebrew calendar, or 6241 in the Egyptian calendar, or even 8 CAUAC as in the Mayan calendar. In this way it becomes just another year, and the question is not about a cycle of time that exists outside of us, but about a cycle of life that exists inside of us. Then the question becomes what is our responsibility, not what will happen.

I am a believer in free will. I am not a believer in predestination. I think a belief in prophecy robs us of our free will. If you insist in wanting to know that it all comes out all right, you must give up your freedom to affect the outcome and help make it all come out all right.

Now, some people may think that I am not as religious as I used to be, and it is true that on Monday, Wednesday, and Friday I

285

might be an agnostic and on Tuesdays and Thursdays a primitive animist, while partying down on Saturdays and sometimes sitting zazen on Sunday. At no time do I subscribe to any "brand name" religions.

I love the ethical teachings of almost all the religions, and I love the psychedelic testimony of their saints. I do not believe in any of their dogmas.

I think each one of us has a non-shirkable obligation to figure out the world on our own as best we can. The way we behave as a result of that investigation is our real and practiced religion.

I consider myself to be an "ethnic" hippie. I know that the hippies were preceded by the beatniks, the bohemians, the nihilists, Voltaire, and so on back to Socrates, but the wave of the revolution that spoke to me was the hippies. Rock and roll lights my soul and gives a beat to the revolution.

When I was a child, I used to hope for calamities because the world seemed so sewed up and frozen in the status quo. I longed for an earthquake or a blizzard so the world would be malleable. When I became a hippie, my fondest dreams had come true. The world was up for grabs. In the following twenty or thirty years, the Republicans and other forces of evil tried their level best to nail it back down.

This year, Bill Clinton proved that the world is still up for grabs. Thank God. (You should pardon the expression.)

This brings us to here and now. Although this election will change the face of the world, it in no way excuses us from our best efforts. The New Age does not come automatically. It's like when the traveler asked the farmer how his potatoes turned out. The farmer said, "They didn't turn out at all; me and Sal had to dig 'em out."

To me, a great deal of the "New Age" is a waste of time. Much of it seems to pander to self-interest and is material rather than spiritual. I mean "Smell this," "Hear this," "Touch this," "See this," "Taste this." There are more important things. How long has it been since you heard people speak of the future in terms of "great pure effort." That Ross Perot could pull eighteen million votes with the idea of "shared sacrifice" shows that people instinctively understand that service is called for.

The key to the future is service. Part of what made Kennedy great was the idea of the Peace Corps. Part of Clinton's votes came from people who liked the idea of repaying student loans with service. As the world becomes more crowded, each way of making money becomes precious, and money is charged for things that used to be given for free or for love. Service becomes a revolutionary act. It must again become respectable to be an idealist.

My new project is called "Rocinante" after Don Quixote's horse, a vehicle for an incurable idealist. We in Rocinante are embarking on the creation of a project that will include a birth center with a midwifery training facility and a complete senior community living center, ranging from assisted living and adult daycare to a skilled care facility and a hospice for the dying. We believe that we have the experience necessary to design an inexpensive and graceful paradigm that can serve as a model for healthcare for the next century.

This is the wild part. As soon as I let out word of what I was doing, people wrote to me from all over the United States, many of them not just interested in perhaps living on Rocinante, but wanting to confer on doing similar projects where they live. It is the *Zeitgeist*. It is the future growing from the compost of the present.

96

ROXANNE (JEAN) LANIER

Roxanne (Jean) Lanier is a gestalt therapist and poet/philosopher. She writes a regular column for *Creation* magazine and is the author of *The Wisdom of Being Human*, and *Diagnoses and Other Poems*.

Archaeology 5000

Thousands of years from now
how will the makers of our computers
be imagined?
Today we put clothes on ancient kings
buried in the tombs of the world
and give them children, servants,
philosophies, even dreams.
The ancient ones live again
clad and nourished by us.
How will we be adorned
by future minds examining our artifacts?
Will we have dancing shoes
and theatre tickets?
Will those looking for clues
feel our goodness?

In this poem I am expressing the hope that the future will be inhabited by people who have forgiveness and gratitude in their hearts. God knows we will have left behind us plenty of need for forgiveness. Nevertheless, I hope that they will find it in their hearts to understand that we did not always know what we were doing when we polluted our air, destroyed our forests, and contaminated our waters. As they remember what we did, they will advance the race if they can forgive us. This means, of course, that they will have to be *present*, and for that to happen, the awareness of the few will have to become the awareness of the many, and soon. There will have had to be changes, great changes.

In my vision of the future, our technology will have learned to serve the Earth, so that the Earth will have survived and be flourishing. Our long ''Yoga of Science'' will have found its fulfillment in realization—the realization of our deep indebtedness to the Earth, to each other, and to Life itself. This is what will evoke a spirit of gratitude, and where there is gratitude there will be forgiveness. ''Without a vision, the people perish,'' but without gratitude and forgiveness, there will not be the people we are meant to be and have always wanted to be, from the beginning.

97

INGRID NEWKIRK

Ingrid Newkirk is cofounder and national director of People for the Ethical Treatment of Animals, the largest animal rights organization in the United States. She speaks nationally and internationally on animal rights issues and is the author of *Save the Animals!*, *Kids Can Save the Animals!*, and *Free the Animals!*.

An Age of Altruism

In this millennium, our species came down with an awful case of the Gobbles. Science was powerless to help. It was not only too busy wrestling with the common cold and playing mix-and-match with baboon bits, pig parts, and the human body, but, some suspect, it could have been responsible for the outbreak in the first place.

As the disease progressed, we became unbearable. We no longer recognized our friends. We were fidgety. Nature bored us. All we seemed interested in was "stuff." We bought wrecking balls, riding mowers, and bulldozers. Down came everything from the Brazilian rain forest to our own once-beautiful countryside, and up went megamalls and superhighways. We left everyone—from whole human tribes to the forty or so mammals, birds, insects, and reptiles who share a single tree—homeless and deprived of the means with which to sustain themselves. Not that we noticed. We were at the store picking up a cheap leather couch and a bucket of fried chicken (seven pieces for $4.95).

In our heightened delirium, we felt so all-powerful that we decided to reorder the universe. We designed factory farms: acres of metal sheds in which we caged chickens so they could never again spread a wing, and calves so their hooves could not touch the earth. We elevated cows and pigs to near-human status by introducing our own growth genes into them. At the same time we reduced them to machines on meat-production assembly lines.

We were having far too much fun to remember the Golden Rule or to be spooked by talk of cruelty, birth defects, polluted air, fouled oceans, deforestation, dead soil, cancers, and heart disease.

Then, on Columbus Day weekend, 1992, came the first signs the fever might be subsiding. In Washington, thousands of people stood in the rain, humbly reading the panels on the ''Names Project'' quilt. Between commercials for the usual linen sales, the mainstream media discussed the devastating consequences of the European invasion to Native Americans (of all species) and to the land. The only snickers seemed to come from Rush Limbaugh who, everyone understood, could not help himself.

By November, although parts of the country remained infected, over half the U.S. Gobbles victims were over the worst. Without embarrassment, they opened recyclable bottles of organic locally grown wine to celebrate a recovery marked by the election of the first potential vegetarians to the White House. In the District of Columbia the celebrations continued with the defeat of a death-penalty bill, in California with the election of a woman who has devoted her life to championing the rights of the differently abled, and, in Colorado, with bear cubs getting more votes than the National Rifle Association.

With the winds of change in the air, how about a New Millennium commitment? Say, a simple one to eliminate all prejudices based on gender, race, religion, species, size, age, and physical ability.

Picture a riverbank. Envision, on one side, those who recognize the common threads that weave oppressions together as one cloth, people who have stopped making excuses about their nasty habits and behaviors and started trying to change them. On the other side, put those who continue to deprive others of their rights, their dignity, their freedom of movement and expression, even their flesh and their skins. In other words, people with the Gobbles.

Now, a New Millennium challenge. To seize every opportunity to throw lines, build bridges, and do whatever else is necessary to help people across the river. We can succeed if we never ''go along'' with an injustice and if we show there are *always* better options than acts or omissions that hurt others. That is what an Age of Altruism requires of us.

98

VIRGINIA RAMEY MOLLENKOTT

Virginia Ramey Mollenkott, D.Min.Hon., Ph.D., is a feminist theologian and professor of English at William Paterson College of New Jersey. She is the author of many works, including *Godding: Human Responsibility and the Bible, The Divine Feminine,* and *Sensuous Spirituality.*

Truth Outstays Delusion

As the 1991 war in the Persian Gulf was beginning to heat up, I listened to a group of Christian social activists worrying about the possibility of its igniting worldwide conflict and possibly nuclear annihilation. They seemed surprised and relieved when I reminded them that egomaniacal forces are not the only forces operating in this world. Although it is not necessarily church-related, there is a powerful spiritual groundswell, a gradual human awakening, that is acting as a restraint upon the forces of destruction. In the teeth of fear and rage, the power of love is preserving the planet as it approaches the year 2000.

There is an apparent boundary between the all-inclusive Consciousness within which we all live and move, and the self-limiting individual consciousness. But it seems to me that at this moment in history, the apparent boundary is growing thinner and more transparent. AIDS activists report a strong sensation that those who have recently left this planet are leaning back to assist the transition of those soon to follow. Thousands of people consult channelers of down-to-earth spiritual insights that have little in common with occult experimentation or the secret seances of the past. Thousands more are experiencing a new connectedness to the transpersonal, transreligious realm of Spirit, practicing mystical disciplines that may have no traditional religious sanction but nevertheless transform their relationships to people, animals, and the whole universe.

Certain physicists express so much awe at the interconnected web of reality that they sound like theologians. Female and male feminists are working together toward an international partnership society of mutual respect, reciprocity, and the sharing of the good basics of life with everyone everywhere. Advocates of racial harmony and lesbian and gay activists and their friends are inching society toward a more relaxed and loving affirmation of human variety. Environmentalists struggle to preserve what is left of ecological health, aided by the miraculous self-renewal of nature.

These and other forces of positive change inevitably frighten those who have bound themselves to an egocentric and materialistic perspective. Personal cruelty has achieved staggering, chainsaw proportions. Corporate and governmental addiction to profit at the expense of people hideously burgeons. The "dearest freshness deep down things" gasps to maintain itself in a riot of pollution. At national and international levels as well as on the individual level, time-bound ego and eternal Self are on a collision course.

But I have no doubt about which will outlast the other. I have experienced the fact that love is stronger than death. Spirit is more resilient than murky materialism. Truth outstays delusion.

So as I approach the year 2000, when I will be sixty-eight and the world will enter its third millennium, I have no fear. Instead I live in the faith that the acceleration of destructive policies will force humankind to find creative compromises between individualistic and socialistic systems: humane compromises that will resemble neither capitalism run amok nor the state communism that has recently collapsed in eastern Europe. A sustainable community is in our future, for it is a fact that we must "love one another or die."

Fortunately for this planet, millions of spiritual beings yearn toward us, eager to guide us toward a healthier tomorrow. And within each of us, an Inner Guide stands ready to show us how to expand our minds into their all-embracing reality. Despite appearances, "the universe is selving itself" just as it should. And on some level, everything is perfectly all right.

99
FRANK ANDREWS

Frank Andrews, Ph.D., is a professor at the University of California, Santa Cruz, where, in addition to chemistry, he teaches values, psychological unblocking, teaching, and loving. He is the author of *The Art and Practice of Loving*.

Choosing a Path of Loving

Only with the care and love of enough people will humanity make it through its deepening difficulties and forge a world worth living in over the long haul. Any one of us can choose our life to be primarily a path of loving, of appreciating and delighting in the people and activities we encounter day by day. By holding to a loving path, we gradually learn the skills and become experts at loving, just as surely as athletes or musicians gain expertise with practice. The more common alternative path is primarily one of striving to reach goals, of creating circumstances in the world that give us occasional tastes of joy. That choice sets us up for disappointment.

Our highest values may be to attain the spouse and children of our dreams. But even if we attain them, will we have the ability to create the experience of warmth and family intimacy we are so sure will follow? Our highest values may be to attain the house, bank account, and possessions of our dreams. But even if we attain them, will we be able to create the experience of security and satisfaction that was our reason for going after them in the first place? Our highest values may be to achieve fame and power through our job. But even if we attain such success, will we experience pouring our energy and skill into a group of people about whom we care? Reaching a prized goal can be the ultimate frustration when we do not know how to turn the process and its outcome into the experience we felt certain would result.

When we are frustrated by disappointment, but addicted to our belief that success is the only route to life's payoffs, we expand our efforts: have another baby; change this spouse for someone else; get a bigger house, a bigger job, more money. Yet even if we could reach these spiraling goals, we still lack the skills of turning them into experiences of joy and love.

Furthermore, our chance of reaching our goals decreases every year because our society and environment can no longer support humanity's addictive strivings. The overpopulated world refuses to sustain still more people, the stressed environment refuses to support ever higher physical standards of living, and fragile local and world-wide societies punish our emphasis on individual and national competition instead of cooperation and mutual caring.

In contrast, when our highest values guide us onto a path of loving, we begin to see that the world is so rich that it cannot possibly disappoint us. We learn how deeply we can delight in the children we actually have, *our* children, however much they may differ from the ideal children of our dreams. We learn how richly we can build a relationship with the spouse we actually have, *our* spouse, even though he or she does not fit the pictures of the ideal spouse that we held long ago. We find out how to make every action, from our paid employment to washing a plate, into an outpouring of loving energy into people and a world about whom we care deeply.

Our culture has love figured out wrong. Occasionally we have been so overwhelmed with the dazzling beauty, grace, and perfection of a person, work of art, or glimpse of nature that we open our heart in a "Yes!" Then the resulting feeling opens us still more, and we experience the spiraling glories of love. Our mistake is in believing that this overwhelming, reactive love is the only kind of love. We may even feel offended at the thought of approaching the world with our heart already open, scanning deliberately for something to appreciate. "It seems too calculated," we say. It is easier to live a life in which events just happen to us, to which we sin ply react, rather than in which *we* choose how to approach and respo. d to the raw material life offers us.

The path of loving is a lifelong mindfulness practice in which our purpose is always to appreciate the circumstances of the moment, whatever they may be. On this path, as with any mindfulness practice, we monitor our attention, and whenever we notice that it has wandered away from appreciation, we calmly bring it back. One result of this practice is that the circumstances of life lose their desperate importance. If we do reach one of our goals, that's great, and if we do not we will still get along fine. Our challenge is to create experience that does justice to the many wonders the world inevitably offers us.

There will certainly come times when we will not be able to appreciate the circumstances at hand. This will not throw us off our path, provided we determine that in such times there must be lessons to be learned. If I cannot play pieces in four sharps, it does not mean I must give up playing the piano. It just means I have something more to learn.

None of us has any idea how deeply a person can live in love, because none of us has been raised by adults who were expert lovers in a society that valued and taught appreciating above all else. The loving path, the path with heart, is available to each one of us at any time, if we but choose it. By choosing it we enrich and ennoble our own life, and deepen the role of loving in our culture.

Throughout recorded history, spiritual leaders have urged us to love. We thought they were asking something so special or so difficult that we figured their words could not apply to us. Who would have thought that we *could* follow their path by approaching each moment from the question, "How deeply can I appreciate this?" It is a conceptually simple approach, age-old, and fully worthy of our lifelong commitment.

100

JOHN ROBBINS

John Robbins is the author of the Pulitzer Prize-nominated *Diet For A New America* and of *May All Be Fed* and the coauthor of *In Search of Balance*. He is the founder and president of EarthSave Foundation, headquartered in Santa Cruz, California.

Something Beyond Hope

I am often saddened by the lack of love in the world. And I am frightened that the world we may be creating, the one we will leave as our legacy to our children, may not be one in which the best of being human is possible. I am afraid that the future is not hopeful, unless by some miracle enough of us manage to learn to infuse our lives, both public and private, with a spirit of compassion. Throughout most of history, if the historical record is any indication, it has been only isolated and rare people whose lives have stood as public statements testifying to the power of love. Most of us, most of the time, simply muddle onward, our lives not particularly illuminated by any sense of greater purpose than our own immediate needs. But I think that in the days to come, more and more of us will be experiencing a need to make our lives consistent with the deeper potential of the human experience. We will see that we have opportunities to help to create, in whatever sphere of action we find ourselves, a world based on an awareness of the interconnectedness of all living beings.

> *A peaceful, just and joyful society will be built by*
> *people who have traded their consumerism for connection*
> *with themselves, with other people, and with their world.*
> —Tom Atlee

It seems to me that what is happening as we approach the end of the second millennium is that the action of the evolutionary life force is bringing about a shift in values and in perception. In the old way of seeing, the natural world is viewed as a collection of commodities; it is made up of inventory for us to convert into revenue. The world, according to this viewpoint, is made up of objects that are there for us to use. Living in such a context of meaning, we have learned to objectify virtually everything. We have learned to use each other, to use our bodies, to use whatever we can get our hands on in the feverish quest to become something our society calls "successful." No wonder we are destroying our life-support systems; no wonder we have become strangers to the possibility of genuine community. We have defined "success" as the ability to consume.

The challenge that now exists in each of our lives is to create a new model and vision of who we are and what we can be and do. The old definition of power, the one that has shaped us and continues to influence us greatly, has to do primarily with control and domination. What needs to be born in each of our lives is a new kind of power, one that expresses our respect for what lies outside of our grasp and control, for the Great Mystery, for other people, for wilderness, for the natural world, for the whole Earth community.

Personally, I look at the global crisis of our time as the historical agent that can help to awaken the human spirit to its interdependence on other forms of life, and thus toward its essential wholeness. Something that has burdened humanity for eons is finally becoming so oppressive that it will be shrugged off. We have lived for so long now with only a partial involvement of our hearts, with so little reverence and sense of the sacred, that it has come to this: We have brought about a world wherein we can see the consequences of this attitude. We can see now the results of humanity's historical refusal to respect and cherish life.

Given the vast list of ecological disasters our species has perpetrated on the Earth, and given humankind's dismal historical record when it comes to living in peace and harmony, I sometimes wonder how we can realistically retain any sense of hope. Perhaps we can't. Perhaps something beyond hope is required.

Hope is the belief that things will get better, just as fear is the belief that things will get worse. I don't know how things will go in the future, but if I have any sense of the flow of our times it is this: By taking a stand on behalf of life in the present, we can develop a sense of integrity and identity that does not depend on separation, but instead is an offering to the common source of all that has life.

Peace Pilgrim was fond of saying that as we live according to the light we have, we open ourselves to more light. To me this means that we can get a renewed sense of promise and purpose from participating in the possibility of transformation. I don't know what the life force of this planet has up its sleeve, but I sense it has something to do with the development in each of us of the ability to live with love, responsibility, joy, and wisdom.

101
CATHERINE INGRAM

Catherine Ingram is the author of *In the Footsteps of Gandhi: Conversations With Spiritual/Social Activists.* As a journalist, she has for the past decade specialized in issues of social activism, meditation, psychology, and consciousness. She is a cofounder of the Insight Meditation Society in Barre, Massachusetts, and of the Unrepresented Nations and Peoples Organization in The Hague, Netherlands.

The Directive Power of Love

There came a point in my life a few years ago, when I looked around at our world and decided that there was no longer any reason to live. I felt that life had become degraded beyond anything I or the apocalyptic visionaries of Hollywood had ever imagined, for it seemed that humans had spoiled everything—the air, the land, the water. Almost all living systems and creatures were threatened, and no place, no matter how remote, was untouched. Even space was filling up with our junk, and one could no longer, on a clear night, dream on that great wilderness without seeing satellites or airplanes crossing the sky. In many places one could no longer even view the night sky through the haze of pollution. I saw that humans were more and more likely to lead subhuman lives; there were increasing numbers of people living in starvation, squalor, and disease, who would accept this fate, having known no other. Even those in rich countries, like my own, lived in a quiet and often repressed fear of the future, yet persisted in the consumption of resources that was killing it. All sense of meaning drained from life. What was the evolutionary point of this death march? I entered a depression that lasted more than a year. To think of the future was unbearable.

As is often true with turmoil, hitting bottom can be a point of epiphany. For me this came in the form of a series of realizations—transcendent in nature, but including the suffering of our world. I saw that on the larger screen, the big picture, no one goes anywhere. Worlds are created and dissolved back into the void, back into the silence from which they temporarily sprang, just as our own short lives dissolve back into their eternal source. These perceptions were experiential, not intellectual, for I had heard teachings about them for twenty years, yet had previously remained locked in the cellar of my mind and conditioning, a domain with which I had become all too familiar. Now I had opened the door to discover a vast silent sky of light, "a shimmering Void," in which all my little hopes and fears and, indeed, everything else arose and fell like tiny pin drops in an ocean. Expanding the view in this way relieved my constricted feelings of both personal and worldly suffering.

Some might say this is contraindicated in our present time of urgency. But these experiences also produced a sense of awe for this great mystery and a heartbreaking love for its manifestation in myriad forms, each one holding so desperately, so precariously, so colorfully to existence. I believe that it is out of an all-embracing love for this poignant manifestation that we can more likely make the choices and sacrifices needed to alleviate suffering and to steer ourselves in an intelligent direction. To work out of fear of disaster and gloom tends to sap one's strength and cloud the mind. Even if we do not manage to change our present course significantly or soon enough, still we rest eternally in the vastness—our efforts, successes, and failures, as all things, arising and passing away.

102

MARK MATOUSEK

Mark Matousek, a freelance journalist and contributing editor of
Common Boundary magazine, writes frequently about psychology and
spirituality.

Man Thinks, God Laughs

When my guru, Mother Meera, was asked by a university
professor about the future of the planet several years ago, she encouraged him not to worry, that the world would survive, that God
would care for his creation. The academic seemed frustrated by this
answer, put off, I suspect, by the characteristic simplicity of Mother
Meera's response and her impenetrable calm. Was she suggesting that
evil does not exist? She was not, Mother Meera explained, but rather
that it is beyond the capacity of the human being to resolve this evil—
that it is stronger, darker, wilier than he is—and that his energies are
better spent focusing on the good. "What about nuclear war?" he in-
sisted. Mother Meera smiled and answered, "There's always something."

At face value, the resolute cheerfulness of the enlightened ones,
their blessing of circumstance exactly as it is, can infuriate the ego
devoted to conflict, doomsday, enemies, and despair. Historically, this
serenity has been misinterpreted as naiveté, even foolishness; masters
have been accused of disconnecting themselves from matter, of sacrificing the Earth for eternity. Nothing, of course, could be further from
the truth. Upon reflection, Mother Meera's advice is far more practical, and constructive, than the prevailing movement toward crisis,

pessimism, and hysteria. When Meher Baba said, "Don't worry, be happy," the avatar was issuing not an invitation to mindless complacency but a spiritual mandate of the most penetrating order, knowing that nothing but liberation is of any ultimate use.

The ambivalence one detects in the attitude of many masters toward "changing the world" reflects their superior apprehension of what reality is, their realization that focusing on outer crisis at the expense of inner discipline—a hazard for many activists—is spiritually, socially, and ecologically futile. Having nothing to prove, enlightened beings never partake in the human thirst for drama (Mother Meera reminds us that the destruction of the world is a human idea, not a Divine one). They tell us to perfect our own tiny plots before venturing into agribusiness. This chastening wisdom, this refusal to incite riots, satisfies the climax-hungry seeker very little. Acceptance is less thrilling than tragedy, after all, but what else can individuals bent on healing our violence possibly suggest?

Overwhelmed by outrage and terror, determined to institute a global change, we cry out that the sky is falling. In response, the awakeners warn us against believing in the darkness, allowing it a home in our unsettled hearts. They assure us that destructive forces will always exist, but never prevail, in a dynamic universe—not even at Auschwitz, not even with bombs in Gaddafi's hands, not even— sad as this would be—if the Earth's population gave up hope. We participate in this destruction, or not, to the degree that we free ourselves from it. But putting the bulk of our energies toward reforming the world is, as a sage once remarked, like trying to straighten out a dog's tail, and just about as permanent.

This is not to suggest that activism is not useful: that we must not continue to struggle against injustice, to work diligently against the pollution of the planet, to fight for education and the freedom of the oppressed. Of course we must. But not as martyrs or self-proclaimed heroes; not in the shadow of some self-fulfilling apocalypse; not so much, in other words, out of terror as out of love.

As His Holiness the Dalai Lama has pointed out, even if the world were doomed—and it is not—the only honorable response would be to work toward the good in the last remaining moments. We are encouraged to act appropriately, to respond selflessly, to endeavor always to keep our hearts open in hell. But to imagine that hell will go away, that the new millennium will (if we just work hard enough) bring an end to danger, to uncertainty, to the simultaneity of agony and joy that is human life, is a form of delusion. The future is fully now, as always. We will see fluctuations, spiralings, mutations—magnificent advances and commensurate declines—but no ultimate resolution in this dimension until we realize God.

This is what Mother Meera knows, taking the full pain of humanity to her breast century after century. The ones like her who suffer most (because they see most clearly) harbor no illusion about the world exploding; the arduousness and complexity of the actual state of affairs allows them no such luxury. They know that there is no easy way out. As *bodhisattvas*, they are simply compelled to return, to help souls forward, despite the dark thing in us that secretly wishes the whole thing to go up in flames. In the face of every argument, every resistance and depression, they advise us to be happy, to do whatever good we can, to leave the rest to God. Tall orders for troublemakers, but good news after all.

103
DAVID LORIMER

David Lorimer, M.A., is director of the Scientific and Medical Network and the author of *Survival?, Whole in One: The Near-Death Experience and the Ethic of Interconnectedness,* and two books on the Bulgarian Gnostic teacher Peter Deneuv.

Light the Gentle Flame of Love

The freshness of the soul must speak in the world.
The force of the spirit must breathe through the world.

The soul is nourished by loving feelings.
The spirit breathes freely through noble aspirations.

The will is strengthened through creative action.

One is the Whole; many are the parts.
When the parts realize their oneness with the Whole,
They embody the Golden Rule,
"Transparent to Transcendence,"
Resonating empathetically.

When Love warms the heart
When Wisdom shines in the mind
Truth stands revealed in Freedom

The future unfolds from within ourselves
Mirrored in myriad fleeting outer forms.

Light disperses the Darkness
Wisdom dispels ignorance
Faith consumes doubt
Hope dissolves despair
Love melts hatred and fear.

One is Truth, many are the words
Inspiring aspiration,
Breathing new life into our perennial hopes.

Nothing new to say; only recollection, restatement.

Listen to the voice of your spirit within.
Sleep not! Forget not!
Light the gentle flame of the force of Love.

104

HAZEL HENDERSON

Hazel Henderson, D.Sc.Hon., is an independent futurist, syndicated columnist, and consultant in over thirty countries. She has published articles in over two hundred journals and is the author of *Creating Alternative Futures, The Politics of the Solar Age,* and *Paradigms in Progress.* She serves on many boards and has been Regent's Lecturer at the University of California, Santa Barbara, and held the Horace Albright Chair in Conservation at the University of California, Berkeley. The following poem is reprinted from her book *Paradigms in Progress* with the permission of Knowledge Systems, Inc.

Cosmic Economics

A work of art
Lies buried in the morning sand.
A sad lover seeks her necklace
Eyes scouring
The glorious, pristine beach
At sunrise.
Remembering the panic of loss
The night before
While walking this same way
Companions joined the search
That moonless hour
Scudding clouds darkening the sky
The lonely lover ponders her loss
Looking for meanings

As GAIA unfolds anew
Her morning splendor
Scurrying crabs in
Glistening pools of watery life
Diving white cranes slice
The breaking surf.

Oh! the ache
Remembering the necklace
Silver and turquoise,
Blazing sun pendant
Of the Zuni People
Fashioned by her lover's hand.
A gift of priceless beauty
From the heart.
Will the shining sand
Give back her hidden treasure?
Oh, cherished hope!
Or is the message deeper?

The giver's heart is full and pure,
Perhaps the soul who finds
The lost gem
Will feel hope and love restored
While contemplating
This sudden fortune.
Lost and Found.
Surely a bond between
Loser and Finder.
Is this the Message?

All gifts must pass
To complete the sacred
Circle of Life.
Loss and Gain are
Narrow Terms,
Eclipsed
In GAIA's cosmic economics.

The lover's search
Is rewarded with a sign:
Two majestic feathers
Lie in the sand
Discarded by a busy pelican.
Feathers of water birds
Are sacred to the Zuni People.
These gifts will now pass
From ocean to ancient
Desert Heartland.

Treasures are everywhere
For all who worship GAIA's plenitude,
Nothing is ever lost.
A part of both lovers
Now forever in this place.
When we re-member Universal Love
We rejoice
In letting all gifts pass.

GAIA does not need
To hoard her riches,
Nor do we.
Cast gladly all our gifts
Upon the water,
Sandy beaches, deserts, too,
Necklaces, bracelets,
Pots and arrowheads,
Glorious weavings, colors
Let them blend
Into the teeming
Multitudinous
Tapestries of Life
In Universal Giving.

105

HAL ZINA BENNETT

Hal Zina Bennett, Ph.D., has helped make possible over twenty books, more than half of them coauthored with leading teachers and healers of our time, including *The Well Body Book; Well Body, Well Earth; The Holotropic Mind; Change Your Mind, Change Your Life;* and most recently his own *Zuni Fetishes: Using Native American Objects for Meditation, Reflection and Insight.*

Honoring Our Power

"It was the best of times, it was the worst of times," Charles Dickens told us nearly 150 years ago. And these words may remind us that in our lives here on planet Earth, the forces we label good and evil, war and peace, humane and inhumane, violence and gentleness, hopefulness and hopelessness, greed and compassion are constantly with us. Always have been. They are expressions of our humanness. Our struggles with these are nothing new, providing lessons on our way to more fully realizing our true purpose.

We have wrestled into our custody the power to destroy whole continents, to annihilate all life on our planet. We have made powerful medicine to cheat death and bring comfort, as well as to meddle dangerously with the building blocks of nature. We have plumbed the creative powers of the human spirit, to abruptly face the best and the worst of our collective self.

Through our power we can challenge the lesser gods, competing with their boundless destructiveness, or we can embrace the love of our Creator. In the new millennium, the goal is to accept full responsibility for our power. The person with the biggest gun can use it to feed the needs of the ego or honor our oneness. Likewise, those with the power to heal can dedicate their handiwork to peace and love, or trade it only for temporary and all-too-fleeting personal gain.

Limiting our power to insatiable, ego-driven, transitory, temporal gains sadly diminishes our collective power, turning it against us all. In the new millennium we will learn to make new choices to benefit the All rather than the few. Out of this, we will begin to understand why giving generously with love ultimately provides us all with a wealth beyond our wildest imaginings. How much more wonderful it would be for the entire world to walk in peace, surrounded by beauty, than to be confined to even the most lush private gardens, barricaded with electric fences, and guarded by armed sentries! These choices are the essence of the gift we are offered.

One of my teachers, Awahakeewah, himself a craftsman, once confronted me at a dark moment in my life. He reminded me that I am only the custodian of creativity; it is not a personal possession like a car or a house. It is an extension of the Creator and Source of All. At the time, I had been unable to write for several months and was deeply depressed. ''Your creativity is not your own,'' Awahakeewah told me. ''You're only a minor vehicle for expressing what you cannot know on your own, no more than a flower or a shaft of grain. Honor Spirit! Get the hell out of its way!''

The message was clear. I had been asking not to serve that Creative Source but to use what I thought was my creativity for personal gain that ultimately would not have served anyone very well. Today, contemplating the new millennium, with all the global crises that we must address, I cannot help but think of Awahakeewah's words—to get out of the way of the creative spirit that moves in each of us. We do this by taking every opportunity to choose peace instead of conflict, love instead of hate, oneness instead of selfishness. In each moment throughout the day, we can choose to ride this evolutionary wave or thrash about wildly in a futile effort to escape it.

Clearly, our greatest crises—the environment, war waged over centuries-old grudges, famines, AIDS, the spreading of worldwide epidemics, living with great stockpiles of dangerous chemicals and nuclear wastes, et cetera, et cetera—are ones we ourselves have made. To look unflinchingly upon these and *own them unequivocally*, as proof of our power, is the first step toward a solution; to deny them is to deny our own power and to submit to our own self-destruction.

So much happening in our lifetimes seems like an evolutionary detour; but perhaps this path has been the only one we could find on the way to acknowledging and honoring our power. Perhaps only by confronting the worst of our potential are we able to understand how powerful we really are—and that if we are to truly delight in the gift of life that has been given us we must choose to use our creativity in the service of love, not fear. And in this revelation we might see that our true power is found in abandoning our fear.

The hope of the new millennium lies in deepening our understanding of our abilities as gods—wrathful and selfish or forgiving and loving. Twenty-some years ago, Joni Mitchell sang that we are "stardust" and "golden" and that "we've got to get ourselves back to the garden." And yet, I think the secret is to learn that we have never left the Garden; it is impossible to leave. We look around us and see the blooms and scions of the seeds we have planted here. And in contemplating all this, we must be as patient with ourselves as with those we would define as the enemies of this Garden; we have planted a crop whose beauty can only be found beneath the color, and we are only beginning to know and appreciate what that is. The biggest lesson of all, to borrow a thought from André Gide, is that *we must understand too quickly.*

106

DANAAN PARRY

Danaan Parry is a clinical psychologist and founder of the Earthstewards Network. He is known around the world for his ability to bring together conflicted cultures to heal the Earth and to become friends in the process. He is the author of the best-selling *Essene Book of Days*, *the Earth-stewards Handbook*, and *Warriors of the Heart*. The following is an excerpt from *Warriors of the Heart*.

A Vision of Love

"Is there no vision of love to bind us together?"

I feel so blessed to be working in a field that allows me to see the massive positive changes that are occurring on our planet. Not only am I in close networking contact with hundreds of groups doing hundreds of effective programs for global understanding, but I also get to visit every corner of the globe. In *every* place I go there are large numbers of people who are working diligently and joyfully for a better world for us all. It *IS* happening. You will not read about most of it or see it on television, because most media have not yet grown beyond the need for sensationalism, and because the nature of this positive change process is necessarily "grassroots," close to the earth, word of mouth, done by "just folks" and not by big shots. Its great strength and resiliency is in its dispersed, decentralized structure. This global grassroots wave of positive change is a hologram, not a pyramid. In a hologram every point is the center, and the old pyramid power structures cannot destroy a new model of power where every person is the center.

From my hands-on experience of this global shift comes my Vision of Love. It is a practical, real-life vision that is already beginning to happen. This is no pie-in-the-sky fantasy of a planet of white-robed light-beings coming to earth to rescue us and take us to that big hot tub in the sky. This is a vision of real people learning to experience their oneness through their differences.

Give Your Gift

Do you know about the concept of the "trim-tab"? Well, on every ship there is a rudder, right? On large ships, it takes a very big rudder to make the ship go in the right direction. This big rudder requires a lot of power to move it—chains, pulleys, motors, and servomechanisms. You alone could not budge that massive rudder without huge systems helping you to do it.

But, on every rudder of every large ship, there is a trim-tab. It is a small piece of metal attached to the rear of the rudder. It smooths out the fluctuations in the course of the ship, and without it set just right, the ship will wander back and forth, on and off its course. Because it is so small and because it is positioned in the right place on the rudder for maximum effect, it requires *very* little power to move it. You, one person, could do it all by yourself. You do not need to get large systems to do it for you.

Every one of us has a "trim-tab." Each of us has a gift to give that is our personal "trim-tab" to help our ship (spaceship Earth) get "on course." You don't need to ask permission to use it. You don't need to get approval from "them" to use it. In fact, you are the only one who *can* use it and *we need you to start using it! Now!*

What is your trim-tab? Are you a masseuse? Use that gift to heal the world. Let go of "safe" and find a way to massage the pregnant belly of a woman in Leningrad. Go to West Virginia and rub the feet of an old black man and don't say, "I'm here to heal you"; rather say, "Let me sit at your feet, grandfather, and rub them as you teach me what I must learn."

Are you an accountant, graphics artist, computer operator, or computer programmer? Get up and go work with Amnesty International or Food First or a local drug-rehabilitation center or a mediation center or any of the many organizations in your area who are *doing* something. Help them to be more effective and more loving. Don't do it forever, just for a while. Go make a difference with the tools that you have and let it change you. Then, come back and do it where you were planted (in your neighborhood and family) and transform that, too. *Be* the Vision of Love. You do it by sharing what is right in front of you. It is the sharing, it is the courage to open your boundaries and invite others to open theirs that heals the world. It is the *means* that count, not the ends.

I am always asked, "How?" "How can I do it? I don't even know how to get started." Stop asking that powerless, inhibiting question. Own your own power; change this Vision to make it *your* Vision of Love. Start telling people about your dream. Start looking for open doors, relevant organizations, leads. Start opening yourself to "trouble." The way will be shown when *you* show that you are serious about walking your talk.

107

LARRY DOSSEY

Larry Dossey, M.D., is a physician of internal medicine, a principal organizer of the Dallas Diagnostic Association, and former chief of staff of Medical City Dallas Hospital. He lectures widely in the United States and abroad, has published numerous articles, and is author of four books, including *Space, Time & Medicine, Beyond Illness, Recovering the Soul,* and *Meaning & Medicine.*

Choosing a Way of Being

"Except during the nine months before he draws his first breath, no man manages his affairs as well as a tree does."
—George Bernard Shaw

"The world is not to be put in order, the world is order incarnate. It is for us to put ourselves in unison with this order."
—Henry Miller

"He who is too busy doing good finds no time to be good."
—Rabindranath Tagore

"People do not need to think so much what they should do, but rather how they should be."
—Meister Eckhart

"Nothing is more fatal to health than overcare of it."
—Benjamin Franklin

I am not eager, bold
Or strong—all that is past.
I am ready not to do,
At last, at last!
—Saint Peter Canisius

"You can't put it together."
—First Whole Earth Catalog

These comments are part of a collective awareness that the world is, and has always been, too complex to be "fixed," even by the best, most well-intended minds. Never before has this fact been more apparent. Not only do experts not agree about solutions, they are not even in agreement about the problems. For many scientists the greenhouse effect remains an unsubstantiated fantasy; the "carrying capacity" of the planet is said to be billions more persons than the current world population; and, in general, predictions of Armageddon are frequently described as wild exaggerations, since, it is claimed, our technology can theoretically solve any currently identifiable problem. Because of these wild disagreements among so-called experts, it does not seem probable that scientific, political, and public opinion can be galvanized into the kind of action needed to meet the global problems that are the concerns of most of the people contributing to this book.

This may not be as forlorn a situation as it may seem. The height of folly, it seems to me, would be to proceed as if we *knew* what to do. Our greatest contribution to "saving the Earth" might well be a moratorium on doing—i.e., stopping, at least for a moment, the aggressive, robust, rough-and-ready kind of doing that seems to characterize the Western approach to problems of all types, and reappraising our place in the cosmic scheme.

There is solid experimental evidence suggesting that ways of being may be more potent than ways of doing in changing the state of the world. In these experiments the intervener does not try to steer the system in any particular direction. These studies involve societies of humans as well as "lower" organisms such as plants and micro-organisms. This evidence is not particularly popular among New Agers, however, because of the incessant proclivity of Westerners to take action, to tell the world what to do. These observations are sometimes interpreted by activists as unforgivable passivity, as giving up. They are not. They are simply an acknowledgment that we humans, besotted by our rigid notions of causality and linear time, have lost touch with how health comes about—both our own health and that of the planet.

So I find myself tiring of talk of "progress," whether it comes from materialistic scientists infatuated by a soulless technology, or whether it comes from those bent on saving the Earth. Sure, I'll continue to recycle, think green, and not have kids. But I also shall continue to feel that the wisdom of the planet so completely dwarfs my or anyone else's intelligence that my best and most proper response is not that of the repairman but noninterference. And I shall continue to pray that Lao-Tzu was right: "Practice not-doing and everything will fall into place."

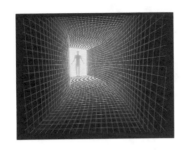

LIVING IN PEACE
AND HARMONY

108

JOHN WHITE

John W. White, M.A.T., is an internationally known author, editor, and educator in the fields of consciousness research, parascience, and higher human development. He is the author of *The Meeting of Science and Spirit, Pole Shift, A Practical Guide to Death and Dying,* and *Everything You Want to Know about TM.* He also has edited a number of anthologies, and dozens of articles and reviews by John White have appeared in popular magazines and major newspapers.

A New World Order

"History is the externalization of the idea of freedom."
—Hegel

"Civilization totters, but it totters steadily onward."
—H. G. Wells

These quotations succinctly give my view of the future. I am profoundly hopeful that humanity will survive looming disasters and will continue to play its destined role in the Grand Design of Creation, which is growth to liberation and godhood.

Do I have fears about the future? Of course. I fear the inevitable twists and turns we will take as we seek to play God rather than realizing our true nature as "always already God." So there will be more Hitlers and Husseins, more Stalins and Mao Zedongs, more McCarthys and Jim Joneses. The present stage of human evolution, which is characterized by the emergence of fully functioning ego in the masses, ensures that. Until *Homo noeticus* is firmly established as the dominant species of planet Earth (and nearby terraformed planets) several hundred years from now, there will be war and oppression and exploitation and various ego-engendered tribulations and afflictions of the innocent. The slicker forms will be scams by well-educated, polite men and women in positions of power who seek personal gain in ways that will make the banking and other financial swindles of today look like stealing from a kid's lemonade stand. There will be more covert action by governments seeking to consolidate power behind a facade of public service. There will be more drugs and AIDS-like plagues. There will be terrorism, gang violence, and criminal activity. There will be racial, ethnic, and religious divisions and prejudice. There will be self-centered hedonism and indifference to suffering.

But there also will be increasing numbers of people entering the transpersonal realm who work selflessly and steadfastly for human well-being. They will increase not only their numbers but also their *proportion* of the spectrum of human consciousness because that is where evolution and the life force is taking us. So we will see a politics of liberation based on genuine understanding of the transcendent dimension of human affairs; we can call that *liberative* politics, because it recognizes the best values of both the liberal and conservative approaches to social action and combines them with an emphasis upon increasing the sphere of individual freedom in a context of social membership. We also will see *transpersonal patriotism*—as distinguished from redneck jingoism—emerge in the community of nations. Through transpersonal patriotism, enlightened self-interest will be pursued in a fashion that honors history and diversity while building unity and removing institutional forms of bondage and barriers to equality.

Already the change of consciousness around the planet has placed enormous moral restraint on governments. The recent Persian Gulf War is dramatic evidence of that and of what the future holds. In 1991, a united front of world leaders and governments faced down a mass murderer-oil field arsonist trying to arm himself with nuclear-tipped long-range missiles, and it worked through a forum that over-arched them all—the United Nations. The diplomatic effort President Bush launched to work through the UN is laudable because the UN, for the first time in history, was not militarily impotent. More than 100,000 coalition sorties were flown against Iraq, yet the "collateral damage" (to use a military euphemism) was quite small in terms of civilian casualties and loss of cultural and religious sites. That degree of care for a civilian populace is unprecedented in the history of warfare; it bodes well for the future.

The restructuring of the Soviet Union, economically and politically, is further dramatic proof that the human hunger for freedom and authentic self-expression is fundamental to our psychological makeup. Democratic reform will continue around the world, despite the occasional emergence of tyrants and juntas.

This brings me to the "new world order." There are two aspects to it, as in all human activities: action and intention. One can do the right thing or the wrong thing for the right reason or the wrong reason.

A new world order is inevitable; the question is: What kind and controlled by whom? I expect economic confederations and cultural blocs of nations to emerge. The surge of nationalistic independence sweeping the former Communist bloc—indicative of the emergence of ego as separate self-sense among the masses—will moderate, and new economic-political alliances will emerge. Just as tribes were superseded by city-states, city-states by feudal fiefdoms, and feudal fiefdoms by nations, so will nations be superseded by confederations and regional unions such as the European Economic Community, until in the distant future—coincident with the elevation of *Homo noeticus* to species dominance—a true world culture founded in love and spiritual wisdom will emerge. At that time, the extraterrestrial embargo on planet Earth will be lifted and humanity will be openly welcomed into galactic society.

In the meantime, there will be political and economic cabals by power groups to secure control of society through various psychological and financial means. They will speak appealing words, such as "environmentalism" and "human rights" and "democracy," and they will often do the right thing because they accurately perceive the "course of human events." But they will not do the right things for the right reasons because they will see in political, not spiritual, terms. Rather, they will be secretly working for world domination through the front organizations of supranational groups whose leadership is either duped or covertly employed by the power groups. Their goal will be a new world order rather than a new world community.

Those dangers to human freedom will be omnipresent for a while, but they will not succeed, simply because the Transcendental Source and Divine Intelligence of Creation has deemed it so. I do not have space here to counter the argument that I am wearing rose-colored glasses, except to ask two questions. First, is it not completely evident that humanity has ascended to its present status because of an inherent urge for truth and freedom, despite the grotesque byways some members of the species have taken, and that the urge for truth and freedom is stronger among us than ever? Second, is it not completely evident that grace is guiding human affairs, so that we will someday be able to say to the misguided among us, as did Joseph to his brothers when they came to him in Egypt for rescue after selling him into slavery, "You intended it for evil, but God intended it for good"?

In *The Meeting of Science and Spirit*, I point out that we humans are on our way back to godhead—back to conscious realization of that which evoked us in the first place and which has been our true identity throughout every step of the drama in which we play the part of lost souls. It is a journey that occurs in stages, in evolutionary steps. We are now beginning to take a giant step into a new aeon. Yes, there are dangers. Yes, we must be cautious. But with an opening of the wisdom eye to match an opening of the heart, that journey will be completed, despite the setbacks and stupidity and willful abuse of ourselves and our world that await us along the way.

109

ADAM CURLE

Adam Curle was trained at Oxford in the social sciences, which he has applied to problems of poverty, education, oppression, and conflict resolution, mainly in economically deprived countries of Asia and Africa, though most recently in ex-Yugoslavia. This work has led to a number of books, including *True Justice* and *Mystics and Militants*, and university posts in several countries.

Steering the World Away from Violence

I was born in France within sound of the guns of World War I. My mother had arranged my birth like this because she was not only a francophile, but had deep sympathy with the troops of both sides engaged in the horrors of trench warfare.

When I was three, immediately after the end of hostilities, she took me back to France to instill in me a horror of war. I still remember the shattered towns in which we stayed, the fields pockmarked with shell holes, and the trenches still littered with fragments of equipment and rags of clothing. This did not prevent me from taking part in World War II, but thereafter my involvement with wars was only as a would-be peacemaker. Altogether I have spent more than a third of my life deeply implicated in eight wars, all desperate, and some very long lasting, and a couple of others somewhat less so.

The apparent causes of these conflicts obviously differed, but the usual underlying reason was that one group was oppressing another, depriving it of the means to satisfy its basic needs—physical, cultural, economic, and as a community with a sense of identity. The oppressors gained an advantage, normally economic, from their oppression, clinging to their supremacy with violence. For their part, the oppressed struggled with equal violence to attain what they considered their rights.

But violence corrupts all who practice it. The oppressors are greedy; the oppressed, dominated at first by a sense of injustice, become greedy for the lifestyle of the oppressors. All are deluded, believing that what is gained, or retained, by violence brings happiness. The struggle generates a distorted perception—a demonization—of the enemy that clouds the feelings and makes any reasonable settlement even harder to achieve. All too often the behavior of the oppressed, when victorious, degenerates into that of those they have vanquished. This is the way the world has been particularly since the end of World War II, during which time there have been some 150 wars.

However, although our great institutions—the states, the armies, the industries geared to making lethal weapons—dominate society, their hold over the minds of more and more individuals is weakening. The belief that human problems can be resolved by violence is fading as a new type of institution comes into maturity—the great international organs of the United Nations. But also a subtler and more fundamental change seems to have occurred in our hearts and our awareness; we sense the interconnectedness of all peoples, indeed of all life. How different are the young people of today from those with whom I grew up!

In my own work of trying to work toward more peaceful relationships through nonviolence, mediation, and reconciliation, I have moved away from questions of technique and method. These are of course important, but no more so than they are to a pianist whose true greatness reflects her musicianship, and whose musicianship is the measure of her whole being.

More and more it seems to me that my work must be much less a matter of helping people how to *do*, than how to *be*. There are, of course, some general principles, which are not much more than common sense and the fruits of experience. But these are of small avail unless we, the people trying to steer the world away from violence, do all we can to develop our humanity to the full. This involves working to expand our consciousness more and more from self- to other-awareness and indeed beyond, to include all life. And perhaps the best we can do for those others is to share as much of this as we can with them, *to be with them in this widening sphere of awareness.*

I realize now how much my mother, though using quite different words, knew about this, but it took me over seventy years to appreciate her wisdom. I hope my grandchildren—the whole world's grandchildren—will learn more quickly.

110

JIM BOHLEN

Jim Bohlen is a political/environmental activist who cofounded Greenpeace and the Green Party of Canada. Through the Greengrass Institute, he is involved in building an international nongovernment organization to lobby for global environmental governance.

The Case for Global Environmental Governance

The prevailing nation-state system of governance does not include the atmosphere and most of the planet's oceans. Consequently, enormous elements of the global ecosystem are open to ungoverned exploitation. This anarchic arrangement has lead to a dramatic deterioration of these global commons. The crash of fish stocks and the evidence of human-caused global climate change is grim testimony to the damage being imposed upon the very life-support systems of Earth.

The June 1992 United Nations Conference in Rio concerning environment and development demonstrated to the watching world that virtually no nation-state is willing to relinquish its sovereignty in the common interest of all. Even where the very survival of the entire planet is potentially at risk. George Bush, president of the United States, articulated this ecological *Götterdämmerung* by saying, "I will sign no agreement that in any way serves to diminish the American way of life."

A Way Out

This irresponsible intransigence indicates the necessity for establishing legally enforceable global governance over the transboundary life-support systems of the Earth. By what process can this be achieved?

Nation states, large and small, strong and weak, appear willing to relinquish some sovereignty in return for perceived economic advantages. This is evidenced by the formation of larger entities, such as the European Common Market and, more recently, the North American Free Trade Agreement. Similar moves are presently being contemplated in the Western Pacific Region, where Japan leads the way.

The same process of relinquishing some sovereignty to achieve a mutually beneficial objective ought to be applied to protecting the global environmental commons. The mechanics for achieving governance is obviously via the United Nations. That organization can effectively achieve it by simply obtaining agreement to expand the definition of security to include protection of the global environment.

What's the Holdup?

"It ain't easy, being green," to paraphrase the cartoon character Kermit the Frog. It will not be a simple matter to chart a course of conduct in respect to protecting the oceans and the atmosphere. It will affect virtually every resource user in every nation. Agricultural practices that permit discharges of herbicides, pesticides, and nitrogenous fertilizer into the water will have to be sharply curtailed. Incineration of garbage, burning of fossil fuels, use of ozone depleting chemicals, all of which substantially contribute to the greenhouse effect that causes global climate change, will need to be reduced or stopped altogether.

It is rapidly becoming evident that living in harmony with nature imposes limits to what we can safely do and use in pursuit of our material goals. The industrialized nations can no longer sequester eighty percent of the world's resources to satisfy the wants of twenty percent of the world's population. We need to share our good fortune with the billions who have almost nothing, with no prospects for gaining some relief from their poverty. To accomplish this goal, we need to define for ourselves what is a lifestyle of material sufficiency and then reorganize the engines of production and distribution to fulfill global needs.

It is predictable that those presently in power will vigorously resist these ecologically driven imperatives, for they challenge the status quo. Therefore, it is up to us, concerned citizens of this one Earth, to do all we can to press for the needed reforms so that a guaranteed healthy planet will be passed along to future generations.

328

To achieve this goal we need to organize a powerful lobby with the objective of pressuring our governments to support the notion that the concept of global security must be expanded to include protection of the environment. This demand would include a call for restructuring the United Nations decision-making process that presently shuts out the public.

Nothing in this appeal is meant to diminish the importance of engaging in local action to preserve one's environment. The evolution of ecologically responsible communities is essential to the task of building a sustainable global society.

ROY FINCH

Roy Finch, Ph.D., is former professor of philosophy at Sarah Lawrence College and at the City University of New York Hunter College and Graduate Center. He is the author of *Wittgenstein—the Early Philosophy* and *Wittgenstein—the Later Philosophy* and editor of the series *Conversations with the Great.*

Visiting and Leaving Troy

i

Standing in—the sign said—the ruins of Troy
With more than ten cities beneath our feet,
No water in sight, no place for the Greek ships,
The most important thing that day was a frog.

Children had found it in the parking lot,
Had brought it to the ticket office,
Enjoyed it more than the ruins. The day was hot
And shabby, as in Schliemann's time, and Troy's.

Impossible to relate the heap we saw
Of mounds and holes to anything we had read
Or knew. We looked in vain for—even a hint of—
Topless towers and *Menaleus upon the walls.*

Credit it to Homer. Troy was always real
In the imagination. He made it, and poet

After poet, to bewitch schoolboys and teach them
Honor and fatality of war after war.

Also to teach that imagination rules
With infatuations of triumph and doom.
A good war, said the philosopher, can justify
a whole lifetime of wicked despair.

No wonder that Schliemann had his wife
Read aloud from the epic to remind them
Of what they were doing in that god-forsaken place,
With chronic lack of funds and fractious locals.

What *were* they doing? Layer upon layer:
There was Troy; there was Homer; there were poets;
There was Schliemann; there was the frog.
Such stories, it seems, are never finished.

But, remember this: the Greeks could always see
The ships which reminded them of home.
Yet stayed nine years. Now the water is silted up.
Fate casts no spell. The place is no longer there.

ii

We are leaving Troy this afternoon—
Not the grandeur, clang of spears and shields,
And far-off cries of men at War,
Not the ageless tellings in children's books,

Nor yet Schliemann's find, city upon city
(Entrance through souvenir shop with indefinite
Designs, incomprehensible maps and brochures,
Courtesy Turkish government, via Hong Kong).

Fill in what you please: Helen, trade, pirates,
History, patriarchy, economics,
Mythic archetypes, ideological dramas.
There is room for it and more. Take it.

What we are leaving is the old fatality,
The long drum roll of the undead, unkind past,
The headlong slide into inevitability,
That human condition of being a man.

To be a man was to stay there—nine years—
Never to surrender to reason or thought.
To accept the burden of killing and dying
(Sweet and decorous to die, blood-lust killing).

Sad immortality on distant shores,
In steaming jungles or blazing deserts,
Heroic youth, flag-draped coffins, fresh remains,
Sons altared to ancient necessity.

This story no longer bears the telling,
No longer holds. What poet can hymn
Mass destruction? What epic lies in
Dresden, Hiroshima, or Auschwitz?

Science has spoiled the honor of war,
As it has spoiled the sacrifice of Abraham.
An older voice is heard: the Ancient Mother,
Demanding unity of earth and humanity,

Calling the heroes home from Troy.

112

RICHARD FALK

Richard Falk, Ph.D., has been a member of the Princeton faculty since 1961. He has written books on international law and prospects for a just and sustainable world, and has long been associated with the World Order Models Project. Among his books are *A Study of Future Worlds* and *Explorations at the Edge of Time*.

International Law: A Mask for Geopoliticians, a Shield for Citizens, a Tablet of Commandments to Shape a Just World Order

Often, misleadingly, there is a public impression that reliance on international law and international institutions is inherently desirable, especially as compared to states acting on their own. Without becoming cynical, it is important to be critical, which means identifying the troubling, and hopeful, elements associated with the various roles being played by international law in the historical frame of the present and near future.

To begin with, to an unprecedented degree, international law is currently more prominent than it has ever been before. This prominence is partly expressive of long-term trends toward complexity and interdependence, perhaps most evident in relation to the evolution of the world economy and efforts to protect the environment (especially the global commons). Such prominence also reflects post-Cold War realities, the possibilities for cooperation among leading states even in matters of peace and security, and the practical relevance of the United Nations as an arena for the making of global policy under such circumstances. Perhaps nothing expresses this trend more forcefully than the high visibility that is given in this period to the negotiation and ratification of important international treaties—the North American Free Trade Agreement, the Maastricht Treaty (on European monetary affairs), and the General Agreement on Trade and Tariffs (GATT).

But prominence is no assurance of performance. Recourse to the United Nations during the Gulf Crisis in 1990 illustrated both the prominence of international legal approaches in this new global setting and the degree to which geopolitics is alive and well, manipulating the agenda on behalf of the specific, often selfish, objectives of big states. What the United Nations Security Council achieved in response to Iraq's aggression against Kuwait was to mandate the United States government and its partners to wage war without any restrictions on the scale of means employed. True, Iraq was obliged to withdraw from Kuwait and was seemingly deprived of its capacity to threaten other states in the region. In this central respect, the promise of collective security was kept. Unlike the period of the League of Nations, when responses to aggression were feeble and disillusioning, or during the Cold War, when the UN was paralyzed in responding to most war/ peace issues, the response to the Gulf War demonstrated that the UN could be effective. What was not demonstrated was whether the UN could be both effective *and* legitimate (that is, adhering to its own charter, avoiding war to the extent possible, acting collectively in the carrying out of decisions as well as in their authorization, avoiding double standards and selective enforcement).

There is, then, a tension between *geopolitics* (greater power dominance) and *geogovernance* (world authority within a democratic constitutional order) that is expressed in relation to the language and behavior of law-oriented undertakings. Are these undertakings of global actors mainly providing vehicles for existing structures of power and privilege in the world? Can such undertakings be brought under democratic controls to an increasing degree, making states, corporations, banks, and markets accountable for compliance with international legal standards and empowering citizens and their associations to implement these standards in appropriate tribunals and through participation in the workings of international organizations? Western Europe has moved impressively, if insufficiently, ahead on several fronts: In human rights settings, citizens can appeal to regional institutions for protection against abuses, including those committed by their own government; in relation to regional policy, the directly elected European Parliament, although lacking governmental authority, suggests the possibility of a representative legislative process beyond the reach of territorial states. Much more needs to be done to achieve democratic control over the instrument of law in the struggle to promote human rights, nonviolence, environmental safety, and the economic and cultural well-being of all peoples.

Nothing will be accomplished without political initiatives rooted in civil society and organized transnationally. Two areas of constructive popular pressure can be mentioned. First of all, the United Nations needs to be restructured to make it more independent from geopolitical forces and more reflective of changes in the world that have occurred in the almost half-century since its establishment. A concrete idea would be to add "a moral superpower" to the Security Council, selected by a commission composed of former winners of the Nobel Peace Prize, to serve for a term of five years. The purpose of this position would be to emphasize that morality is as important as is the association of power with military capabilities and wealth.

A second area would be to give citizens legal access to domestic courts to challenge the legality of foreign policy by reference to the norms of international law. This legal empowerment would acknowledge the relevance of the Rule of Law *beyond* as well as *within* the borders of sovereign states. Possessing the capability to confine foreign policy to an objective reading of international law framework would be a breakthrough in constitutional rights and would disempower large states from using force at their discretion.

From a professional perspective, lawyers with these sorts of outlook have started to organize transnationally. In 1992, the International Association of Lawyers Against Nuclear Arms (IALANA), founded a few years ago, launched (in collaboration with other NGOs, including the main initiative of medical professionals, Physicians for the Prevention of Nuclear War) The World Court Project. Its goal is to persuade the United Nations General Assembly to seek from the World Court in The Hague an Advisory Opinion to establish that the threat or use of nuclear weapons is always in violation of international law, a determination which if made would add weight to the overall struggle to abolish all weaponry of mass destruction.

This brief overview suggests both the menace of international law at the disposal of existing centers of military and economic power and the promise of international law at the disposal of democratic social forces. The balance is now weighted heavily in a geopolitical direction. Whether it can be redirected on behalf of the great historical project of equitable and sustainable geogovernance is the decisive challenge facing both the specific profession of law and the far broader reality of an emergent transnational democracy.

113
MICHAEL HARBOTTLE

Brigadier Michael Harbottle, O.B.E., is a former chief of staff of the United Nations Peacekeeping Force in Cyprus. He is the author or coauthor of a number of books on international peacekeeping, including the *Peacekeeper's Handbook*. He has been a senior lecturer in peace studies at universities in England, Canada, and South Africa, and in 1983 he and his wife, Eirwen, founded the Centre for International Peacebuilding. He is a founder-member of Generals for Peace and Disarmament.

Proper Soldiering:
People and the Planet First

In 1966 I was appointed chief of staff of the United Nations Peacekeeping Force in Cyprus. After twenty-nine years of service in the British army, this was to be a turning point in my life, not only in terms of experience, but in my whole approach to militarist doctrine. My task as a peacekeeper was not to enforce solutions on those involved in conflict but to assist them in finding those solutions without resorting to violence. We did this in many ways by interpositioning the UN soldiers between the combatants at critical times in areas of direct confrontation, but mostly through negotiation, mediation, and conciliation. Every member of the force was involved, from the most junior soldier up to the force commander. As proof, the fighting was brought to an end after four and a half years without the UN firing one round of ammunition.

This service with the UN was so compelling and worthwhile that at its end I resigned from the British army. No way could I return to a stereotype of the past, which I had come to see as a retrograde and negative approach to the resolution of conflicts, like that of Northern Ireland.

The Centre for International Peacebuilding, which my wife and I established in 1983, is designed to facilitate opportunities for people of different nations, particularly those of western and eastern Europe, to interact and interrelate, combining their professional experience and expertise in joint projects that, besides benefiting our global society, will overcome the prejudices and "enemy" images dominating the political scene at the time.

This was our vision in 1983, one which has not diminished over the years but rather has been enhanced. Enough has happened in the meantime to encourage one to believe that attitudes are beginning to change in military thinking with regard to the interpretation of security and the revisions in doctrine and strategy required. At the armed forces' institutions in a number of countries, serious thought is being given to how military resources could be more widely applied to a more holistic concept of security. More and more countries are coming around to the idea of involving their armed forces in their national environmental conservation programs. Senior officers in Britain's armed forces, who in the next few years will hold the highest positions at the top of their professions, are beginning to recognize that a new philosophy of service is needed whereby the armed forces can serve their community and society as a whole, in a more constructive way. It no longer makes any sense to train for war 365 days a year when the resources that the armed forces have on offer, professional and technical, could be applied to a broader-based potential.

A year ago I published "What is Proper Soldiering: Centre for International Peacebuilding," which outlined a new perspective of the role of armed forces in the 1990s, advocating a three-dimensional commitment besides that of national defense: UN peacekeeping/peacebuilding, international disaster relief, and environmental security. The military infrastructure and its considerable technical capabilities could be used to "fight" for the survival of our planet. Great attention has been given to this document internationally because it represents a positive approach to the resolution of the present dilemma facing the armed forces in many countries in terms of future doctrine and military strategy. It is a vision that extends the possibilities for greater global security and stability, for the perspective calls for international interaction and the joining of forces to deal with environmental problems that know no boundaries or borders. The essence of peacebuilding would thus be encouraged and military confrontation replaced by cooperation.

Peacebuilding, after much arguing, has at last been recognized as a crucial part of conflict resolution. Peacemaking (diplomatic) and peacekeeping (military) can achieve only so much, but as long as the fundamental causes of a conflict exist, peacemaking and peacekeeping can only be a peripheral and temporary expedient. Peacebuilding tackles the roots of the conflict, reestablishing the social, economic, and intercommunication structures between communities or states, rebuilding confidence, restoring the administrative structures that have been broken down—all of which have to be successfully accomplished before a conflict can be said to have ended. Peacebuilding has a place in all the dimensions of conflict resolution: in the preventive diplomacy or pre-action stage, within the peacemaking and peacekeeping process, and in the post-action phase when it is needed most of all. To date, even though peacebuilding has become an acceptable practice for the UN and is seen to be a part of the process of the peaceful settlement of disputes, it still has to be tried. But in the future I do believe that its potential will be fully justified, and UN operations will be mounted with joint military/civilian components for peacemaking, peacekeeping, and peacebuilding.

In 1985 I entered an essay competition arranged by the *Christian Science Monitor* with the theme "How Peace Came to the World in the Year 2010." My entry was subsequently published as one of their selected essays in a book of the same name. In my essay I used the practical experience and thinking of our Centre for International Peacebuilding and the group Generals for Peace and Disarmament in offering a proposition by which peace and stability could come to the world through interstate and intrastate peacebuilding. Since then we have moved forward along this road, and, though intrastate conflicts are rampant, there is a growing awareness that security and stability are not achievable through violence or the barrel of a gun, but rather that if a peaceable and survivable world is to come about, it has to be through the way in which people respond to one another and to the fact that people and the planet are more important than politics and nationalism. It is a vital ingredient to this process that we all learn to understand and accept the differences in geopolitical perspectives of peace and security as viewed by and related to different regions of the world. The quicker we do so the better we can respond to the North American Indian's philosophy of "having to walk a mile in another man's moccasins before one can know what he is saying."

114

KEN KEYES, JR.

Ken Keyes, Jr., is a leading figure in the fields of personal growth and world peace. He is the author of a dozen books, including the best-selling *Handbook to Higher Consciousness* and *The Hundredth Monkey*, and is founder of the Ken Keyes College in Coos Bay, Oregon.

Plenty and Security for
All through International Law

If humanity is to enjoy the third millennium, there are certain directions that we should take as quickly as possible before it is too late.

Our species faces extinction unless we go beyond the international anarchy of about two hundred nations scattered around the globe—each of which tends to regard its interests as more important than all the rest of the people on this Earth. The demise of *Homo sapiens* may come from the evermore efficient killing devices that our military-industrial complex is creating every day. More and more nations have nuclear weapons. All nations today are capable of making poison gas. Other effective methods of mass killing are being improved or invented. Both our lives and our pocketbooks today are in great jeopardy as we go toward the third millennium.

You would not think of living in a city without the protection of laws, courts, and enforcement. Yet we live in a "Wild West world." Law and order came to the Wild West when people demanded that the pistols be taken off the hips of the people and given to a sheriff who would protect everyone. Harry Truman said, "When Kansas and Colorado have a quarrel over water in the Arkansas River, they don't call out the National Guard in each state and go to war over it. They bring suit in the Supreme Court of the United States and abide by the decision. There isn't a reason in the world why we cannot do that internationally . . . . It will be just as easy for nations to get along in a republic of the world as it is for you to get along in the republic of the United States." The nations of this world must develop a system of mutual security through laws, courts, and enforcement that enables countries to safely disarm. In the last century, no democracy has declared war on another democracy. Perhaps we can amend the United Nations charter to provide all the democracies with the defense and ecological protection they are not getting today.

We must solve international disagreements *legally* rather than *lethally*. We must have international laws enacted by elected representatives of the people, an international police force trained to enforce the laws, and international courts to decide who is innocent or guilty. Today our international anarchy leaves humanity naked and defenseless before any dictator who can get his hands on a bunch of weapons.

Weapons are fast. The slow way to eliminate humanity is by environmental degradation. It is only in the twentieth century that we began to seriously impact the quality of our food, air, and water. Unless we simplify our lifestyles and as consumers use less fuel, energy, lumber, newsprint, hydroflourocarbons, and so on, we will gradually diminish the Earth's ability to sustain us.

International problems must have international institutions to solve them. Our global ecology must be protected by enforced international laws. No nation alone can do the job. *It is fortunate that both the problems of war and ecology can be solved by a single solution—enforced international law.*

A life primarily motivated by trying to find enough security, enough sensations, and enough power, pride, prestige, and money is not deeply fulfilling. Those who are happiest on Earth understand the limitations of the material plane alone to give us a really satisfying life. Whether an individual has discovered it or not, we all have within us a higher self that can only be satisfied through service to others. A mind preoccupied with its own security, sensation, and power is like a body that is nurtured only by cotton candy. The deeper satisfactions require us to place increasing amounts of energy into appreciating others, understanding others, cooperating with others, and giving generously of our time and our resources to others. As has been said, "It is through giving that we receive."

The development of understanding and compassion is essential to our highest happiness. We cannot always approve the words and actions of other people (sometimes we must even oppose them). But behind it all, we can always realize that they are simply trying to feel good, capable, loved, beautiful, or worthwhile (either skillfully or unskillfully). As strange as it may seem, both the bank robber and the schoolteacher are alike. They both want to feel secure financially. The vast difference between their actions lies in their level of skill in doing so. Even though we must clash with and oppose what someone may be doing in the moment, we can always extend our compassion by realizing that they are just unskillfully trying to get what all of our human hearts want—a life on Earth that feels good.

At this point in history, our species seems to be at a crucial point in its journey. *Homo sapiens* has only been on Earth for several thousand generations. We have created the ability to destroy ourselves. Or through both international law and creating understanding, caring, compassion, and heart feeling toward all of our human family on earth, we can create the joy, fulfillment, and happiness that is our birthright.

115

ROBERT MULLER

Robert Muller is emeritus chancellor of The University of Peace in Costa Rica and former assistant secretary general of the United Nations. His World Core Curriculum for education is being adopted by schools around the globe and earned the 1989 UNESCO Education Peace Prize. He is the author of several books, including *What War Taught Me About Peace*, *The Birth of a Global Civilization*, and *First Lady of the World*.

Dream for the Next Millennium

I dream
That on 1 January 2000
The whole world will stand still
In prayer, awe and gratitude
For our beautiful, heavenly Earth
And for the miracle of human life.

I dream
That young and old, rich and poor,
Black and white,
Peoples from North and South,
From East and West,
From all beliefs and cultures
Will join their hands, minds and hearts
In an unprecedented, universal
Bimillennium Celebration of Life.

I dream
That the year 2000
Will be declared World Year of Thanksgiving
By the United Nations.

I dream
That during the year 2000
Innumerable celebrations and events
Will take place all over the globe
To gauge the long road covered by humanity
To study our mistakes
And to plan the feats
Still to be accomplished
For the full flowering of the human race
In peace, justice and happiness.

I dream
That the few remaining years
To the Bimillennium
Be devoted by all humans, nations and institutions
To unparalleled thinking, action,
Inspiration, elevation,
Determination and love
To solve our remaining problems
And to achieve
A peaceful, united human family on Earth.

I dream
That the third millennium
Will be declared
And made
Humanity's First Millennium of Peace.

116
ELIZABETH ATWOOD LAWRENCE

Elizabeth Atwood Lawrence, D.V.M., Ph.D., is a veterinarian as well as an anthropologist, and is professor of environmental studies at Tufts University School of Veterinary Medicine. Dr. Lawrence is the author of numerous articles and three books, including *Rodeo: An Anthropologist Looks at the Wild and the Tame*, *Hoofbeats and Society*, and *His Very Silence Speaks: Comanche—The Horse Who Survived Custer's Last Stand*.

The Owl's Call: A Meditation on Interspecies Reciprocity

Several times during recent political campaign speeches, President George Bush assured his listeners that "people are more important than owls." Deriding his rivals, the Democratic challengers for president and vice president, Mr. Bush even ventured to warn the American people: "Elect my opponents, and we'll be up to our necks in owls!" The president's overriding certainty, his strident and persistent references to owls as an election issue, and his ultimatum that countless jobs are doomed if owls are saved are strongly evocative of speculation about humankind and nature and the precarious relationship between them as the end of the second millennium approaches.

Key questions arise: Must we choose? Is it us or them, people or owls, humans versus animals, the tame versus the wild, culture versus nature? Or is there still time and do we possess the ingenuity to find ways of simultaneously appreciating and preserving the interests of both? Can balance be established and maintained, can humanity find a harmonious place within the natural world?

Specifically at stake in the current controversy is the northern spotted owl, endangered denizen of the vast, magnificent old-growth Western forests upon which the species is totally dependent and with which its life cycle is intimately interwoven. Large and spectacular, yet uncommon and retiring, found only deep within its dense woodland sanctuary, this bird is an appropriate symbol of the age-old dilemma surrounding human interaction with nature. Evidently President Bush and those whose support he was acknowledging or seeking are convinced that owls are antithetical to jobs, and believe that no law or agency has the right to place the survival of what Bush called "that little furry-feathered guy" ahead of people's livelihood.

On a practical level, arguments center around whether or not the Endangered Species Act allows sufficient consideration of the economic costs of preserving biodiversity. Sacrificing the owl by destroying its forest habitat for lumber, however, will not insure jobs for very long. As pointed out in a *New York Times* editorial (September 21, 1992), further clear-cutting is only a short-term remedy and, if continued at the present rate, could annihilate the old-growth forests in fifteen years, ending not only the loggers' work but also the sustainable jobs associated with recreation and tourism. Other factors involving business decisions and market forces such as the exportation of raw timber to Japan, automation, and a shift in investment capital to the South by the big timber companies may well have been more detrimental to the loggers' employment than the ban on cutting trees to preserve owls.

A solution to the current owl problem, as it represents a microcosm of many such conflicts, must involve reconciliation between human interests and conditions required for the bird's survival. Thus this particular situation highlights the need for a clear path for the twenty-first century. In the face of pressing human concerns, we must learn to take account of the rights of other forms of life to share this earth with us. To do so, we must reexamine the basic ideology of our society that has so long dictated that human desires and immediate gains are paramount and that we have an imperative for unquestioned domination of the natural world. A most profound change must come in viewing animals not as mere instruments for human exploitation but as possessing intrinsic value.

In the case of the owl, as with other creatures, it must be perceived through the lens of our whole being—not as a frivolous and expendable caricature for amusement or as a scientific specimen for classification. Fortunately, there are precedents. In ancient Greece, Athena, Goddess of Wisdom, took council from an owl who was her constant companion. And out of the Celtic tradition comes Merlin, the great sage and teacher who also obtained knowledge and instruction from an owl. A dramatic painting by a contemporary Kiowa-Comanche artist, Blackbear Bosin, entitled "Of the Owl's Telling" depicts a Plains Indian warrior who is seeking a vision receiving the message of an owl perched on his shoulder. Indeed almost every known culture has revered the owl, endowing it with deep-level significance on aesthetic and spiritual planes. Thus the unique bird brings into focus the sharp distinction between strictly pragmatic considerations and profound meanings that emanate from that same portion of human consciousness that gives rise to art, poetry, and myth.

Owls' capacities, wondrous in the biological sense, become even more so under the influence of the mind, which transforms ordinary observations into metaphor that elucidates the human condition as part of nature and infuses mortal existence with significance beyond the mundane. Under the resulting enchantment, all forms of life are kin and share many attributes with their relatives. Most importantly, animals are recognized as having characteristics not possessed by people, fostering a complementary relationship rather than one in which the nonhuman is inferior.

Owls' unique set of traits have made them, for virtually all peoples, more than a distinctive group of avian predators. Their unusual capacity for keen vision in the dark has always evoked deep admiration and gave rise to the idea that the brilliance of the owls' shining eyes must be attributable to an inner light, a magic glow that guides them at night when most other beings are virtually sightless. Since, as a skilled nocturnal hunter, the owl can travel safely and surely through the darkness of night, it became known as a guide on the human journey to the afterlife. For the darkness of night is often an allegory for the darkness of death, and the passage to the hereafter is dark and dangerous. The owl became a link with the supernatural world, not only as a messenger of death and a predictor of fatality or misfortune, but also as a source of knowledge about the afterlife. By seeing more clearly, the owl also seems to know more profoundly than other creatures, including humans. In many cultures, the owl is the embodiment of wisdom.

Other biological characteristics contribute to the bird's reputation for sagacity. Its absolutely silent flight and soundless motions when capturing prey have an association with uncanny skill and premeditation. Observations of the nocturnal owl's stillness and somber mien during the day add to its image of quietness. Long diurnal periods of physical inactivity, during which the owl appears to experience inward-directed contemplation, reinforce the idea of unusual knowledge coupled with self-discipline. Its air of aloofness, a perceived withdrawal from earthly concerns, helps to transform the owl into a scholar, even an ascetic, whose spirit is master over its body and who concentrates not on the physical world but on eternal truths. New graduates, professors, philosophers, magistrates, and others who are perceived to have special intellectual powers are symbolized by the "wise old owl" wearing academic gown and spectacles, who has the ability to make discerning judgments.

Sobriety is paramount. As a seeker of privacy, solitude, and secluded places, the bird is emblematic of a passion for books and learning and of libraries as quiet places for study. The owl's vigilance allows it to stay awake all night while most creatures sleep, suggesting the soul's immortality. Its eerie voice is often somber and solemn, befitting a partaker of the divine mystery. Looking to the owl as interpreter of supernatural messages, bearer of spirits, and guardian of souls, doctors, priests, and shamans of various cultures have often courted the owl's favor, asking for guidance in the healing arts.

No matter how effective our stewardship of the living earth, it is doubtful we will ever be "up to our necks" in owls. But on the threshold of the third millennium, we can learn from the bird who has been almost universally regarded as a sacred font of wisdom. Members of an ancient group that predated humankind on earth, owls have not generally been hunted or domesticated. Rather they have remained wild and remote inhabitors of yet-unconquered domains. Inspiring the human imagination, they evoke fear, awe, or respect, and continue to express and symbolize profound thoughts and emotions. Uniting science and poetry through their eyes' inner light that is celebrated by both realms, the spotted owl calls us not to make a choice between pragmatism and beauty, between people and animals, but to restore reciprocity between humankind and the natural world and to work tirelessly at the task of bringing our species into harmony with all forms of life who share the planet.

117

MICHAEL W. FOX

Michael W. Fox, D.V.M., Ph.D., is a vice president (Bioethics and Farm Animals section) of The Humane Society of the United States, is on the board of directors of the Center for Respect for Life and Environment, and is a vice president of Humane Society International. He has authored over forty books, is a contributing editor to *McCall's Magazine*, and has a nationwide syndicated newspaper column entitled "Ask Your Animal Doctor." Among his many books are *Inhumane Society: The American Way of Exploiting Animals*, *Returning to Eden: Animal Rights and Human Responsibility*, and *Understanding Your Pet*.

Steps Toward a Humane Society

Millions of people enjoy the company of companion animals and the birds and other creatures in their gardens and community parks. But except for the occasional visit to the zoo or a drive into the country where one might see a few cows and horses (since most farm animals are kept indoors in "factory" farms), we are not generally aware of the degree to which society depends upon exploiting animals. And we are also ignorant of how much of a burden we have become to the animal kingdom. Indeed, modern society is responsible for nothing less than a holocaust of the animal kingdom. Animal suffering and extinction is symptomatic of a destructive relationship with the rest of creation that may well terminate in our own extinction and is linked today with the disintegration of the atmosphere and the increasingly dysfunctional condition of both the Earth and industrial civilization.

Now is a time of reckoning for each of us to make an honest

and thorough inventory of how we singly and collectively cause harm, suffering to other creatures, and destruction of the natural world that is fast becoming an industrialized wasteland. Religious leaders are saying that this reckoning is important for our redemption as more environmentalists contend that it is essential for our future survival. Half a century ago Mahatma Gandhi said that "the greatness of a nation and its moral progress can be judged by the way in which its animals are treated." The spiritual insight of St. Francis of Assisi made him call all creatures our brothers and sisters, and he called for a true democracy that embraced all of creation in respect and reverence. But today animals are treated as mere commodities by a consumer society that is consuming the world. As Albert Schweitzer advised, without a reverence for all life, we will never enjoy world peace. The fate of the animals will be ours also. Compassion is a boundless ethic, and if we exclude animals or certain species from this circle of ethical concern and responsibility, we are guilty of a chauvinism that animal rightists rightly term "speciesism." Politically it is nothing less than biological fascism.

While millions of people love their animal companions, enjoy Nature, and are concerned about the protection of endangered species like the panda bear, the humpback whale, the bald eagle, and the African elephant, evil flourishes where good people do nothing. Only when we look at our personal and collective inventories and realize to what degree animals are exploited and suffer directly and indirectly from habitat destruction, do we realize how extensive our impact is on the animal kingdom.

The suffering and sad demise of the animal kingdom can be stopped, as it must for our own redemption and for the future and integrity of Earth's creation. Simply sending a donation to an animal protection or conservation organization or putting one's fur coat in mothballs is not enough. Our lifestyles, consumer habits, recreational activities, and even the practice of medicine and allied animal research, as well as agricultural practices that rely on harmful chemicals and intensive, drug-dependent methods of livestock and poultry production, must all be changed. In helping liberate animals from the cruel tyranny of industrialism, consumerism, and scientific imperialism, we will be helping ourselves also. Such altruism is enlightened self-interest.

Two notions must be put to rest. One is that animals were created for humanity's use and that we have God-given dominion to exploit them as we choose (Genesis 1:26). The other is that since animals prey on each other, it is natural and not unethical for humans to exploit fellow creatures. First, the original meaning of *dominion* is from the Hebrew root verb *yorade,* which means literally "to come down to, to have communion with." It is an injunction to humane, compassionate care. As to the second notion, there are now 5.3 billion people on Earth and 3.6 billion livestock, far too many of us to live as predators since the planet is too small. And it is suffering the consequences of overpopulation and overconsumption. The more livestock we raise and consume, the less land is available for wildlife, whose extinction rate accelerates as a consequence.

Some people are skeptical because they feel it is too late to make a difference. But it is never too late and the challenge never too great when there is a unified spirit of concern, which is the only foundation for a community of hope. As overwhelming as the task may seem to make the world a better place for our children and for fellow creatures, we can all make a difference because we have the power of choice. We can choose not to buy furs and ivory, soak our lawns with weed killer, or eat "factory" raised pork and veal. My book *Inhumane Society* not only documents the extent of animal suffering and environmental destruction in the world today; it also offers many choices and empowers us all to make a difference for the good of all.

Our own well-being, and of generations to come, depends on everyone recognizing that animals have interests, feelings, a will to live, and are worthy of our respect and concern. As we destroy their habitats, so we destroy "our" environment and life-support systems; as we crush their spirits to serve our own ends, so we demean our own. Human well-being, animal well-being, and the well-being of the natural world are one and the same. We are all one. When we take care of Earth's creatures and creation, the Earth will take care of us. Our arrogance, nonsubsistence needs, and scientific powers should not lead us to think otherwise, since we have neither the wisdom nor the technology to create an alternative life-support system at Nature's expense. As history will show, in the process of trying to do so, we destroy our own humanity, which cannot be fulfilled at the expense of the rest of Earth's creation.

118

BERNARD E. ROLLIN

Bernard E. Rollin, Ph.D., is professor of philosophy, professor of physiology and biophysics, and director of bioethical planning at Colorado State University. He is the author of over 130 articles and six books, including *The Unheeded Cry,: Animal Consciousness, Animal Pain, and Science* and *Animal Rights and Human Morality*. He has lectured all over the world.

Animal Rights—Preserving an Ancient Contract

It is accepted "wisdom" among the agricultural and research communities that those who advocate for the recognition and the codification in law of rights for animals are radicals and extremists. Opponents of animal rights further maintain that concern for animals is a misguided urban phenomenon, a decadent creature of wealth and leisure, growing out of humanity's ever-increasing distance from its agricultural roots.

In truth, both of the above claims are grossly inaccurate. In the first place, if the concern for animal rights were strictly or even primarily a fringe phenomenon, it could enjoy no social efficaciousness. As a Texas cowboy once said to me: "Hell doc, if it were just the radicals, we could shoot the sons of bitches." It is certainly the case that the most radical proponents shout the loudest, grab the most media coverage, and state the position in its most extreme form, but that is true of any social movement.

Nonetheless, for any movement to be effective, its most hyperbolic rhetoric must reflect to some extent what Plato calls "recollection'' in the hearts and minds of mainstream people. And, while most people in society are not yet ready to give up all animal use, they are uncomfortable with the naked exploitation that has characterized animal use since World War II, with the advent of industrialized agriculture and large-scale use of animals in scientific research and testing. According to a *Parents Magazine* survey, while some eighty percent of the public believe that animals can be used in agriculture, the same percentage also believe that these animals have rights.

The thrust for articulating and encoding these rights in law— for ''writing them large,'' in Plato's felicitous phrase—is, if one chooses to use these categories, far more conservative than it is radical. As far back as the earliest domestication of animals, as is the case today, the overwhelming use of animals has been agricultural. Prior to World War II, the keeping of agricultural animals—be it for food, animal products, fiber, locomotion, or power—has been a matter of *husbandry*, nurturing and augmenting the animal's ability to thrive and flourish in an environment for which its biological nature is suited. This sort of agriculture represented a primordial contract between humans and animals, still expressed by extensive (i.e., open space) ranchers of the West, the last traditional husbandrymen in the United States, as ''We take care of the animals, and they take care of us.''

The husbandry imperative expressed in this dictum was a near-perfect amalgam of ethics and prudence. Self-interest bonded with morality to assure that animals lived essentially happy lives or, at least, did not suffer at human hands. Such agriculture is about putting square pegs in square holes; round pegs in round holes. In such a world, it was quite plausible that the only social ethic regarding animal treatment was the minimalist prohibition of deviant, intentional, willful cruelty. The hurting of animals by humans was minimized by the absolute requirement of husbandry.

With the advent of both high-technology agriculture and large-scale animal research in the mid-twentieth century, the contract was broken. Much of science was about hurting animals to cure disease and advance knowledge. More important, the rise of such technology as antibiotics and vaccines allowed the placing of square pegs in round holes and round pegs in square holes, while producers profited and animals suffered by the thwarting of their natures. As the university departmental nomenclature betokens, ''animal husbandry'' became ''animal science.''

The demand for animal rights began in the mid-1960s, when society became aware of how contemporary agriculture spurns the ancient contract. The concerns that demand articulates is echoed by the traditional rancher agriculturalists we mentioned earlier, the vast majority of whom despise industrialized agriculture as much or more than do "urban radicals." Of the six or so thousand ranchers in Colorado, Wyoming, Montana, Nevada, Alberta, and elsewhere to whom I have lectured in the past six years, over ninety-eight percent assert that animals have rights. As one rancher put it: "If I had to raise animals the way the chicken people do, I'd get the hell out of the business."

Thus, concern for assuring that animals used by humans live happy lives is neither fringe, nor exclusively urban. It is, in fact, an urgent cry for reasserting the age-old bond with animals forged by prudence into ethics in the face of radical technology, whose only inherent values are efficiency and productivity.

119

LAURA A. MORETTI

Laura A. Moretti is founder and editor of the award-winning *The Animals' Voice Magazine*, an international publication focusing on the rights of animals.

Home is a Wounded Heart

I floated lazily downstream on a makeshift raft I had created, the hot afternoon sun tanning my young skin, bees buzzing the honeysuckle that grew along its banks, a green-eyed dragonfly hovering before my hand-shielded face. There weren't any other sounds for miles, just the running water emptying into tranquil pools that slowed the raft and spun it slowly before picking up a mesmerizing speed again in the shallows. Overhead, the sky was cloudless and translucent blue. My thoughts were lost in its vastness; only my heel touching the lukewarm water brought me back to Earth.

I had that memory last night, watching television; how different it was from the reality of another world: children, as young as I was then, scrambled for footing on the muddied banks of a Faroese island, grappling with their elders for the ropes that had caught a pilot whale in its death throes. The animal, groaning in agony, its head gruesomely severed behind the blowhole, thrashed violently in the blood-tainted waters, among its dead and dying companions, but to no avail. There were dozens of hands on the ropes, too much muscle, not enough strength left in the great, dying whale; even so, the heart was pumping blood, not into the creature's brain where it was demanded, but into its nose and lungs, into the waters that had once given it life.

354

And my heart broke again. As it had done eighteen years earlier, watching a seal pup writhe in the blood-splattered snow beneath the sealer's weighted boot. For every step forward, there seems to be two back. Yes, take heart, I hear, that such footage makes it onto the airwaves at all; the good people of planet Earth will not turn away from the injustices exposed to them. . .

But nothing, I cried, but *nothing* makes up for the murder of one single being; nothing brings back life, not even the good people of planet Earth and their glorified technology and so-called progress; nothing gives life *but* life, and nothing brings back life—but *nothing*.

As strong as I am—and after eighteen years, I think sometimes I am too strong, too casual about it, too proud that I am able to endure the death of another; be motivated by it, I mean, and put in another fourteen-hour day on behalf of death and dying—I am still moved, still heartbroken and sickened—dear God, am I *sickened*—with the empathy I feel with that one and single and solitary being in the throes of dying.

I could have turned the channel. It would have been that easy. I could have muted the sound, thanks to remote control, and shut out its screaming, the way only a whale can scream. But I couldn't. I'd be damned if that animal died alone; to turn away would have made me as guilty as if my own hands were on the ropes that held that dying creature at bay.

Take heart? It is a long way from lazy raft rides in the neighborhood creek bed; my heel touching the lukewarm water today would only bring painful visions of blood-red seas—this, the price of enlightenment.

We who work for the lives of others live in the shadow of the death of others. This is our way, not by choice, but by demand. Better to have a wounded heart, a sick and hurting heart, than to have no heart at all, to feel for nothing, to care for no one, to live for death. The world is ailing. Every morning when we awaken, there is a whale thrashing, a monkey screaming, a lone wolf howling in the back of our minds. There is no escape from enlightenment, from truth, no escape from what lies beyond the morning sparrow's song. Not for us, those of us who work for the lives of others.

But shut our eyes? We cannot. Wish that we could? We would not. We know that healing and change begin with the truth.

And the truth begins with a broken heart.

Keep fighting the good fight.

120

CHARLES MAGEL

Charles Magel, Ph.D., is emeritus professor of philosophy, Moorhead State University, Moorhead, Minnesota. He is author of *Keyguide to Information Sources in Animal Rights* and *A Bibliography on Animal Rights and Related Matters* and the editor of J. Howard Moore's *The Universal Kinship*.

Animal Slavery Will End in the Twenty-First Century

The first time I offered a course at Moorhead State University attacking animal slavery, in 1977, it was my opinion it would require at least two centuries to remove the chains of animal bondage. By 1985, approximately one thousand students had attended my classes. Intensive dialogue with students convinced me that perhaps only one century would be needed. Today, in 1993, I am convinced that by the year 2050, animal slavery will be abolished.

Most people do not view animals as slaves, nor do they view owners of such slaves as slaveholders. But the animal owner really is a slaveholder, and the owned animal really is a slave. Slavery can be defined as a relationship in which one individual (slaveholder) has exclusive control and use of the life and activities of another individual (slave). This definition captures the essence of both human and animal slavery. The histories of both are fascinating. For the Western reader a study of human slavery could well concentrate on ancient Greece and Rome as well as the rest of Europe and the Americas. The history of animal slavery would require a study of the domestication of animals, which probably began about 10,000 B.C. in Western Asia or the Middle East. I suspect most people find it strange to view the domestication of animals as the enslavement of animals, but such is an implication of the definition of slavery. We human slaveholders have practiced exclusive control over and use of animal slaves in many ways: for labor, for food, for clothing, for entertainment, for tests on the safety of drugs and chemicals, for experiments, and so on.

Thomas Jefferson, an owner of human slaves, inserted in the Declaration of Independence the moral principle that destroyed the theoretical basis of human slavery: All humans have an equal right to life, liberty, and the pursuit of happiness. But it took an Abraham Lincoln, and nearly a century, to burst the chains.

Today, in 1993, we find the theoretical basis of animal slavery similarly destroyed. Peter Singer, Australian philosopher and author of *Animal Liberation* (1975, 1990), has effectively shown that all sentient animals—human and nonhuman—are entitled to equal consideration of their pleasures, pains, interests, and desires. Tom Regan, American philosopher and author of *The Case for Animal Rights* (1983), has demonstrated that given we humans have rights to life and liberty and the pursuit of happiness, it necessarily follows that animals also have these same rights. Peter Singer and Tom Regan and others—such as Henry Salt, *Animals' Rights* (1892); J. Howard Moore, *The Universal Kinship* (1906); Richard Ryder, *Victims of Science* (1975); Andrew Linzey, *Animal Rights* (1976); Stephen Clark, *The Moral Status of Animals* (1977); Bernard Rollin, *Animal Rights and Human Morality* (1981); Paul Taylor, *Respect for Nature* (1986); and Steve Sapontzis, *Morals, Reason, and Animals* (1987)—are the Thomas Jeffersons of the twentieth century. What we now need are twenty-first century Abraham Lincolns to unshackle the fetters of the animal slaves. It will not be long!

SPIRITUALITY

121

DAVID G. BENNER

David G. Benner, Ph.D., is a clinical psychologist with current faculty appointments at the University of Toronto and Redeemer College. He is the author or editor of nine books on psychology and religion, including *Psychotherapy and the Spiritual Quest*.

The Priority of the Spiritual

The vantage point from which I stand and crane my neck to get a view into the next millennium is that of a practitioner and teacher of the art of psychotherapy. But I am a psychotherapist who is not satisfied with the common current views of the nature of human problems encountered by myself and my peers. My perspective on the problems now commonly facing men and women in the late twentieth century shapes my view of the future.

It is my conviction that most of the problems in living that are presented to those of us who find our vocation in the mental health professions in the late twentieth century should be understood to be spiritual, not mental. Prior to the present century, these problems in living were the concern of religious soul-care specialists. However, the rise of science and the subsequent decline of organized religion has witnessed the evolution of the care of souls into the cure of minds, and the new specialists for these matters are the secular priests of modernity, the psychotherapists.

Just how well psychotherapists are equipped to handle the demands of soul care is a matter of some debate. But unless the spiritual nature of our most basic yearnings and anxieties can be recognized, there is little hope for the efficacy of the helping interventions. The basic human need for connection with the transcendent and for an identity found in this relationship can only become more apparent in the next millennium. The bankruptcy of materialistic philosophies should be obvious to any astute observer of the human condition in the last decades of the twentieth century. But with futurologists such as Charles Handy telling us that our children will likely have a lifetime total work experience of no more than 50,000 hours (this in contrast to a present lifetime average of 100,000 hours) while at the same time living on average for approximately 100 years, it is quite clear that the first generation of young adults in the third millennium will experience even more acute need for a reason for living that transcends success and personal happiness.

Embarking on this new era, what humans need more clearly than ever before is spiritual groundedness. As a Christian, I affirm the unique possibilities of discovering both this groundedness and our place in the cosmos in the life, death, and resurrection of Jesus Christ. But proponents of various religious traditions must learn to talk, and even more importantly, to listen to each other as we seek to discern spiritual truth and find new ways of making these ultimate realities relevant and accessible to people.

There is every reason to believe that the developments in science and technology that we will witness in the next twenty-five years will make those of the last several centuries pale by comparison. But will the human experience in these decades be better or simply easier? We may have a life of more comfort, stimulation, choice, and even leisure, and we will, in all probability, live longer. But will our lives have more purpose, direction, and ultimate fulfillment? Science and technology, the great hope of the last several centuries, cannot provide these things. Nor can education, at least not as it is presently conducted. Only religion has the possibility of answering these deepest human needs, and consequently it is absolutely urgent for us to reevaluate its place in both personal and public life.

The only life ultimately worth living is the one that is integrated around some reference point outside of itself. And, as psychologists of religion are increasingly recognizing, the more transcendent this point of reference is, the more adequate the resulting integration and life direction. This, then, is our challenge as we head into the third millennium—the rediscovery of the ancient truths of our spiritual traditions and the working out of these truths in the age that we prepare to enter.

122
JACQUELYN SMALL

Jacquelyn Small has degrees in psychology and clinical social work, and is the author of *Becoming Naturally Therapeutic, Awakening in Time,* and *Transformers, The Artists of Self-Creation.* She is the founder and codirector of Eupsychia Inc. in Austin, Texas, which offers programs in transformation psychology and transpersonal addiction recovery.

Service at the Closing of an Age

Today, we are on the brink of the closing of an entire era in human history, and a paradigm shift is occurring that is shaking loose the very ground of our perceptual reality. At such appointed times in our earth's unfolding saga, a whole new dimension of consciousness enters into time, pushing aside the familiar turn in all areas of our lives. When completing a great cycle such as this, we must all be prepared for a "destiny transfer," which can be experienced as a total shake-up of the life we have known. We are moving into a new dimension of the Self, and therefore, the entire "storyline" and roles we have been identified with that were literally holding our reality in place are beginning to dissipate. And we are left with a feeling of "hanging in the dangle." For a while now, there may be no sign of a safety net beneath our precarious existence to help settle our nerves.

The Self, on its evolutionary journey, is taking a leap. And quite a leap it is! For to move forward now, beyond our confusion and doubt, requires a dropping of the familiar and hurling ourselves forward into the great unknown. Science and its two-hundred-year hold on our brains, has been serving as our God. But now our scientific theories are too limited to explain us. It is as though we have outgrown our own minds, and no longer know what to trust as real, or how to control the outcome. For many, this is quite an untenable state of affairs.

It appears that we are passing out of an age that was governed by the personalistic life in which materialism was our Lord and entering into a larger Reality, one in which our conscious awareness is anchored in the impersonal life and a greater "plan" for humanity. To be "impersonal," however, does not mean that we become cold, aloof, and unfeeling. The impersonal Self has disentangled emotionally from others through an attitude of nonattachment, yet feels an abiding compassion for all of creation. From this cleared-out perspective, we have stepped in to a higher identity and no longer take our little upsets so personally. No longer are we living life, we feel; *life is now living us!* To make this shift from the personal to the impersonal life is the difficult challenge of "surrender" that all great minds have taught is the only way to live. For our human history has shown us quite plainly that all unconscious egoistic living ends in total disillusionment and despair.

At the closing of an age, the sacred archetypal process of disidentification moves in, demanding that we release *in form* all that from which we have gained our identity during the past cycle. An alchemical process naturally ensues, during which the essence is squeezed out of each experience and relationship we had taken on, and the contents and roles that no longer contain life for us will dissolve. All will be placed on the auction stand, ready to be evaluated for what truth each part of our old identity holds for our advancing soul. The unifying Self, which is both the creator and completor of all our experiences, will reveal the passing cycle in its entirety—its spiritual purpose, ways that we have grown or gotten stuck, the lessons learned or failed. Whatever is exposed that is not to be carried forward into the next cycle is called out so it can be named, disidentified with, and released. All must come up for review so we can choose and thereby co-create a future that we truly desire. We are emptying out, which is often experienced as "running dry."

At this planetary dark night most people are focusing with anxiety and sadness on all that is falling away, not yet aware of the emerging new life, and are paralyzed by a deep sense of loss. Without a context for understanding this process, people fall into apathy or despair, too frightened to carry on.

Yet, from somewhere deep within us, we welcome this coming change. The pain of our world is the loss of legitimacy of a spiritual perspective and our greater identity as spiritual beings. We have lost our memory of the heaven-wide Reality in which we all truly belong. Our essential nature, it seems, is more that of a mystic than a scientist, so without touching the sacred and beautiful in life, we cannot survive. When the dreamer in us dies, and the magical, mystical view of life falls into disrespect, our creativity loses force, and so does our zest for living. So, not unlike our more natural animal friends, we are all getting ready to migrate, in search of a new feeding ground; as spiritual beings, we are starving for spiritual food.

The task at hand during this next decade is to build a bridge between the personal and the impersonal life by co-creating sacred spaces for Spirit to do Her "psychospiritual" work of completion. We must come together in the safety of loving groups so we can question, or even fall apart if need be, without the fear of judgment, while undergoing these major "let go's" in our mental, emotional, and physical lives. We need to grieve our losses, and own our dysfunctions and forgive them, for that is the human part, while simultaneously learning to recognize and embody our new and awaiting higher identity. With gentle group support we will discover that all our experiences, even the hurtful ones, served a sacred purpose for the unfolding life of Spirit.

So today, a new kind of philanthropist is entering upon the scene, to guide us through this disquieting "threshold of tomorrow." This new breed of server is emerging now to accompany us through the overlap between two worlds, the chasm of the heart. These ordinary folk are seasoned travelers upon the path of direct experience, people who have "gone first," already having hit bottom from their old ways—and survived! They know only one thing in order to serve: how to keep the faith and trust in the process while birthing the new life. By holding steady while the masses plummet into the natural chaos of rapid change, they serve by simply "doing their Being." They remind us that it is okay to die, knowing that living goes on beyond our fears and disbelief.

The human/spiritual heart is the bridge between the personal and impersonal life. We enter into this sacred chamber to redeem "the Promise" that we can honor all aspects of ourselves, even our shadowy parts. It is from this heartspace, but naked and raw, that we are made fresh and innocent once more. Our redemption lies in this recognition that it is all worked for the good of the whole. And from this safe and accepting space we can together nurture our dreams of the future, the subjective life where our hearts truly thrive. Our task, then, is to remain conscious of the full participation of both the ego and the soul who together create a third and higher possibility. Since two dimensions of consciousness are blending into one, evolution insists that we claim our hybrid nature, that we are both/and, and never either/or. Otherwise dualism would grab us once more and we would be thrown right back into the old ego-centered ways.

Drawn from my work in our psychospiritual retreats with hundreds who are consciously making their way into the new, the following can serve as reminders for making the shift more smoothly, each to be enacted according to your own inner guidance and natural style:

- Be willing to note your resistance, then say "I am willing" and surrender to whatever your existence brings you each moment of every day.
- Align your personal desires with what is good for the whole.
- Synthesize the seed harvest from your past and carry with you that which you truly value, with a willingness to release all else.
- Challenge humanity's outmoded forms in whatever places you know are within your sphere of influence in the world.
- Hold the tension between conflicting ideals by continually reminding others of the good in all seemingly opposing views.
- Think creatively and image your ideal future and life's work, according to your own inspired dreams and messages from inner guides and teachers.
- Become a model of authentic living for a world that is starved for truth.

Many today are feeling this yearning to serve in this new and simple way. Perhaps it is indeed "in the stars" or in our genes that at these appointed times we will hear a wake-up call to take up our stations and stand tall in this exciting "adventure in consciousness." For there must always be a few who hold steady for the masses, so that when the old world ends there will be a bedrock upon which to do our work for the creation of the new. And may we all be joyfully encouraged during the challenging times ahead by these words of the Tibetan Master Djwhal Khul:

> Nothing under heaven can arrest the progress of the human soul on its long pilgrimage from darkness to light, from the unreal to the real, from death to immortality, and from ignorance to wisdom.

123

DAVID STEINDL-RAST

Brother David Steindl-Rast, Ph.D., has been a monk of Mount Saviour Monastery in the Finger Lake region of New York State since 1953, and after twelve years of formal training received permission to practice Zen with Buddhist masters. Although he spends the better part of the year in seclusion, he has lectured extensively on all five continents and has contributed to a wide range of books and periodicals. His current books include *Gratefulness, A Listening Heart,* and *Belonging to the Universe.*

Rediscovering Common Sense

At the end of a century or of a millennium, people in the past may have had an image of themselves as sailing excitedly into a new era—the wind of history swelling their sails. Our collective self-image, as we approach the year 2000, differs from that dream. Ours is a nightmare: alone on an immense ocean, we cling to debris; shipwrecked, we are adrift toward ultimate disaster.

This image seems widespread enough to challenge us. It haunts me often enough to make me face it and ask: Well, what would I do if I woke up and found that nightmare to be reality? I would panic. That could mean a quick and relatively easy demise. But things might drag on. My panic might wear off. What then? I would have to face the situation.

I could imagine saying to myself, "David, this is it" (a phrase that sometimes brings me to my senses). "Be present here now" (I owe this one to Ram Dass). "Be true to your Self" (this one comes from Alcoholics Anonymous, but I like to spell Self with a capital S—

to think of spelling while clinging to a plank afloat on the high seas might add a touch of humor).

Come to myself/Self (and humor always helps that process), I might get playful and imagine that this was just an exercise at an Esalen awareness workshop: "Give yourself to it, David!" I would begin to notice: The horizon narrows when I sink down into a trough between swells; when the surge lifts me up, the horizon expands. It is vast. Down again. Up again. Ah, the water is carrying me. I might recall reading that seawater is similar in its consistency to the amniotic fluid in which I was bobbing up and down like this before I was born. This would give me a sense of belonging. Maybe the millions of sea creatures down there not far from me in the deep would begin to seem to me like sisters and brothers. They would soon be feasting on me, but it would be a party.

Then night would raise above me a dome of innumerable stars —awe-inspiring. That awe would make me forget my plight. I would forget myself in contemplating space so immense that I was lost in its vastness—lost, and yet my eyes, the eyes of the universe seeing itself: a cosmos come to itself in my heart. (Not even Maslow could have guessed that my shipwreck would climax in a peak experience. A happy ending of sorts, after all.)

But back to the start. Before its wreck, the ship of our human endeavor bore its name proudly on its bow: "Common Sense" (that sense of universal communion through which alone everything makes sense). This ship was wrecked, not in a crash, but by slow, almost imperceptible disintegration. Shall we allegorize further? Its mast was the uprightness of being true to oneself. It splintered when we became used to a brazenness no longer ashamed of putting profit above personal integrity. The ship's hull was compassion, holding together all with all. It shattered when we lost the sense of being one family with all others—humans, animals, plants, minerals—and started exploiting them. The sail was awe, swelled by wind of the Spirit. It ripped to shreds when we lost cosmic reverence.

All this can be said without allegory. The universal condition in which we find ourselves in this decade before the year 2000 is alienation. We have lost Common Sense; we have lost our sense of belonging to self/Self, to the Earth Household, and to Ultimate Reality (by any name). When this happens to a world, it is shipwrecked and adrift. But here allegory breaks down; we can never piece the ship together again. Yet we can find access to Common Sense again and again. To regain this access is the great challenge. We can rise to this challenge in any situation.

Even the crisis of finding myself adrift and abandoned can shock me into coming to "mySelf." In the freedom that is "just another word for nothing left to lose," I can rediscover universal belonging. Confronted with the ultimate limit, I can become aware of the limitless horizon around me and within me. This rediscovery of Common Sense is our last, our only chance to escape annihilation. It may or may not equip us to sail into a new age, as in the ancient dream. But even if we should still be clinging to our plank when the year 2000 dawns, we might, as in my nightmare's happy ending, remain adrift and yet be where we ultimately belong.

124

RAIMON PANIKKAR

Raimon Panikkar, D.Th., D.Sc., Ph.D., is emeritus professor of religious studies at the University of California and an ordained Catholic priest. He has written about three hundred articles and thirty books, including *The Silence of God*, *Myth, Faith and Hermeneutics*, *The Vedic Experience*, and *The Intrareligious Dialogue*.

On the Threshold of Tomorrow

To speak of a global crisis is a cliché—nonetheless an obvious truth. Parents do not know what to say to their children; two-thirds of humanity are living an economically wretched life; and the other third suffers from depressions, ambitions, fears, and worse scourges. Most of the non-Western cultures are infected by a complex of inferiority that contributes to their actual inferiority. Life on Earth is threatened, and if we go on sliding on the myth of history wanting to cross "the threshold of tomorrow" by "progressing" toward the future, there will be soon not much time left for life.

We have reached the bottom. And this may trigger a revelatory experience—if we have eyes to see and ears to hear. It is the revelation that the economic problem is not just economics, the political troubles not mere political corruption, the technological cancer not a sheer moral question (of a better use), the scientific quandaries not only a scientific question, the ecological situation not solved by a better treatment of resources. More, not even the human problem is an exclusive human affair.

This revelation is the disclosure, on a higher spiral than previously, that we need to reestablish both a divine friendship with the cosmic and a cosmic awareness of the divine.

A *comotheandric* insight is emerging all over the world: We are all engaged in an adventure that concerns not only the human destiny, but the divine and cosmic dimensions of reality as well. Out of the darkness of our times, and at the price of an unimaginable amount of suffering, a new/old awareness is dawning upon us. It is our responsibility to live up to this challenge and to contribute to overcoming—not to denying—the prevalent two-dimensional view of reality —as if time and space were all that there is. We should awaken to our *theanthropocosmic* dignity.

I sum it all up suggesting that we should sit—not sleep—on the *threshold*!

125
BONNIE GREENWELL

Bonnie Greenwell, Ph.D., is a transpersonal psychotherapist special-
izing in spiritual emergence issues. She teaches at the Institute of Transpersonal Psychology, writes and lectures extensively on kundalini experiences, and is the author of *Energies of Transformation: A Guide to the
Kundalini Process*. She is a founding member and co-coordinator of the
Kundalini Research Network.

Chaos and Transition:
Patterns for a Stronger Species

Before I began to do research as a doctoral student and then
specialize in working with people who had experienced kundalini
awakenings, I never imagined the extraordinary range of multidimensional experiences I would encounter, or that this work, which I
thought was very individual and personal, would lead me into refram-
ing the nature of world events.

I now do therapy and consult with people who have had
powerful light and visionary experiences, who remember past lives
as clearly as most of us remember breakfast, who channel light beings
who are trying to raise consciousness on the planet, who have traversed
other-dimensional worlds, who have had encounters with extrater-
restrials or other-dimensional teachers, who demonstrate uncanny
psychic awareness, and who are undergoing major energetic and emotional transformations accompanied by expanded consciousness. These
life-changing phenomena are occurring across all cultures and ideologies, judging from letters I receive from all over the world. The peo-

ple having these experiences are often successful, healthy, and highly educated people thrown into a paradigm beyond their belief system, who find themselves struggling with the twofold task of functioning in society and honoring an expanded awareness of unitive consciousness.

Today I believe that like a dry creek bed filling slowly with melted mountain snow, the battered human spirit is receiving a regenerative flow of spiritual consciousness to help us set a new directive for our collective work as a species. This is happening across the planet, as thousands of individuals are drawn to look inward for deeper experiences, and then find themselves faced with the need to integrate transformative changes and radical new paradigms regarding the nature of human consciousness and existence. Many of us witnessed similar shifts as a result of drug experimentation in the sixties.

Today it is happening with fantastic diversification and more integration, often as a consequence of spiritual practices using contemplation, visualization, meditation, drumming, chanting, asana, and breathing exercises. Kundalini awakening and other spiritual experiences may occur through deep psychotherapeutic or body therapy processes; near-death experiences; breathwork practices; in relationship to the energy of teachers, therapists, or lovers; and even spontaneously through dreams, crisis, concentration, and biofeedback. Some people report inexplicable nighttime awakenings into electrifying energy and light fields.

Kundalini is the creative energy and consciousness said by the ancient Indians to be coiled at the base of the spine. It is the residual of the energy/consciousness blueprint that distributes prana through the body and causes life to animate the fetus. When it awakens there is a definite physical sensation that may be experienced in three intensities—with the slow spiral movement of a snake winding upward through the body, as a steady stream of energy, or with a sudden explosive power like a geyser erupting. This experience may trigger energy, heat, pain, emotional changes, physical problems, visionary experiences, psychic openings, expanded creativity, and many other events. In a full awakening it is the beginning of a lifetime of change in the physical, emotional, and spiritual condition that has the potential to lead to liberation. Some yogic masters state that kundalini awakening changes the cellular structure and the brain. Sri Aurobindo and Pandit Gopi Krishna felt its awakening could lead to a greater evolution of the human species.

Many psychics and teachers claim that the planet may also be having a kundalini awakening. Our species may be in the throes of a transformation so profound that our present consciousness cannot even fathom it. We are faced with collective powers that overwhelm our capacity as a group to contain them, and consequently we have become fragmented and thus even less able to cope with the immediate needs of our time. This is, of course, destabilizing, and fear even further immobilizes us.

Despair is understandable. Fear is natural. Anger makes sense in the face of all of the chaos of the present era. But those who do depth therapy, and who attempt to heal the wounds of the psyche, also recognize that there is a powerful potential for evolution amidst chaos. Those who achieve transformation are those who are able to endure and turn inward, holding an intention for wholeness or transcendence. They are willing to be co-creators of their future by taking new risks and making new choices. They open their hearts rather than turning away from the pain. And they are willing to go through whatever is their fate and work through their own limitations. This stirs the psyche into new insight, new spiritual energy, and new potential.

It seems today that millions of people are experiencing a kind of trauma and cleansing at some level of their psyche. Those who find an inner strength, a mastery of their individual self, or the freedom of the universal Self at the core of their humanity will survive to build a new system with a new vision—probably a planetary vision, a humanistic vision, built on the foundation of understanding the errors of the past and recognizing the potential for the species in a new paradigm.

When a sufficient number of people across the global community make a full transition to a new vision, we will stop imposing trauma on one another and become capable of working cooperatively on perspectives and solutions to help us cope with the natural traumas of our planet. What I have seen in recent years among the individuals I have watched in spiritual crisis, as well as in the teachings of nearly every channeled master, in the messages of other-dimensional beings reported by thousands of people, and in the writings or lectures of every highly developed spiritual teacher from Teilhard de Chardin to Satya Sai Baba is the same message—this is an age of great cleansing and great transition on the planet, and it will be painful, and it is essential to a coming new age of greater wisdom and harmony. Underneath the message is a clear implication that we all have work to do to become strong enough to cope, and wise enough to proceed, amidst all of the challenges of the coming years.

126
PETER A. CAMPBELL

Reverend Peter A. Campbell, Ph.D., is cofounder and resource development coordinator of the Institute for Bio-Spiritual Research in Coulterville, California, and the coauthor of *Bio-Spirituality: Focusing as a Way to Grow.*

The "Dearest Freshness Deep Down Things"

The issue for human survival during the third millennium is neither understanding, nor prediction or control (our well-worn tools of scientific method used for mastering the environment). Rather, it is learning the language of "spirit" and "grace" as these emerge within our body's unique way of knowing. The challenge is no longer domination, but "incarnation!" In the words of Marshall McLuhan, we must "re-enter the tribal night," but this time with our eyes open. The human body itself is our barely recognized doorway into the next age of consciousness.

The question for those at the threshold of this third millennium is whether we will fritter away time with endless speculation about the age to come, or turn to the more immediate task of honing the actual tools that can lead us into the next stage of human development. As a species we are finally awakening to the mystery of "communion." But before growing into such wholeness together and with our planet, we must first discover it by entering within ourselves.

Ours is a decisive moment of conversion, not just individually but as a species. The quest for security can either perpetuate age-old patterns of domination and control, or challenge us to take, as

Christopher Fry has said, "The longest stride of soul folk ever took./Affairs are now soul size./The enterprise/Is exploration into God." With the coming of a third millennium, we enter an era of "bio-spirituality," the life of spirit as this arises from within the human organism itself.

What we need today in order to evolve is not some further multiplication of cognitive information, but "processes" that effectively reveal our body sense for the wholeness that we seek. We require not more analysis but the practical knowing of "How?" to touch the inner movement of spirit and grace as these can be felt in our bodies. We have found a simple, effective, teachable process called "Focusing" that allows this to happen. It is easily learned by children as well as adults. Focusing is a process that opens the world of spirit because it involves an incarnation, an entering into rather than dominion over feelings and emotions that are the stuff of building isolation or communion.

Most of us have learned, and learned well, the language of conquest. Now we must embark together on a journey into the dark night of our fears, our loneliness, our unresolved anger and guilt. The ancient Greeks had a word to describe this spectacle of evolving wholeness. They named it *musterion*. In the New Testament this special word is translated into Latin as *sacramentum*. Our bodies are truly sacramental —not at all what they appear on the surface, but holy places of grace and spirit where the catalyst for evolution lies at the core of our deepest fears and longings, our awesome vulnerabilities. Here we cannot understand. We may never predict. We are totally unable to control.

The poet Gerard Manly Hopkins reminds us of the "dearest freshness deep down things." The third millennium offers a time of spirit and grace, a bio-spiritual journey where by entering into the vulnerability in our body we can experience the resurrection!

127

JOHN DAVIDSON

John Davidson graduated from Cambridge University with an honors degree in natural sciences and worked for seventeen years in the University's Department of Applied Mathematics and Theoretical Physics. Since 1984, he has written a series of books on science and mysticism, including *Subtle Energy* and *The Web of Life*, which express the feeling that all human experiences lies within the framework of a great mystic reality.

This Moment is Our Window into Immortality

$\mathbf{A}$n Indian friend of mine, an Urdu poet as it chances, included a brief poem with his New Year's greetings card one year. "Everyone," he mused, "is wishing each other a Happy New Year. But I see nothing new about it . . . The planet is old. Nature is old. Man is old. Human strengths and weaknesses are old. The mind is old. The soul is old. Even God is old. Where is the newness of it? Yet with what fervor everyone wishes a Happy New Year upon the other. What," he asked, "is this New Year all about?" The answer, as my friend well knew, lies locked up within the mystery of time.

There is no doubt that physically we live enveloped in a realm of space and time. All that happens within the realm of sense takes place in space and time. But where is this time, this space? Is it outside, as what we call the world? Maybe, but what is "outside"? Can we really differentiate between the perception and the thing perceived? Philosophers have chewed the question over many times, for nobody denies that the perception—the experience—of every outer thing is to be found within—within our own mind.

Our experience of the world lies within ourselves. And this is true of every incarnate being, human or otherwise, for perception is personal, per se. Furthermore, differing species—bats, bees, dolphins, and the rest—have radically differing perceptions of what we call the world. And the differences lie in the perceptions—in the senses, yes, but also in the mind. Yet clearly, all perceive some common ground, else there would be no "world" at all to which we relate. Somehow, all living beings are in this thing *together.*

We can say that we are shareholders in the existence of the world of space and time—a world that exists by virtue of a myriad of mental shareholdings: the shareholdings of all the souls inhabiting this realm. In fact, we are all its dynamic co-creators. This, incidentally, is the substrate to the law of *karma.*

Sages of the mystic path have said—so very frequently—that time, space, and all things that change therein are an illusion. They are *maya:* a play or dance of the Supreme One. The One is the Supreme Source and Reality, the Universal Inner Life or Consciousness of all, the Immortal, Uncreated, Self-existent One. It is the Universal Mind, they say, who divides and diversifies the One into the manyness in which we find our lives enmeshed. The Universal Mind, then, is the architect of time and space, the weaver of the great web of illusion over the face of the One. And our human mind is but one aspect or part of the Universal Mind, just as the soul—the real Self or pure consciousness—is a drop or particle of the Divine. And the mind, the source of the illusion, lies within us, just as the soul, the essence of Reality, does so, too.

This, then, is the source of the illusion that tomorrow will bring fulfillment of our heart's desire, tomorrow—or the next day—will bring our "Happy New Year." This is the ceaseless treadmill of desire and time, the two so closely intertwined in an endless "chasing of the wind."

But if tomorrow is only an illusion, a phantasm of the mind, dividing the present into past and future, what is this sense of immanence and imminence that so many of us feel? Why does *this* moment feel so important? And why do we feel that something big is so close to us, so close to happening?

The feeling arises because this moment is our window into immortality, and there is nothing bigger than that. This moment is eternity, right now. *It is all we ever have.* Immortality is that which lies *beyond* time, it is not a forever *in* time. Therefore, at every moment in our lives—in our consciousness—we are presented with the opportunity either to move inward toward the immortal, unchanging, ever-present One, or to move outward into time—into unconsciousness, into unreality, into illusion, into *maya*, into the never-ending dance of time.

God is here, present within us now. God is the origin of this sense of immanence. We float and live and move in God, whether we know it or not. Our being is never away from God's Great Being, for the drop only exists by virtue of God's Ocean.

Consequently, it is always a Happy New Year. We are always on the "threshold of tomorrow." But we have to know where and how to find it, for that New Year and that "tomorrow" are right now.

God is the One: we the faithful, submitting-yet-dynamic, loving drops. Let us awaken into our new dawn, seeking and finding the living, loving Light within! This alone will give true meaning to our time here, for this, most surely, is the purpose of time.

128

FREDERICK FRANCK

Frederick Franck, M.D., Ph.D., is an artist and writer whose paintings and drawings are part of the permanent collections of more than twenty museums in the United States, Europe, and Japan. He has written over a dozen books, including *The Zen of Seeing, The Awakened Eye,* and *To Be Human Against All Odds.*

A New "Stripped" Spirituality

I have lived through almost this entire century from before World War I. I miraculously survived the era of murderous tyrannies, of Mussolini's Fascism, Hitler's Nazism, Stalin's Communism, of extermination camps and gulags, the criminal insanity of Hiroshima-Nagasaki, the oversaturation of the globe with nuclear murder machinery. I was still around to see Communism collapse after sacrificing millions of lives for the brilliant future that never came, to watch the liberation of eastern Europe at once converting itself into religio-ethnic mayhem. It would be all too naive to project on its threshold a twenty-first century of peace and happiness.

Is there no hope then? I believe there is, but it requires a miracle of faith in the human potential for sanity. I see glimpses of hope in the ever-wider awakening of my contemporaries to the seriousness of the present ecological crisis, to the abject nihilism, the demonic aspects of a society dominated by technocratic hubris in conjunction with the amoral power of the jumbo corporations in their obsession with quick profits at any price.

Hope is only justified provided this awakening would grow

into the groundswell that would force a turnabout at the base from "business as usual," that would overcome that petit bourgeois nostalgia, that panic in the face of inevitable change, which six decades ago made the psychoses of Nazism triumphant.

I cannot help thinking, gazing into my crystal ball, that the *conditio sine qua non* for a livable future would require a newly "stripped" or "poor" spirituality that, without being at all incompatible with the traditional religions, may well be the nightmare of its authoritarian institutions. This "stripped" religiosity would have as its main article of faith, that in each one born human there lies—genetically transmitted—the thirst for, the thrust to, the potentiality to grow to full human status. This full human status is characterized by an insight into one's own life process, which opens the way to the first stirrings of empathy with the life processes of other beings and consequently to universal compassion.

It would imply that the arbitrary interruption of the others' maturation to the potential fully human status stands convicted as the ultimate abomination.

A second point of faith is that openness to the sacred that our technological delusions have disregarded with horrifying results: the sacredness of the biosphere, the total interdependence of all beings it encompasses. Whether this sacredness is expressed in pan-en-theistic (not to be confused with pantheistic) terms, compatible with the Abrahamic religions and Brahmanism, or in nontheistic concepts as in Mahayana Buddhism, is of secondary importance.

129

VALERIE ANDREWS

Valerie Andrews is the author of *A Passion for This Earth: Exploring a New Partnership of Man, Woman and Nature*. She is currently writing a screenplay and finishing a novel called *Reinventing Your Life*.

The Liturgy of Surrender

How do you create a future? By making love to the body of the Earth and to the beloved, by receiving what is "other" with humility and grace.

And by tending to the inner life, by seeding the eternal dialogue between Earth and Spirit, between God and Spirit, between God and our still unformed humanity.

The novelist Nikos Kazantzakis said there are prayers for three kinds of souls:

Oh Lord, I am a fragile twig, do not bend me or I will break.

Oh Lord, I am a tender sapling. Bend me—but not too hard for I might break.

Oh Lord, I am a mighty oak; bend me and who cares if I break!

If we are lucky we *will* break, and in the process discover a ˥ew way of being.

˩ future is a sense of radical newness given to those who ˙ave enough to surrender and regrow themselves. As St.

Paul said, "Where I am weak, there I am strong." Paradoxically, this is the point of revelation and discovery.

When I face my terror, I am raised above it. When I embrace the fertile darkness, I am redeemed. When I die unto the moment, I see through it, to eternity. This cycle of surrender and becoming is our earthly liturgy.

I have discovered this by living the life of the body, by observing animals and plants, by watching the way the soul of the world is manifest in all living things.

We become truly ourselves when we open to the deeper force of evolution. We are the benefactors of this grace, to the degree that we learn to honor it, to celebrate its hidden workings.

To my mind, the future is built on unceasing prayer and adoration. On a willingness "to suffer"—which means to allow a greater force to penetrate our lives.

We create the future through an intensely private act: the decision to offer ourselves up, to burn and be consumed like wood, to die a thousand times in the seasons of our lives.

We are made anew like the grass, the rivers, and the trees. Yet there is also something that *we* make as we offer ourselves up, like impassioned lovers, to the fire of creation. Moment by moment, the future of the world is shaped by our conscious sacrifice.

130
LAMA CHAGDUD RINPOCHE

Lama Chagdud Rinpoche, a highly realized master of Vajrayana Buddhism and the Great Perfection, is also an artist, poet, and Tibetan physician. Having fled Tibet in 1959 during the Chinese invasion, he worked for twenty years in refugee camps in Nepal and India, where his practice of meditation, inseparable from selfless activity, sustained his work.

A Prayer for Bliss and Joy

To all beings in general, who gather without being summoned,
and especially to the many beings reborn
through the virtuous power of their previous good actions:
Let these words fall on the blossoming *utpala* petals of your
ears.
The lotus of my body bloomed in a place
where the root of all benefit and well-being, the Buddha's
teachings, flourished,
a cool land completely surrounded by rings of snow mountains,
a realm of activity for the exalted and sublime one
[Avalokiteśhvara] whose compassionate eyes never close.
I offer for your delight this advice from one who has had the
good fortune
to be nurtured by authentic deities and qualified lamas.
For all of us mortal beings assembled together here,
due to the various forces of karma previously gathered
we dance in the procession of appearances—pleasant, painful,
and neutral—

driven mad by the seductive demons of distraction,
tightly bound by the confining shackles of hope and fear.
We beings who are tormented by unbearable suffering
today have slightly opened our two eyes of transcendent
    wisdom;
not wishing for quarrel, disease, famine, and war,
we do not surrender our power to the feeble forces of selfish
    desires
but seek to follow straightforwardly the sublime path to
    excellence.
With this the first light of bliss and joy dawns,
as we sing our song of joy and dance our dance of happiness.

His Holiness the Dalai Lama, who directs us to the path of
    peace and happiness,
and other holders of the teachings, spiritual mentors whose
    affection for us does not depend on personal acquaintance,
journey in all countries without discrimination,
radiating the sunlight of the sacred and profoundly meaningful
    Buddhadharma
and causing the lotus beds of love and affection in the minds of
    intelligent people to bloom fully.
With this second instance of bliss and joy,
we sing our song of joy and dance our dance of happiness.

In this world we have a multiplicity of religious traditions;
without being corrupted by arrogant obsession with our own
    traditions, all of us
should use our discriminating intelligence, like wingèd bees
    sipping nectar,
gathering the distilled essence from the flower beds of other
    fine traditions
to share skillfully with other beings the honey we have
    gathered.
With this result, the third instance of bliss and joy,
we sing our song of joy and dance our dance of happiness.

Henceforth and at all times,
light the lamp of clarity in places of darkness!
Liberate the foe of your anger with the weapon of love!
Seize beings headed down wrong paths with the hook of
    compassion!

Diligently don the armor of patience that protects you!
Hold to your own place, that of the ruler of undistracted
  intrinsic awareness!
Dedicate any virtue you bring about to all beings!
I pray that this vision of benefit and happiness may unfold
  forever.

I, the old Tibetan named Chagdud,
have written this message; everyone, please look upon it
  favorably.

131
LEX HIXON

Jikai Lex Hixon is studying for Dharma succession in the Soto lineage under Tetsugen, Sensei—Bernie Glassman, who serves the homeless and AIDS patients of Yonkers, New York. Lex is a practitioner in five sacred traditions and the author of several books, including *Heart of the Koran, Great Swan: Meetings with Ramakrishna,* and *Mother of the Buddhas: Meditation on the Prajnaparamita Sutra.*

The Morning Star of Enlightenment

Koan:

From beneath the Bodhi Tree, Shakyamuni directly perceives the morning star and is enlightened, exclaiming: "I, the broad earth, and all conscious beings are simultaneously enlightened and manifest the Great Way together."

Comment:

The amber autumn full moon sets at dawn, balancing on the black rock palisade, reflecting across the wide river. As beloved Master Keizan proclaims, our true nature stands like an eighty-thousand-foot precipice within each movement, within each perception.

Seeing directly and immediately—this alone is the morning star of enlightenment that unveils universal Buddhahood. The Bodhi Tree is our precious human body. Awakening, we cry spontaneously: "I am the living universe. I am the six realms of transmigration—

elemental, animal, etheric, human, subtle, and divine. All this, working together harmoniously, is enlightenment." There are no separate sentient beings, yet the enlightened way naturally and tenderly serves sentient beings. How? By lifting them into enlightenment.

Leaving the palace of convention at nineteen, practicing adamantine sitting, enlightened at thirty, for the remaining forty-nine years of his life, Shakyamuni is never alone. He is continuously giving the gift of Dharma, both through his words of truth, abundantly diverse, and through the silent evidence of his actions—simply walking, standing, sitting, lying down.

Never alone. This means oneness. Nothing separate is there to be known. Great Compassion is simply the absence of separateness. This unique compassion without subject or object manifests directly from the wisdom of enlightenment. Total inclusiveness. There is no way to approach it, cultivate it, or even be aware of it.

All the noble Shakyamuni needs now are robe and alms-bowl. When there is no more sense of being a separate individual, what needs can there be that are not spontaneously fulfilled? This is the meaning of every *vinaya* discipline, every form of external or internal renunciation.

Shakyamuni resembles any humble old monk. Who can perceive that he is actually all mountains and rivers of the universe? He is our eye and we are his eye. This discerning eye is not two, not one. It is our entire being. Where is Shakyamuni now? Where are we? Where are the worlds of multiplicity?

The lion's roar, "I am Buddha; I am awake; all beings are awake," is not a statement by Shakyamuni, not a perception belonging to Shakyamuni. Rather, Shakyamuni Buddha and all Awakened Ones come forth from this primordial "I am." The entire cosmos comes forth moment by moment from this one fundamental innate mind of clear light. With great kindness, Master Keizan, Mother of Soto Zen, presents us the record of the unveiling of this boundless clarity through fifty generations—the drama of Dharma succession, the untransmittable transmission of light.

When Shakyamuni pulled up the boundless net, all the openings in the net, all phenomena, were also liberated. Did this happen 2,500 years ago? If so, it is not the pure principle of enlightenment. There is no cosmos apart from Shakyamuni and no Shakyamuni apart from this burgeoning cosmos, this pupil of his wisdom eye. Our very skin, nerves, and senses are the morning star of enlightenment, yet enlightenment has absolutely nothing to do with skin, nerves, senses, or Buddha Dharma. Although both sides are true, leave both sides behind! There is only limitless awareness in this hermitage.

A wonderful old plum tree stands deep in the garden. It is more ancient than the memory of our ancestors. It appears more like a giant rock than a tree. Is it still alive? Yes! A green branch springs from the dark, gnarled trunk. This branch suddenly manifests thorns. Thorns on a plum tree? Impossible! Separate sentient beings on the Tree of Enlightenment? Impossible! Yet they continue to manifest, right before our eyes.

Now the plum branch is timelessly bearing fragrant blossoms. Miraculously, fruit also appears—not just the delicious plums of Buddhism, but awakened guides and holy prophets, women and men of all sacred traditions, flourishing on a single branch.

Poem

What magnificence! What splendor!
The morning star is everywhere.
At this very moment,
Shakyamuni Buddha is seeing.
We all practice peacefully
the fullness of the Great Way.

132

DAVID FRAWLEY

David Frawley (Vamadeva Shastri), D.O.M., is a modern proponent of
the Vedic system of knowledge, which is the oldest spiritual tradition
of India and perhaps the entire world. His books include *Gods, Sages
and Kings: Vedic Secrets of Ancient Civilization* and *From the River of
Heaven: Hindu and Vedic Knowledge for the Modern Age.* He is the
director of the American Institute of Vedic Studies based in Santa Fe,
New Mexico.

Living in Recognition of the Infinite

According to the yogis of the Himalayas, human beings have
lived on this planet for hundreds of thousands of years. During this
period there have been many cycles of civilization, of which the present humanity is only one episode. Some of these civilizations have
been more advanced than ours, and many have achieved spiritual
greatness. Others have destroyed themselves through the abuse of
power and knowledge. What we call history is thus just what little of
the past that our myopic vision is as yet able to recognize. We are
neither the first, the last, nor the greatest of civilizations. Those we
know of in history are only a few of the civilizations too many to number. Yet today, as is not uncommon for the arrogance of the human
mind, we believe that ours is the greatest of all civilizations and that
we have been given dominion over the Earth to use or abuse as suits
our temporary inclinations.

Today we are trapped in a materialistic and technological view
of the world. Even religion we mainly use for political and economic

advantage. Ours is the age of the machine in which both nature and the human being are being reduced, if not destroyed. We look outward for truth and happiness and have nearly lost all sense of the internal mysteries. We have reduced everything to a formula, equation, or a name. We have still not yet learned to control our population, to respect our planet, or not to use mere words, titles, and beliefs to divide people into warring camps.

In truth, as spiritual beings, we live in eternity. Time is just the illusion of our thought process as it plays upon the outward-looking senses. Our culture has no place to evolve or progress to except into the timeless. In eternity there is no advance or retreat, no success or failure, no final frontier, and certainly nothing to conquer. Yet it is not the eternal that we are seeking but what makes the most money, provides the most pleasure, or merely gets us through the next election.

Therefore it is time that we humbled ourselves and revised our vision of things. We are little better than creatures of a day, at best no more beautiful than flowers, and at worst—which is the direction we appear to be striving in—a blight upon the planet. We have not yet answered the fundamental questions of life. Our culture still does not know whether there is immortality, or what the nature of the Divine may be, if it exists at all. All of our marvelous information and technological expertise cannot touch the issues that really concern us at the level of the heart. If we look to discover these deeper truths, it is to our ancient scriptures or Oriental gurus that we must look, not to our modern scientists or our computer banks.

There is no end of the world coming. Life has an unlimited power to renew itself, though certainly we can damage our planet further and bring this cycle of civilization to a premature end. There is no miraculous golden age around the corner either. Our problems must be solved through hard work and clear thinking. No alien entity, deity, or avatar can remove them for us apart from our own sincere efforts. This does not mean there is no grace or magic to move us forward but that we must discover it through a change in how we live on a daily basis. We must learn to live once more in respect for the sacred nature of all life and in recognition of the infinite, compared to which whatever we achieve remains only a votive offering.

133

STEPHAN A. HOELLER

Stephan A. Hoeller is bishop of the Ecclesia Gnostica, a church of Gnostic descent. He is the author of several works on Gnosticism, especially in its relationship to Jungian psychology, including *The Gnostic Jung and the Seven Sermons to the Dead, Jung and the Lost Gospels, Freedom: Alchemy for a Voluntary Society,* and *The Royal Road.* He is a frequent contributor to *Gnosis* and *Quest* magazines and lectures worldwide on Gnostic and other esoteric topics.

A Gnostic View of the Future

I am a Gnostic. It was in my childhood, when the comforting orthodoxies of tradition seemed to fail a world suffering the Second World War's shattering blows, that the first glimpse of Gnosticism came to me, with its disclosure of long-forgotten truths. So overwhelmingly deep was its ancient hold upon my mind that I became a relentless gatherer of information about every aspect of this ancient tradition and eventually resolved to dedicate my life to its revival and dissemination.

The vision of the future that discloses itself to the view of the Gnostic is not a collective one. The future, therefore, to me is individual. It has to do with the fate of individual selfhood and only in a derivative sense with the future events taking place on the dark and sorrowful planet upon which we live at present. Gnosis is knowledge. And so it is on knowledge—not on belief, or projection, or wishful thinking—that one such as I relies in order to envision the future. I feel that I possess a certain kind of knowledge, based on my experience of realms terrestrial and spiritual, that reveals to me the origin of things, that discloses to me the true character of life in this world of matter and flesh and also the destiny of my true selfhood beyond all materiality and embodied existence.

Viscerally, instinctively, intuitively, I feel life in this world of matter, space, and time to be a failed and flawed work, vitiated and corrupted in its most fundamental structures. Mainstream Christianity has given recognition to this insight with its doctrine of the fall. Gautama, the Buddha, expressed it well when he said that earthly life is suffering, from which only a radical awakening of the spirit can liberate us and transport us to Nirvana. While others may debate such insights, I know them to be true.

But these radically negative recognitions regarding all creation —from the distant stars to the deteriorating cells of the body—are accompanied by an equally radical certainty that is an organic part of the Gnostic vision: the conviction that within me dwells a mysterious thing that does not participate in the curse and the emptiness of this world. Within me, and indeed in all human souls, there dwells a secret fire, a spark, a ray of light emanating from the true, the ultimate Deity —that distant, yet mysteriously ever-present Stranger, who in a paradoxical way is also our only true friend in our condition of exile.

What then is the future? Or, more properly, what is my future? What is the future of any and all who wake up to the recognition that they are exiles from worlds of boundless light and love and power, living in a dark place of suffering? Our task and thus our future is to regain our lost homeland by renouncing the snares of the powers that rule this world, to rediscover our unity with the transcendental realm of existence, to find again the kingdom of that original, ancient, and alien Light, the scattered and lost sparks of which we are.

These recognitions are brought to us by our own Gnosis and by the Gnostic tradition. The terms "Gnosis" and "Gnostic" may seem vague, encompassing numerous diverse meanings. Gnostics were always encouraged to express the ineffable realities they glimpsed in any and all ways suitable to them at the time. Still, there always was a common agreement among Gnostics about the nature of this world and about the possibility of attaining to a life greater and richer than the one we dwell in at present.

How then may our task be fulfilled, our future realized? Am I, are we, strong and wise enough to accomplish a work of such tremendous magnitude; can we overcome the great difficulties that stand in our way? Yes, because we are not alone. We receive help if we possess the humility to accept it.

We have not been left unaided in the wretchedness in which

we have become involved. Manifestations of the Truth in human form have come to us repeatedly: Buddha, Zarathustra, Mani, Jesus. These Messengers have the capacity to arouse our sleeping souls to awareness of our plight and to bestow the grace that will assist in the task of overcoming the inertia our ignorance has laid upon us. Equipped with wakefulness and grace, we shall rise on high, leaving the weary phantoms of this world forever behind. Shining beyond all our dreams of glory and perfection, we will enter the world of Infinite Light, nay, we will become that light ourselves. While thus undergoing redemption from terrestrial limitation, we need not fear for the welfare of this world, nor for that of the beings living in it. Every time a human soul attains to liberation, the flaw in the world is thereby diminished. Freeing our souls by Gnosis is the best way we Gnostics know whereby to improve conditions in this world. Thus it has been during the first two millennia and shall be in the third.

Such is the future declared to me and to others by Gnosis. Understandably, it is not a future than can be partaken of by all at any time. Only those who have come to see the worthlessness of earthly aims and who have glimpsed the glories of their potential future state can realize this future at this time. The invitation to these recognitions is ever with us, though the response to the invitation must come from every individual soul.

134

GEORGE TREVELYAN

Sir George Trevelyan's field of action since the war has been adult education, most recently as founder/president of the Wrekin Trust, an educational foundation concerned with the spiritual nature of humankind and the universe. He is now retired, but continues to lecture widely and is author of several books, including *Exploration into God* and *Summons to a High Crusade.*

The Coming of Light

A new millennium! Humanity has always felt that somehow something dramatic will happen to the world as it reaches a new thousand years.

Geographers and geologists can warn us of earth changes in the coming decades, and a wider dimension is indicated by the vision and understanding of the sensitives and seers. Planet Earth is to be seen as a living being with, in a true sense, its own consciousness. Indeed, there is a deep truth in the concept that ours is a planet of freedom and free will and that humankind has been given this setting as a school for the evolving of consciousness.

We know that we each have our guardian angel and a higher Self. But these beings may not interfere with our freedom of choice. We may get dragged down in striving to satisfy our desires, but in time will come the deep conviction that the real goal for each soul is to come back consciously to God in freedom, ultimately becoming a co-creator in the great pattern of the living universe. We flounder around with our ambitions, desires, and fears, but a time comes when, like the prodigal son, we "come to ourselves" and say "I will go back to my father."

That Biblical parable is profoundly relevant to our present age. Indeed, there may be much breakdown and confusion in the coming changes. Many will lose their bodies. Note the phrase, for it gives the true picture: The entity in you and me, that which can say "I AM," is a spiritual being, a droplet of divinity, and as such is imperishable. Do not identify with the body. It is the marvelously designed mobile temple to house the immortal and evolving spirit in its earth experience. People tend nowadays tacitly to assume that body and matter are primary. We are challenged to reverse the picture.

You are a spiritual being, immortal and imperishable. You belong to the world of spirit and have descended of intent into the prepared vehicle of a body, a "temple" of great beauty that enables you to sojourn for a while in the heavy vibrations of the world of matter, in order to learn the lessons that personality can teach.

Planet Earth is the wonderfully designed training school for souls. Given freedom we do as we like, spurred on by ego and self-gratification, and in the process we often hurt others and thus may need to come back to Earth again and again. The concept of reincarnation assuredly makes sense!

Though all this may seem theoretical, it is in fact of burning significance to us as we face the possible changes in our lifetime. We may be sure that if we are indeed dedicated to the coming of the light, which is, of course, the Second Coming of the Christ, we shall in crisis be watched over and helped by the invisible beings. They will never enforce a course of action, but will guide us into situations in which we can take the decisions in the light of Love.

Let change come (we cannot stop it!), but know that you are in continuous touch with the higher Self and guiding angel, who will be very close in time of crisis. We are making a breakthrough into something quite new—indeed it may be incomprehensible to our current understanding. But this is the great adventure of our time and is indeed exploration into God.

135

ANN FARADAY

Ann Faraday, the first English postgraduate to receive a Ph.D. in dream research, is author of *Dream Power* and *The Dream Game*. She is a leading member of the Australian Transpersonal Psychology Association in Sydney.

Toward a No-Self Psychology

All my thoughts, hopes, and fears about the future have changed radically since I fell asleep one night in October, 1985, and woke up next morning without a self. I don't know what happened to it, but it never returned.

This should have been an occasion for some regret, since I quite like my self—a self born long ago when I first discovered that other people did not automatically share my private inner space and could not intrude on it without my permission. Since then I had worked hard on my self to make it a good one, mainly by praying to God to remove the bad thoughts and feelings surrounding it. I soon came to think in terms of my higher Self and lower self—and hoped that God would always love and forgive me so long as I at least aspired toward the higher and abjured the lower. The higher Self, I decided, was probably my Soul, which would eventually unite with God and live happily ever after.

So it came as somewhat of a surprise in later life to learn that the Soul is not to be sought in the heavens but in the depths of the psyche, especially in the ''lower'' or ''shadow'' part, which I had tried so hard to disown. Through psychotherapy and dream work, I discovered that far from diminishing my self, all those buried fears, guilts, and "weaknesses" brought a welcome softness and subtlety to life. In fact they led me on to even deeper "archetypal" encounters that expanded the boundaries of self into the greater collective psyche of humankind. What had begun as a journey of purification had become one of completion or "individuation," and I looked forward to attaining what Jung called Wholeness/the Self/God before too long; all I needed, or so I thought, were just a few finishing touches.

In the meantime, in true human potential fashion, I was furthering all this growth by "taking care of" and "looking after" whichever self I happened to be into at the time. I no longer berated my self for making mistakes and was usually able to say "no" without feeling guilty. All things considered, including many years of meditation practice, I rated myself at around level 3.5 on the transpersonal ladder of enlightenment.

It was at this point in my imagined psycho-spiritual development that I lost my self. To compound the irony, before going to sleep that night in October, 1985, I had actually done a "self-remembering" exercise for precisely the opposite purpose—to center my energies in such a firm and clear sense of self that it would continue into the dreaming process instead of getting lost in it, thereby giving me a "lucid" dream in which I was aware of dreaming. I went off dutifully repeating the words, "I am, I am, I am . . ." and was more than a little astonished to awaken some hours later, laughing because the pundits had got it wrong: The truth was much more like "I am not." I was emerging from a state of consciousness without any "I" or "self" at all, a state that can only be described as pure consciousness. I cannot even really say I experienced it, because there was no experiencer and "no-thing" to experience.

And far from being a matter for regret, this loss of self came as a distinct relief. In fact, when bits and pieces of my old identity— hopes, fears, goals, memories, spiritual aspirations, and all the rest— began to re-collect as I woke, I tried to fight them off, in much the same way, perhaps, as the reluctant survivors of near-death experiences resist return to life's "little boxes." But unlike those survivors, I brought back no blissful sense of Divine Presence or a mission to accomplish, nor even intimations of immortality—just a total inner and outer "Emptyness" that has remained ever since.

This may not sound like a happy state of affairs to psychotherapists, who would probably see it as evidence of midlife crisis or incipient psychosis. But it is far more interesting than that. I experience this "Empty-ness" as a boundless arena in which life continually manifests and plays, rising and falling, constantly changing, always transient, and therefore ever-new. Sometimes I feel I could sit forever, knowing myself not only as a fluid manifestation of life within the arena, but also as the "Empty-ness" that holds it. If this is psychosis, everybody should have one, and the world would be a far more serene place for it.

After all this, I see no special significance in the approach of a new millennium, but as a psychologist, my hopes would go something like this:

1) I would challenge the ancient creed that developing a strong self-sense is essential in rearing children with adequate strength for living. Surely it is possible to encourage them to find "fluid identity" within the constantly changing play of life, not seeking permanence of any kind, particularly that of self. Perhaps we could even teach them to see and enjoy themselves as unique "non-entities," instead of separate hidebound selves obsessed with their own survival.

2) In psychotherapy, I would hope for a radically new approach to those who suffer from "inner emptiness." Instead of working toward filling that void with new purpose, direction, and meaning, I would aim to assist sufferers to go even deeper into that "Empty-ness" and discover its true nature. I would actively discourage all ideas of "inner journeying" toward wholeness, or "paths to enlightenment." These serve merely to postpone happiness here and now and build up the self-illusion.

3) In the spiritual domain, I would fire all gurus and transpersonal psychologists who use stage-by-stage models of "self-development" (explaining experiences like mine as fifth-level transient *nirvikalpa-samadhi*—or whatever). And I'd like to see the term *self* with a capital *'S'*—Self-actualization, Self-realization, Self-transcendence—expunged from psychological and spiritual literature, reserving the word strictly for the empirical self of everyday life. It is the whole obfuscating *concept* of "self" that needs to be transcended, for in my experience there has never really been any self to transform, actualize, realize, or transcend.

4) Finally, as a dream researcher, I would like to see more work done on the liberating power of sleep (a condition much-maligned in spiritual traditions, despite the Upanishadic statement that every night in deep sleep we go to the feet of Brahman. Shakespeare called sleep "the death of each day's life"—and if there are occasions when the self-sense relaxes and the body-mind opens to "Empty-ness" during sleep, as I now suspect, then it may well be "chief nourisher at Life's feast."

136

STEVEN M. ROSEN

Steven M. Rosen, Ph.D., is professor of psychology at the College of Staten Island/City University of New York. His philosophical essays have appeared in a variety of forums, and he is author of *The Moebius Seed,* a conceptual novel exploring the theme of human transformation or extinction.

The Plight of Odysseus

> *He tarries at the threshold.*
> *He delays.*
> *He sets out with trepidations clinging to her memory, leaves but*
> *does not.*
> *Odysseus does not know that his moment of departure will bring*
> *him.*
> *home to Her.*

This poetic passage came to me all in a rush—a rare even in my long labor to articulate what I feel about the human dilemma, circa 2000 A.D. Let me build on it as my way of adding my voice to the chorus assembled for this promising endeavor.

Contemplating the poem retrospectively, I believe it may be taken as a metaphor for the challenge of human growth and development, human maturation and fulfillment. I am speaking less here of the life history of any *particular* human being, than of humankind in general, humankind as such.

"He tarries at the threshold, he delays." "Odysseus" is reluctant to sever the bonds of impulse and instinct, to exit the womblike enclosure of "her" embrace and take the first steps toward individuation, toward fulfilling humanity's potential.

When he finally sets out, Odysseus does so with "trepidations," he "leaves but does not." In what sense does he leave? He takes definite strides toward his autonomy. And yet, he is "clinging to her memory." Since it is this above all else that Odysseus wishes to deny, he tells himself he simply has put her behind him. It is this "oedipal fabrication" that makes his departure a *falsehood,* and said pseudo-liberation is what lies at the heart of the crises presently confronting us. Down through the centuries, our pretense at individuality has grown evermore pronounced, so that now, the illusion of isolation is so complete and compelling that we are unhinged by it. What accompanies our contemporary sense of alienation, estrangement, and existential despair? The desperate denials, the projection and posturing, the care-less detachment, the abuse of self and other, the "emptiness," "nothingness," raging addiction—the living death that threatens an end to all life.

The truth of the matter is that a paradox operates here. As long as we effect the "oedipal posture" of *simple* autonomy, *simple* self-subsistence, as long as we perpetuate the illusion that we are divided from nature and each other *as opposed to* being united—that is, as long as we dualistically cleave independence from dependence, proclaiming the former and denying the latter—we remain unwittingly, destructively independent. In truth, there is just no simple dividing of division and unity, and one-sided "declarations of independence" only betray the lack thereof. To gain our independence in earnest, it seems we must sense, own, and knowingly embrace the bodily depths of our dependence (here there can be no independence *from*). The individuation that would come with such an act of "withdrawing our projections" (as Jung would have put it) would amount to dwelling in the paradox of being fully alone and fully all one.

Or putting it differently, the true taking leave *is* the true coming home—the moment of "Odysseus'" true departure that brings him "home to Her."

Postscript on our prospects for the "future": In view of the portentous fragmentation besetting us today, we well might ask *when* the needed realization may come. Can we be optimistic about the "future"? Will "Odysseus' homecoming" happen "in time"? The event in question surely will not happen *in* time (in, say, five months, or five years), since it will mark an *end* of time. Time— in its "oedipal," linear manifestation—is what divides us, projecting the "future" beyond our reach. "Tomorrow" must also be NOW.

137

KENNETH RING

Kenneth Ring, Ph.D., is professor of psychology at the University of Connecticut and cofounder and past president of the International Association for Near-Death Studies. He is the author of three books concerned with near-death experiences and other extraordinary encounters, including *Life at Death, Heading Toward Omega,* and *The Omega Project.*

Taking the Long View

It may not be a happy time in history, but the course of our prospective evolution as a species still fills me with optimism. Thus, when the calamities of everyday life and the dour forecasts of the pundits for this decade combine to depress our spirits, it may help to take the long view.

It is easy, of course, to get lost in the welter of one's own personal—or indeed the world's seemingly intractable—problems, but if one can climb to higher ground, something more promising, I believe, can be seen emerging on the horizon of our future.

For the past fifteen years, I have been studying persons who have found themselves, often without warning or preparation, caught up in an extraordinary encounter of some kind that ushers them into a supersensory world of radiant beauty and perfect love. Many of these individuals have undergone what we today call a ''near-death experience,'' and, as we now know, for most of them, their lives will never be the same again. Lately, I have also been researching persons who had had other kinds of extraordinary encounters, such as UFO-related episodes, which may be marked by very different features than near-death experiences, but which also leave lasting psychic traces on those who report them.

We have known for years that such experiences can bring about major psychological changes in people, but only now are we beginning to see how momentous and wide-ranging these transformations may be. For example, in my new book, *The Omega Project*, I have reported on evidence that there may well be important *psychophysical* changes—changes in physiological functioning, in neurological systems, and in brain structure—in the aftermath of extraordinary encounters such as near-death experiences and UFO-related incidents. These changes are highly consistent across both groups and imply a refinement of the nervous system and a corresponding expansion in states of mental awareness. Moreover, there is evidence that these psychophysical effects may be mediated by an activation of the *kundalini*, held by many theorists to be the evolutionary energy underlying humanity's ascent into higher states of consciousness.

We also know that literally millions of persons over the globe have had such experiences, and there is a fairly widespread belief that their numbers are increasing. But what is especially heartening is that our latest findings suggest that some aspects of the kind of transformation that these extraordinary encounters tend to bring about is *not limited to those who have had them*. For example, we have now discovered that persons who merely become *interested in* near-death experiences also show a marked shift toward greater compassion toward others, a lessened emphasis on materialistic values, and a heightened ecological concern. Moreover, more than eighty percent of such persons report that since becoming interested in near-death experiences, they have a diminished fear of death and are more convinced in life after death. Though they have not themselves had a near-death experience, they seem to see and treat the world as if they had. Similar effects hold for those who have come to have an interest in UFO phenomena.

What does this mean? In terms of notions like Sheldrake's hypothesis of morphic resonance, perhaps the field for this kind of consciousness is beginning to spread throughout an informed humanity like a benign virus and is starting to transform the collective psyche of the human race in much-needed ways. My friend John White is fond of saying that we will not have a better world until we have better people in it. Could it be that, in the midst of our seemingly dark decade, such persons are being, as it were, ''mass produced'' through the instrumentality of such pervasive extraordinary encounters, and that their effects are starting to ripple throughout that portion of the human race that is drawn to wonder about the meaning of such experiences? Perhaps, however, to reap their benefits, we do not really have to figure them out, much less have one ourselves; perhaps for this, all we have to do is open our hearts to them.

Perhaps in this way, the forces of evolution may yet save us from the sorrowful end that a limited historical vision would forecast for the human species.

138

JOHN WREN-LEWIS

John Wren-Lewis, a former leading British scientific futurist and initiator of the 1960s "death of God" movement, now lives in retirement in Australia, where he is an honorary associate of Sydney University's School of Religious Studies and engaged in research on the subject of the following essay for a forthcoming book, *The 9.15 to Nirvana.*

Dying to Reclaim the Aquarian Vision

Though I put no faith in astrology or special dates, I think the turn of the millennium could witness the kind of radical change in human life that was envisaged in the 1960s as the dawning of the Age of Aquarius, though along lines never previously considered.

Back then, when psychedelics failed to bring the democratization of mystical enlightenment and consequent hoped-for greening of the world, spiritual pundits claimed vindication of their aristocratic traditions. Our psychochemical experiments served, they argued, to demonstrate that lasting enlightenment is an Olympian achievement reserved for spiritual champions; the rest of us have to be content to spend an indefinite number of lifetimes in discipleship, or else give up mystical hopes altogether and find what niches we can in the power-establishment. But now, from a quite unexpected quarter, an entirely different kind of reason for Aquarian democratic hope has emerged.

The medieval Zen mystic Bassui Tokusho described enlightenment as "feeling like one come back from the dead," and similar assertions occur in basic mystical literature from all cultures. In the systems evolved by pundits and theologians, this is interpreted to mean that

405

enlightenment requires "dying to self" or "sacrifice of the ego," involving a long struggle against narcissism, "the monkey mind," and the ego's fear of annihilation. Pundits of human-potential persuasion represent this process as the highest stage of personal growth, in which the personality transcends itself after heroic fight against regressive egoic tendencies.

Nowadays, however, people from all walks of life are coming back from the dead in a more literal sense. Thanks to improvements in resuscitation technology, substantial numbers all around the world are being rescued from the very brink in extreme medical emergencies. And afterward, quite a few of us, including some like me with no prior belief in mysticism, have found ourselves living in a state of consciousness where "egoic" preoccupations no longer dominate life, even though we have done nothing to discipline self-concern. We still have the sense of self, but it is now experienced as just part of universal aliveness, not a central anxiety.

The phenomenon has begun to receive both scholarly and popular attention during the past decade, under a quasi-official medical name "near-death experience" or NDE. Its full significance is often missed, however, because media reports tend to focus on the fact that some whose lives have been changed in this way describe visions that seem like glimpses of the soul leaving the body and entering another world where supernatural beings and deceased relatives are encountered. NDEs have been hailed as powerful new evidence for the immateriality of personal consciousness and its survival beyond the grave—and that may be so. But to see them primarily in that light is to do less than justice to some of the life changes that have occurred.

Most people throughout history have taken survival beyond the grave for granted, yet have been every bit as ego-preoccupied as any modern Westerner—witness the rampancy of anxiety-driven behavior in every known human society. The really revolutionary significance of NDEs, including some like mine that involve no visions, is that on occasion they produce *a lasting change in consciousness itself*, a qualitative shift that reduces anxiety in a way that not even the most convinced belief can do. Psychologists who have studied the phenomenon internationally have actually stated that in the most profound cases it amounts to a mystical opening, with wide individual variations of intensity but a common factor, best described as a continuing sense of the eternal ground of being.

After my own rescue from death-by-poisoning in 1983, I felt as if something like a cataract had been removed from my brain. This has allowed me, for nine years now, to experience the full wonder and depth of life-in-each-moment in a way I had never imagined in my wildest dreams during my previous sixty years, not even in psychedelic adventures. And from this depth perspective there is no attachment to personal concerns, because the satisfaction of merely existing far outshines the transitory pleasures that come from getting my individual preferences met. To my amazement, it even transforms the pains that come when life goes against my personal inclinations.

The mere fact that such opening can occur without any spiritual discipline presents a fundamental challenge to the aristocratic or "growth" model of enlightenment. No doubt pundits will try to evade this challenge, either by saying that it is not real enlightenment or by asserting that we must have been "old souls" who were already prepared by work done in previous incarnations. But anyone with firsthand experience of eternity-consciousness knows it is the pearl of great price, no matter what other pearls there may be to come from life's infinite ocean—and there is no way even umpteen lifetimes could have prepared us for it, because it is just not like that at all.

Perhaps the most extraordinary thing about it is that it does not *feel* in the least bit extraordinary or "high." It feels so absolutely natural that I continually wonder how on earth I contrived to live for sixty years without noticing that I was just a focus of infinite aliveness, eternity's game of John Wren-Lewising along the time line, quite possibly for only a finite term, which is quite okay. It is as if the NDE jerked me out of a collective nightmare in which individuality seemed to mean separateness and struggle to survive, when in truth it is an arbitrary convention, like lines of latitude on maps.

One cannot, of course, recommend dicing with death as a *way* to mystical awakening; ethical problems aside, many people rescued from the brink report no special experience or life change. What NDEs *do* offer is a significant clue to the nature of the "waking dream" that blocks out awareness of eternity in so-called ordinary human life. If this trance can on occasion be broken simply by close encounter with death, it must be produced by something like a hyperactivity of the "protective instincts" that are meant to maintain the game of individuality by avoiding death as long as possible. Post-NDE lives offer vital evidence that the game actually functions more efficiently without that "anxious thought of tomorrow" that ordinarily blocks awareness of "eternity now."

Enlightenment, then, means liberation from a program malfunction, whereas reifying that malfunction by calling it "ego" and trying to discipline it serves only to reinforce it. From my own experience, I believe the survival drive gets switched off during very close encounters with death, and as a result its spell over consciousness is broken on "coming back from the dead." What we need now is to set all ancient traditions to one side and do some real experimental research into less drastic ways of soothing the hyperactive survival drive. Therein, I believe, lies real hope for the dawning of the Age of Aquarius.

RECOVERING SPIRITUAL PRACTICE

139

RICHARD ROHR

Franciscan Father Richard Rohr is founder of the New Jerusalem Community, Cincinnati, Ohio, and founder and animator of the Center for Action and Contemplation, Albuquerque, New Mexico. He is active in peace and social justice work and is known as the country's best-selling religious cassette author. He is author or coauthor of several books, including *Simplicity: The Art of Living, The Wild Man's Journey*, and *Discovering the Enneagram.*

Entering into Mercy

I pray that the church is much smaller in twenty years—and happy to be so. I suspect this is the only way we can regain our integrity and effectiveness as proclaimer of the kingdom: smaller numbers, smaller parishes (communities), smaller bank accounts, smaller programs, fewer clergy, less officialdom, smaller expectations of our capacity for success—a "mustard-seed conspiracy," of sorts. I have come to seriously believe Jesus' teaching about "two or three gathered in my name." Two hundred or three hundred look good, but mean less and less—to one another and to the world.

I hope for more truth, more real edges and influence, more energy for the inward journey, more prophecy, more right-brain intuition, more adoration, more real security, more spiritual and political hope for the human heart—just big enough and strong enough "for all the birds to come and shelter in its branches" (Matthew 13:32). But not so big that we forget, or do not need, or imagine that we Christians are the only tree.

If we continue to emerge as the group most capable of evangelizing culture itself, if we continue to stand in that naked place of the Gospel somewhere between and apart from liberal or conservative, if we continue to be walked on as a bridge, I have every hope that this oldest institution in Western civilization might be satisfied and secure as God's immoral minority. It takes two thousand years of history to grow up to that!

Now our identity is firm enough to prefer discernment over law, pastoring over programming, and the inherent wholeness and rhythm of the wisdom community. By the year 2000 we should be old enough for an adult marriage with Jesus in all his parts and all his pains. We should be free to fail because we can be so secure at the center. We will no longer need to be right or in control, but as never in our infancy, we are now a church capable of speaking truth to power—especially our own. Twenty years from now, I think, we will be a church that is both mystical and political in the same moment. There will be no other way to recognize Jesus. There will be no other reason to stay around.

I hope we will have the courage to stop rewarding and confirming people's egos and calling it morality, ministry, and church. I hope we will have lower expectations of leadership and the institution and, therefore, less need to rebel against it or unnecessarily depend upon it. After all, as Rainer Rilke put it, "There is no place on earth that isn't looking at you. You must change your life." The church cannot make that happen. It can only announce its possibility and offer its risen life as leaven and salt. I always wonder why such a glorious power and privilege is not enough. It is more than I ever hoped for or will ever do!

More than anything else, I hope we will be a people who have entered into mercy and allow others to enter. I once saw God's mercy as patient, benevolent tolerance, a form of forgiveness. Now it has become an understanding, a loving allowing, a willing "breaking of the rules" by the one who made the rules, a wink and a smile, a firm and joyful taking of the hand—while we clutch at our sins and gaze at him in desire and disbelief. So many things have now become signs of this abundant mercy—not grudgingly extended, but patiently offered—to this church and this age. As we grow older, it almost takes more and more humility to receive it.

Time has been gracious to us. The church must be gracious to all the world. And we must be gracious toward such a body and such a task.

140

ARTHUR VERSLUIS

Arthur Versluis, Ph.D., is professor of English at Washburn University in Topeka, Kansas. He is author of numerous books and articles, including *American Transcendentalism and Asian Religions* and the forthcoming *Theosophia: Christian Visionary Spirituality.*

Sophianic Mysticism

This, more than one Christian writer proclaimed during the past century, is the era of Sophia. Sophia, of course, is the Greek word for Divine Wisdom, and refers to the feminine aspect of the Divine. We can find praise of wisdom before the Christian tradition in the Old Testament, but it is with the Gnostics that we find Sophia appearing as a mythological being during the dawn of the Christian era, again appearing to Boethius in prison in the sixth century, again to Dante in the form of Beatrice at the turn of the fourteenth century, again to Jacob Boehme at the turn of the seventeenth century, again to Vladimir Solovyov at the turn of the twentieth century. Sophia has appeared again and again throughout history to inspire and illuminate humanity. I should like to suggest what Sophia can mean to us, now.

It is a commonplace nowadays for feminists to claim that Christianity is exclusively patriarchal, meaning of course thereby, bad. Some feminists have called for a feminine view of God in Christianity, as though this were something human beings ought to invent. But human beings do not invent religion; they experience it. Sophia is not invented by women who require a feminine God; indeed, Sophia has historically been experienced more by men than women. I would argue, in fact, that Sophia is more necessary for men than for women: There is polarity between Christ and women that is complemented, in a sense, by the polarity between Sophia and men. But spirituality cannot be reduced to sexuality.

Traditionally, Sophia as the feminine aspect of the Divine is the complement of the Logos, so much so that Jacob Boehme could entitle a book *Christosophia*. Sophia forms the center of theosophy, the spiritual discipline of which Jacob Boehme is a primary exemplar, but which includes such later authors as John Pordage, Jane Leade, Louis Claude de Saint-Martin, and Franz von Baader. For all of these authors and many others, including members of at least one theosophic group that continued into the twentieth century, Sophia is the mediatrix between God and humankind; she is the medium through whom God brought creation into existence, and through whom we "return" to God.

Modern Christianity is assailed for many reasons these days, and even defenders of traditional Christianity concur that it is close to moribund. Certainly this situation is one reason why Asian religious traditions, not to mention various newfangled cults, find numerous adherents in Europe and America. People hunger for authentic religious experience, and if they do not find in Christianity an authentic spiritual discipline leading to religious experience, then they search it out elsewhere, often in the process mistaking fool's gold for the real thing, to their cost. All too often, modern Christianity appears to be little more than a social phenomenon, a bulwark against the vicissitudes of modern life, a place to meet people, a source of emotional stimulation.

In such a world, Sophianic mysticism may have a very important place. Sophia has always been the inspiration for spiritual renewal. Only now are we discovering how much the theosophy of Jacob Boehme inspired the spiritual revival that swept Europe during the seventeenth and eighteenth century, and how much his theosophy inspired the great artists and scientists of that time, from William Blake to Isaac Newton. But this is always the case: The whole of Western history is one of cyclical decline and renewal. And always the divine feminine has been central to those periods of renewal, be it in fourteenth-century Italy, with Dante, or twentieth-century Russia, with Solovyov and Bulgakov. If you wish to see the source from which will spring the next cycle of spiritual renewal in the West, you likely need look no further than Sophia, Divine Wisdom.

141

GEDDES MACGREGOR

Geddes MacGregor, D.D., D.Phil., *docteur-ès-lettres,* is emeritus distinguished professor of philosophy, University of Southern California, and an Anglican priest. He is the recipient of many awards and is the author of numerous articles and thirty-one books, including the recent *Images of Afterlife: Beliefs from Antiquity to Modern Times* and *Dictionary of Religion and Philosophy.*

Preparing for 2001 through Authentic Prayer

One might possibly argue the case that the close of even a century tends to entail a certain cultural agitation or moral collapse. The literary and artistic style and mood of the 1890s is such that its distinctiveness is sufficiently captured in the phrase *fin de siècle,* which by analogy can serve to express any attitude that is "too-too" sophisticated or refined; the decadence that one expects with a closing decade. True, things do not always work out with the neatness of such expectations. At the time of this writing, cowboy and country values seem to be staging a comeback even as we reap the bitter fruits of the 1960s. No doubt it all depends on the company we keep. Still, no educated person is in any doubt of the meaning of *fin de siècle* in its general application, despite the paradoxes that attend it.

If such paradoxes appear with the ending of a mere century, they are no less likely, to say the least, to be found at the end of a millennium. Historians of the Middle Ages detect something of the kind toward the end of the previous millennium, which must have been a traumatic episode for many. The entire twentieth century, at least from the outbreak of World War on August 4, 1914, may well be seen as a *fin de millénium*, with all the apocalyptic overtones of that term. Undreamed of discoveries and events ensued, of course, but overcast by the hideous carnage of war, the hunger and misery of vast multitudes, the stupidity and folly of racist riots and other senseless violence, and not least the decline in literacy (few even in academic circles can now spell correctly *its/it's*): All these tragedies along with cavalier unconcern for the environment that is our priceless heritage, our gift from God, portend ill for what lies ahead of us. We have been shown (if we needed showing) what clay feet we humans have.

Have we humans prayed enough? Indeed we have. But have we prayed well enough? True prayer is really keeping company with God. What passes for prayer is generally mere descant and counterpoint. We ought to pray, more than for anything else, for a deepening of our self-awareness, an enrichment of our inner life. That is supremely what we need in preparation for the year 2001. Such authentic prayer is not the whole of religion but it is its essence and is often if not generally the ingredient most neglected by Church leaders. If we understood better the nature and unique value of prayer, we should include in our liturgies a thanksgiving for *unanswered* prayer: thanksgiving for the grace of God who in his mercy graciously did *not* answer those foolish prayers of ours.

I find that it is only when I attain such awareness, however minimally, that I become able to discern the true purposes of God in the guidance of my life. Therein is wisdom whose price is indeed far above and infinitely beyond the price of rubies (Proverbs 8:11; Job 28:18). Such wisdom enables me to understand my karmic inheritance and to begin to transcend it.

142

JOHN SEED

John Seed conducts Councils of All Beings and other ReEarthing workshops and is a coauthor of *Thinking Like a Mountain—Towards a Council of All Beings*, where some of the deep ecology rituals alluded to in this essay are described.

For the Earth

Dr. Mustapha Tolba, director-general of the United Nations Environment Program, warned in his introduction to *United Nations World Conservation Strategy* that unless we change course, "we face, by the turn of the century, an environmental catastrophe witnessing devastation as complete, as irreversible as any nuclear holocaust."

Dr. Paul Ehrlich warns us that we are sawing off the branch on which we are sitting.

Dr. David Suzuki, professor of genetics from Toronto and Canada's foremost ecologist, at the Stein Wilderness Festival 1990: "We may have less than ten years before the damage to the Earth's life-support systems reaches the point of no return."

Dr. Raymond Dassman, professor of biology, University of California: "The Third World War has begun: It is being waged against the Earth."

Are we humans really about to extinguish ourselves? Are we really about to destroy the life-spport systems that support complex life on this Earth?

How can this be? What can we do?

Let us dwell for a moment on the route we have taken that has led us here and pray to our ancestors for understanding and guidance.

Bring to mind the 4,000 million years of unbroken success since our adventure into biology began.

Journey back with me. Let us reconstruct, recapitulate, our voyage so that we may remember and harvest the gifts of our ancestors.

Honor first your mother's womb where a single seed from your father united with her egg and then flow back from there through the womb of her mother, and back and back through mother after mother. A few hundred generations and we leave written history behind, metals turn back to soil, agriculture disappears.

We lose control of fire, soon we are back up in trees, and then after a while we drop our opposable thumb and scurry as mammals on the forest floor staying out from under the feet of dinosaurs. Our fur turns back to reptile scales, we slither in and out of the ocean until we are back under the water and free from gravity. Backbones disappear; life becomes simple—a tube of cells, then single cells washed back and forth in ocean currents, until at last we leave the organic and swim in the molecular soup once more.

One thing we know for sure about our ancestors during this vastness is that each and every one of them grew to maturity and managed to reproduce before being consumed. The fact that you are here is absolute proof of this. Can we possibly grasp what this says about our pedigree?

Think for a moment on the implications. Let us dwell with one anonymous female fish. An unbroken chain of DNA leads from her body to yours. She laid a myriad of eggs in her life but only a few survived to reproduce. One of those was your ancestor.

And at each step of the way it was like this—we threw heads every time for 4,000 million years. To throw tails once was to break the chain. Are we *really* about to throw tails? Why? For a microwave oven and an electric toothbrush?

Can we identify with this vast process rather than our race or religion or ideology? Can we represent the accumulated striving of each and every ancestor and bring *this* into our lives? What kind of choices, priorities, and personal and political agendas spring from such a perspective?

Is it really possible to identify with the precious flame passed from fin to claw to paw and now into your trembling hand rather than with this present life alone? How shall we go about this?

Well, one thing for sure, we are not going to be able to *think* our way back to participation in the ancient web.

This bulge above our noses is such a recent innovation. How can we reconnect with the intelligence that ensured our survival before thinking began, the intelligence that has stood the test of time? How can we un-earth, re-member, embody in our lives again the lust for survival that surely characterized us before we became confused by all these thoughts?

I propose that the key lies in ritual. We need to reclaim the rituals that affirm and nourish our interconnectedness, our interbeing with all that is and all that ever was and that ensures our survival.

We "civilized" ones are the first humans ever to have dispensed with the ceremonies and rituals by which *all* previous communities have ensured continued participation in the dance of life. In our "enlightenment," in our arrogance, in our fear of inquisition we uprooted ourselves from the living Earth, from our own Nature, and now wilt and expire.

Unless we learn once more to harmonize our human song with the great symphony from which we emerged and in which we remain inextricably embedded, our evolutionary journey will draw abruptly to a close. We are the last generation of humans to be offered this choice: Soon the damage to the life-support systems will be beyond repair.

143

ANNA HALPRIN

Anna Halprin, Ph.D.Hon., founded the San Francisco Dancers' Workshop Company and cofounded Tamalpa Institute in Marin County, California, where she currently teaches. She leads large community rituals both there and abroad. She has published articles and books and has appeared in movies and on television programs.

Recovering the Lost Language of Dance

There is a long tradition of using ritual dance for the purpose of affecting the world. Western civilization is one of the few cultures that does not use dance in this way. In ancient times and in traditional cultures, dance functioned as the means by which people gathered together in order to confront the challenges of their existence. Dance was used to help hunters gather food, encourage the growth of the crops and their harvest, celebrate birth and marriage, initiate the young, initiate adults into the sacred mysteries, prepare for war, celebrate victory or lament defeat, aid the sick, help the dying on their journey into the land of the dead, and maintain the life of the community on its proper path. Dance was the most important language people knew. It was a language of power and the language of the spirits. It was the language nature understood, the language in which the myths and stories that provided the people with a way to make sense of their experience were told.

In the evolution of Western industrialized culture, people gradually lost the language of dance even as they lost their consciousness of the spiritual and natural worlds. By now we know of the various problems and crises birthed by the alienated consciousness of the age of industrialization. Insulated from nature by a world of technologies, Western culture has deeply disrupted the delicate fabric of life in a way that threatens our continued existence. We also face a thorough dislocation stemming from the same roots and manifesting in crime, disease, confusion, isolation, and the constant threat of war.

The rediscovery of the lost language of dance offers us the very vehicle that people traditionally used to form culture and face their crises. It is time for us to reapproach dance with the attitude our ancestors held, as a vehicle to understanding our relationships to the world. There is no denying that dance had the power to cohere and maintain ancient societies. We now have the opportunity to bring that power to bear on our task of transforming, reuniting, and renewing our society so that we may find harmony among people and between people and the Earth.

It is in this context that we at Tamalpa Institute developed a dance called "Circle the Earth." Circle the Earth is a large-scale dance ritual I have been developing since 1981 in response to the different social issues facing the life of my community. It is an attempt to recapture the essence of ancient ritual in contemporary terms. Circle the Earth is a five- to nine-day workshop process that culminates in a performance for the community. Over the ten years of its existence, the themes of Circle the Earth have evolved from the reclamation of a mountain from a trailside killer, to planetary peace, to the specter of AIDS and life-threatening illness.

Our concept of peace goes well beyond the idea of peace as the absence of war between nations. Peace should be a powerful, creative way of life through which people cooperate to solve their problems and realize their potential. Illness is also seen in a more connected way. If one of us has AIDS, we all have AIDS. The human community and the planet body are reflections of one another and our "cures" will be created through the community actions we take.

Circle the Earth seeks to create bridges where boundaries exist, and to walk across these bridges with one another. It is based on the belief in the efficacy of dance to heal, and in the power of personal stories to forge a collective experience. The philosophy of this dance posits that the human body has infinite wisdom that informs our minds and our experiences and attempts to gain access, at all times, to this body wisdom and use it in the creation of a pertinent, contemporary ritual. An underlying assumption guiding the creation of Circle the Earth is that the body does not lie, and that the stories in our bodies, when they are revealed, are the hidden treasures of our lives, our relationships, and our communities.

I am committed to the revelation of everyone's personal myth within the context of the group myth because I have seen how individual stories shape and create a dance that actually effects change for its participants. The collective mind is not derived from one source but from the investment of the individual's personal ideas and feelings into the larger collective body. Encompassing our diversity is one of the challenges in making a contemporary dance ritual. We are a culture of many people from many places and we often do not have the tools to bridge the gaps between us. A contemporary ritual speaking to our differences will encompass our diversity and place an equal value on everyone's story. A contemporary ritual that speaks to our differences will acknowledge our individual responses to the universal problems facing us.

I believe we can create new dance rituals in the juncture between the individual and the collective body. To do this, we work with the essential language of the body and movement, a language that has not been shaped so specifically by our censoring minds. Dance expresses universal human responses in a form we all share, the movements of the body. Dance gives us new models for our relationships and new understandings of our experiences. Dance can reach into the depths of our bodies and give us back a reflection of the depth of this knowing. When we dance, we cut across the divisions created by our differences and we create an experience in which we can all participate. Dance creates immediate, direct, and powerful experiences that bypass discussion, argument, committee meetings, and difference. Through dance, we can use our individual resources, the stories in our bodies, to subvert the isolation of our culture and build a collective body truly answerable to our human needs.

Circle the Earth is one small part of a long search for the maps we need to take us to the places we want to go. I can imagine many new places to go, and many new dances to do—dances of sexual liberation to remind us of the beauty and life force of the body; women's dances to support our visions; men's dances to channel male energy; dances between mothers and daughters, and fathers and sons, to heal the wounds between us; dances with animals and trees to to remind us we are not the center of the universe but part of its circle; dances to celebrate birth and to mourn death; dances to heal the sick and to celebrate union. I see all of us dancing the hard dances until they become easy, stumbling and tripping over each other until we learn to dance together. I see the creation of these dances as a wonderful possibility and a great hope.

144

JOSHUA HALPERN

Joshua Halpern, M.A., is a writer and drummer. He is the author of *The Ceremonial Circle, Live Your Health,* and *Children of the Dawn.*

Community-Making: The Path of the Drummer

The drum is the most powerful tool human beings have invented to make community. It is not a coincidence that the first thing the colonial invaders did upon arriving on Turtle Island was to confiscate the shaman's drum and outlaw dancing. And then later, as part of the same sickly oppression, they forbid the slaves from drumming—it seemed like a fire broke out in the mainhouse kitchen every time they did. The power of the drum to knit people together so they can work for a common vision is one that no government or technological innovation is ever going to end or exceed.

The path of the drummer is not like other paths. It is unique because it demands the daily solitary discipline of hatha yoga but is a tool for community building, and it becomes necessary to take the energy out, to share the sound. The drummer must have a strong ego but also be able to totally blend. The drummer must have power but also be able to share it. The drummer must have competence but not get hung up in competition.

What I advise as a way to establish yourself in the drum is to gather in a three-couple configuration on the new moon every month for a three-year period—to make a commitment to circle and drum with your friends. Out of such meetings issues forth the best culture for growing an abundant life. From such a meeting ground the couples can clearly dialogue on how to go about creating the kind of work and world they want their children to live in. They can discover whether they can live together, which is essential for those of us who want to live in community, and they can focus on survival, love, peace, and healing.

The company of three viable couples begins with individuals. There is usually much work and time before this can happen, years of practice and struggle. We all have our own way to the path of the drum.

I started drumming when I was seventeen. I studied for a year and then played alone or with a very small group for ten years before taking it out into the wider community. I now have a group of friends who I know through the drum. That is our connection. Our words are sung from the taut hide; our love is expressed through the hallows.

The main thing to learn if you want to begin to drum is how to listen. If you listen to the sounds of the night you will play the pulsations that need to be played. It is not necessary to study other sound systems. It is only imperative to feel, hear, and resonate with the ones of your bio-region, tribe, and family.

How the first drum was made

snake traveler rested on Orion's belt before
spiraling into horizon's mouth to become
spine and hidden essence

snake's friend peasant knelt on the ground
eyes watered the dry seed
the salt made a hot sinewy liquid
snake bathed in it and moved past the cultivated fields
into the rocky barren places
and then into the deep forest

snake walked until he found a large stone
and went beneath it and rested and awoke
while the owls talked in the cold
in the morning of the fifth day of the journey
snake beckoned and uncoiled
and peasant moved into a fetal position
as morning crow began to fly

they went to the water and bathed and prayed
they felt good with each other
they listened as a flowering bush began to blossom

424

they wandered for two more days
on the tenth day they came to a valley filled with empty
   bird nests
hanging from limbs and leaf holds
peasant asked snake "where are the eggs?"
snake looked in the dust

O maker of drums!
Bom!
O Maker of mouths of rivers
Bom Bom!
snake stopped in the dust and laid his skin on the ground
his last words were "make a drum from my taut hide."

O trumpet of the earth
O saxophone of the soul
O wings upon which spirit flies
hear us now
hear our drums.

145

JACQUELINE MANDELL

Jacqueline Mandell teaches Buddhist meditation retreats and seminars internationally. She has lectures at the World Health Organization and Harvard Divinity School. Her biography is included in *Meetings with Remarkable Women: Buddhist Teachers in America, Turning the Wheel: American Women Creating a New Buddhism,* and *Buddhist America.* She is a wife, mother of twins, and a writer.

A Festival of Happiness

Earlier this week our township celebrated its annual Festival of Happiness. My five-year-old daughters, Chloe and Erica, laughed and ran as they followed their friends Yuki-chan and Dai-chan down the narrow Japanese streets. The children dressed in turquoise "happy coats" with large black letters symbolizing happiness on the back, and they pulled a long thick rope attached to a wooden float on wheels.

On top of the float were four boys and girls chanting and loudly beating on a huge drum. Behind the float four men followed carrying a heavy portable shrine. My husband, Allan, was the first American ever to carry this neighborhood's shrine.

The rest of the residents and shopkeepers, standing on the sidewalk, waved to the passing parade. Many offered envelopes of money as the shrine went by their homes. Rest stops with snacks were established along the route and vendors held a bazaar nearby.

The local festival was organized and guided by adults, but the children were the main attraction. There was a week of drum practice before the event as well as the making of colorful flower decorations. A few days later, with the donations, the children's park was freshly painted, noodle dinners were given to the participants, and a party was given for the adults.

My vision for the future:
International harmony.
Intergenerational communication.
Appreciation of differences without judgment.
Sustained community activity.
Giving and receiving happiness.

INDEX

QUEST BOOKS
are published by
The Theosophical Society in America,
Wheaton, Illinois 60189-0270,
a branch of a world organization
dedicated to the promotion of brotherhood and
the encouragement of the study of religion,
philosophy, and science, to the end that man may
better understand himself and his place in
the universe. The Society stands for complete
freedom of individual search and belief.
In the Classics Series well-known
theosophical works are made
available in popular editions.